I0824246

FLAVORS FROM THE SHORE

BLUEWATER GRILL

BLUEWATER
AVALON

BLUEWATER
AVALON

FLAVORS FROM THE SHORE

BLUEWATER GRILL

NOSTALGIC SEAFOOD RECIPES CELEBRATING OUR COASTS & WATERWAYS

JIM ULCICKAS • RICHARD STAUNTON

WITH JAMES O. FRAIOLI

Skyhorse Publishing books may be purchased in bulk at special discounts for sales promotion, corporate gifts, fund-raising, or educational purposes. Special editions can also be created to specifications. For details, contact the Special Sales Department, Skyhorse Publishing, 307 Fifth Avenue, 4th Floor, New York, NY 10016 or info@skyhorsepublishing.com.

Visit our website at www.skyhorsepublishing.com.

Culinary Book Creations LLC
www.culinarybookcreations.com

10 9 8 7 6 5 4 3 2 1

Library of Congress Cataloging-in-Publication Data on file.

Production: James O. Fraioli, Culinary Book Creations LLC
Cover photograph by Tucker + Hossler Photography
Designers: theBookDesigners

Print ISBN: 978-1-5107-8420-8
Ebook ISBN: 978-1-5107-8437-6

Printed in China

To the millions of guests who have graced our doors and created memories of their own in our establishments. Thank you.

CONTENTS

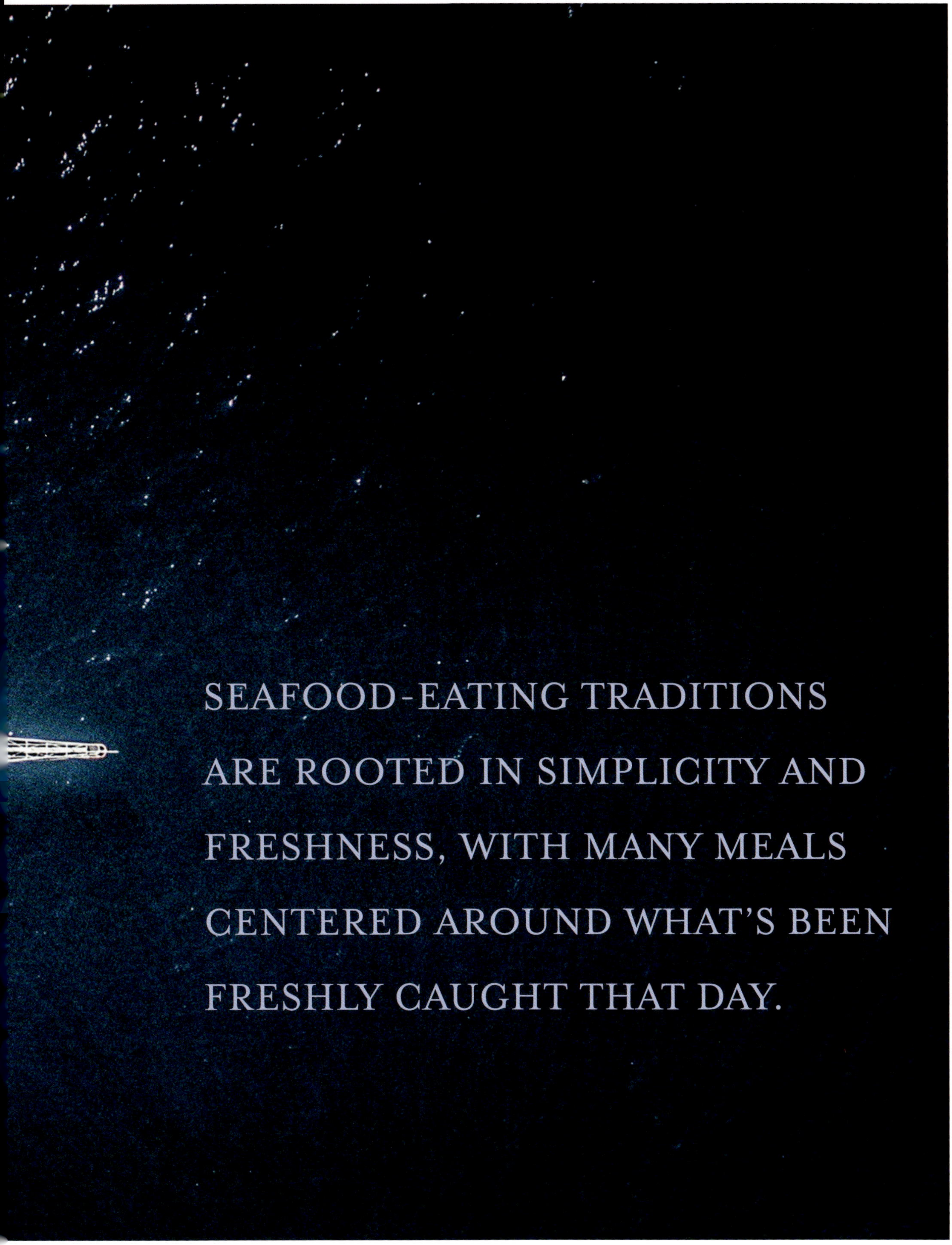

SEAFOOD-EATING TRADITIONS ARE ROOTED IN SIMPLICITY AND FRESHNESS, WITH MANY MEALS CENTERED AROUND WHAT'S BEEN FRESHLY CAUGHT THAT DAY.

PREFACE

BY RICK STAUNTON

Growing up on the Northern Beaches of Sydney in the '60s, '70s, and '80s, the ocean was an integral part of my life. My dad and I would spend countless hours surf fishing, and if we didn't catch anything, we'd head to the local fish-and-chips shop to buy what we should have caught. My weekends and holidays revolved around fishing, spearfishing, and surfing. As I got older, road trips with friends took me up the coast of New South Wales and Queensland. We'd travel all the way to Cairns and the Whitsunday Islands, where the spearfishing was epic—coral trout, wahoo, grouper, and snapper were abundant. We even crossed the country to the West Coast, surfing, spearfishing, and diving for spiny lobster—the best in the world. In Australia, seafood is more than just food—it's a way of life. The country's deep connection to the ocean is reflected in its seafood culture, where simplicity and freshness are key. Whether at a fine-dining restaurant or a local fish market, meals are built around what's freshly caught that day. One of the most cherished traditions is fish-and-chips—crispy battered fish, often barramundi, flathead, or snapper, paired with hot, salty chips, enjoyed at coastal kiosks or beachside cafes with the sound of waves lapping in the background.

My love for oysters was passed down from my dad, who introduced me to Sydney rock oysters—small, flavorful gems that are a local delicacy. These would be freshly shucked and served with a squeeze of lemon, often alongside a chilled glass of Australian white wine. Australia's strong barbecue tradition also celebrates seafood. Family gatherings and beach barbecues featured prawns, lobster, squid, and various types of fish like barramundi, kingfish, snapper, and flathead—grilled whole with a simple seasoning of olive oil, garlic, and lemon. One of my family's traditions was visiting the Sydney Fish Market, one of the largest in the world, where the choice of fresh seafood was, and still is, amazing. The sea provided not only sustenance but also the backdrop for family gatherings, where the flavors of the ocean and the warmth of shared moments came together.

When I moved from Australia to the United States, my love for the ocean and seafood found a new home. My wife's family owned a series of fish market restaurants, and together, we enjoyed countless trips on their fishing boat, *Pilikia*, which doubled as a harpoon boat for swordfish. My family also spent many hours fishing with my father-in-law on the tip of Baja, chasing yellowfin tuna, wahoo, and dorado. These catches would be enjoyed in simple Baja fashion—fresh fish on tortillas with lime, shredded cabbage, and salsas, a perfect reflection of the way the ocean's bounty can bring people together. Just like you'll discover in this wonderful book.

Duke

FROM A BYGONE ERA . . .

. . . TO TODAY

INTRODUCTION

BY JIM ULCICKAS

The title of this book, *Flavors from the Shore: Nostalgic Seafood Recipes Celebrating Our Coasts & Waterways* , is a fundamental principal of Bluewater Grill. We believe food has a unique way of connecting us to our memories, acting as a trigger for recalling emotions, places, and people from our past. By focusing on how food intertwines with personal experiences—whether growing up, on vacation, fishing trips, or family gatherings—the narrative can explore the deep emotional connections people have with their heritage, loved ones, and the simple, meaningful moments that shape their lives. My favorite movie scene is in the animated film *Ratatouille* when snobby French food critic Anton Ego is served a simple peasant-food dish from his childhood. The first bite brings a flashback of childhood memories and love for his mother's cooking. It is this concept that our dedication to food and hospitality is founded on at Bluewater Grill.

I grew up in Massachusetts as a kid with a bucket and a fishing rod, not a bat and ball. I would spend hours hunting for frogs, turtles, and crawdads, fishing for bass, bluegill, and sunfish. In retrospect, the quote on my high school yearbook page—"There is no love more sincere than the love of food"—was a foretelling of my future in the restaurant business.

My Lithuanian grandparents taught me a tradition of growing, raising, producing, and storing food that I exercise to this day. Even though we live in suburban California, we keep fifty chickens, four goats, a pet pig, four beehives, a vineyard, numerous fruit trees, and a large vegetable garden. We have installed solar power and a rainwater capture system. Among my forms of relaxation are bottling, canning, freezing, and fermenting our production.

The biggest influence on my love for food and hospitality was that of my stepfather, Curtis Blake, cofounder of Friendly's restaurants in Springfield, Massachusetts, in 1935. His simple concept was to have "friendly" food, service, and prices. This fundamental concept has translated to our operating philosophy of premium-quality food and service at a reasonable price. It is through this influence that my sister Anne started an ice cream sandwich business which I helped her expand, and I got my first job cooking at Abel's Lobster in Maine. This was followed by a postcollegiate stint at W. R. Grace & Company working in the restaurant division, where I worked in finance, the commissary, purchasing, distribution, and operations. It was this experience in the trenches that taught me the importance of knowing all the elements that make a restaurant successful. In today's competitive and ever-changing landscape, it is important to be aware and address change before you get left behind. It is because of this that Bluewater Grill has remained successful for thirty years and continues

GRILL

LANDROVE

to grow and prosper. It is also the reason we became a leader in sustainability long before it was fashionable. Our purchasing decisions have always been influenced by selecting vendors that are local and observe "best practices" and make decisions based on what is best for the product and the environment and not profit. Bluewater Grill has become a family of eight locations in Southern California and Arizona, focusing on coastal and resort communities. We employ close to one thousand people in the kitchen, as servers, hosts, bartenders, bussers, and managers. It is these people that are Bluewater Grill and that are responsible for our longevity. We share an intense dedication to quality in all aspects of food, service, hospitality, and facility that we call "blocking and tackling." Simply translated, if you execute the basics successfully and consistently, success is the by-product. Operating a restaurant on a busy night is controlled chaos, but with the right people, systems, planning, attention to detail, and a lot of hard work, hot food comes out hot, and cold food comes out cold every single time.

This book is important not only to prepare some of our favorite recipes but to weave the concept into these recipes that ingredients matter. We hope you take the time to source the highest-quality wild or farmed product you can find and reward small producers for their efforts to do the right thing. It may cost a little more and take a little longer but, in the end, the quality will shine through and will make a difference in the result.

THIS BOOK IS IMPORTANT NOT ONLY TO PREPARE SOME OF OUR FAVORITE RECIPES BUT TO WEAVE THE CONCEPT INTO THESE RECIPES THAT INGREDIENTS MATTER.

BLUEWATER
GRILL

PURCHASING, SELECTING & SEAFOOD CARE

Many people in the United States, especially those not living on a coast, lake, or waterway, prefer to cook beef, pork, and poultry as their main sources of animal protein rather than fish. Some reasons for this include not knowing what kind of fish to buy or how to prepare it, or the belief that cooking fish can make a house smell fishy, or because the cook simply doesn't like fish. Yet fish is incredibly nutritious and heart healthy. In fact, fish is more healthful than red meat and even poultry. Species like salmon, mackerel, bluefish, and herring—all oily fish—are rich in omega-3 fatty acids believed to be both heart- and brain-healthy. The benefits of eating seafood have been proven by studies of fish-eating populations, especially those in Japan and Scandinavia. Eating fish also adds variety and interest to anyone's regular diet.

Seafood is different from other types of food because freshness is the key for safety and flavor. To ensure you and your family and friends enjoy the best fish possible, especially when making our mouthwatering recipes ahead, remember these helpful pointers:

SEAFOOD BUYING TIPS

Fish and shellfish should always be purchased fresh or fresh-frozen. Although this may sound like an obvious statement, sometimes the supply chain takes too long to get fresh seafood to local stores, shortening its shelf life so that it appears unappetizing to the consumer. In addition, many types of fish and seafood, including shrimp, squid, and scallops, are not available fresh in many parts of the country, so frozen is the only alternative for these items as well as some varieties of finfish.

The first step is to ask questions. Learn about the various and unfamiliar species being sold and the fishing method used, which this book is intended to help you with. For the more ethically minded, learn the difference between seafood harvested in US waters and those brought in from overseas. All of this plays a vital role in purchasing the most sustainably harvested or farmed and freshest seafood available.

After receiving a little education, and now admiring that delicious piece of fish behind the glass you're eager to prepare for your family and friends, refer to these helpful tips before you make the purchase:

Seafood should never smell fishy. In fact, fresh fish should never have any unusual or offensive odor whatsoever. Always ask to smell the fish before you buy. Don't wait until you're home to discover the seafood you bought is spoiled. This tip refers to

OLD BAY

not only buying fresh fish, but all seafood including shellfish, such as crab and scallops.

If the fish you like has its head still intact, take a moment and inspect the eyes, which should always be clear. Cloudy eyes are a sure sign the fish is not fresh or has been previously frozen. Same with the gills. They should be bright red. Light pink or brown gills indicate a mishandled fish or one that has already spoiled.

Inspect the flesh or meat. Fresh fish should be firm and spring back when touched. If your finger leaves an impression, the meat is soft and has probably deteriorated.

Examine the skin of the fish. The exterior should be clean, and if there are any fins intact, they should look crisp and moist, not discolored or dry, particularly around the edges.

For species such as clams, crab, lobster and the like, buy live whenever possible. This ensures the freshest quality rather than frozen prepackaged products.

When buying live shellfish like clams, mussels, and oysters, the shells should be tightly closed. If they are open, they should close when you touch them. They should also be housed in circulating seawater or held in a cold case. If they are displayed on ice, make sure they are very cold—and alive.

For live crab and lobster, if you don't catch it yourself, they too should be stored in a circulating marine tank. They should be lively, especially when removed from the water. Do not purchase those that are limp and lifeless. If buying cooked crab or lobster, examine their shell. The exterior should be free of cracks and should smell clean and fresh.

If traveling a good distance, have the supermarket or fishmonger add a bag of ice with your seafood purchase. Your fresh fish must stay cold if you want it to remain fresh. Better yet, bring a cooler with some ice when shopping for fresh seafood no matter how far you are traveling. Even a short trip in the summer heat can reduce the quality of your purchase. It is a good idea to complete all your other errands before buying seafood so you can go straight home.

SEAFOOD CARE

Once home, it is best to remove the wrapping from the market and immediately place your seafood in the coldest part of the fridge. Make sure it's not too crowded with other items. The coldest part of the fridge is the back. If you are refrigerating more than one seafood, do not store them together in one container or plate, and do not let the juices from one seafood come in contact with another seafood.

If you find yourself purchasing frozen seafood, keep it frozen until you are ready to prepare and cook it. To properly thaw, defrost in the refrigerator and never at room temperature. Also, plan ahead, as you may need to defrost the day before your dinner party or family gathering.

Live seafood, like clams, crab, or lobster cannot be frozen, but they should last for a couple days if you keep them in an open container on ice in a cool, dark place. (Note: Do not cover the live seafood with ice as marine seafood will quickly die in fresh water.)

Also remember that live seafood needs air to breathe, so always remove them from the bag or container they were sold in. To properly store live shellfish, wrap in damp paper and store in the refrigerator with ice packs to keep as cold as possible, but do not freeze.

You should eat your seafood within three days of purchase if kept fresh, one or two days if kept alive. If you are going to remember one rule when it comes to caring for your seafood, remember this one—fresh seafood is best when consumed the day of purchase. The longer it sits, the quicker it deteriorates, as most fresh seafood has already been in transit four to six days before reaching the market.

If you will not be eating your purchase right away, go ahead and freeze it in a ziptop bag. Most fish species freeze well. You don't want to wait a few days and then decide to freeze. When you're ready to eat, take your fish out of the freezer and place the bag in a bowl of cold water until thawed. We do not recommend freezing live shellfish.

Finally, although we are introducing you to a variety of fish and shellfish—the species we serve at Bluewater Grill—keep in mind many other species are out there for you to try. Feel free to experiment, try those other fish, and see what you like best. Regardless of what you choose, always remember to buy from a reliable source, and always buy fresh whenever possible.

SUSTAINABILITY

We're sure you've heard the term *sustainable seafood*. But what does it mean? In a nutshell, it's seafood, whether fished or farmed correctly, which can exist in the long term without compromising the species' survival or the integrity of the surrounding ecosystem. It also means you—our guest and home cook—have the power to make a difference through the choices you make when purchasing seafood, just like we do at Bluewater Grill. As you make the proper choices, the demand influences the supply, which ultimately brings more sustainable seafood into the marketplace.

Our goal is to bring you those fish and shellfish from well-managed fisheries committed to seafood sustainability—essentially the seafood you'll find throughout the pages of this book—to your kitchen table to be enjoyed by you and your friends and family.

SIGNATURE COCKTAILS AS WE SET SAIL

As avid boaters, we enjoy "boat drinks" when on the water. Our boat drinks consist of cocktails made with rum, tequila, wine, or vodka, served either on the rocks, blended, or frozen. Personally, we prefer rum. In fact, I love rum so much we developed our own rum brand, which we call Catalina Rum Company. We sell the concoction exclusively at our restaurants. We have a light rum from Jamaica and a dark rum from the Dominican Republic with labels designed to commemorate the Catalina Island experience. My two favorite rum drinks in this chapter are the Captain's Mai Tai and Cucumber Mojito.

CATALINA
RUM COMPANY
40%
DARK
CATALINA

RUM CONCOCTIONS

CAPTAIN'S MAI TAI

The mai tai was invented by Victor Jules Bergeron Jr., also known as Trader Vic, in 1944. Bergeron was the owner of a tiki restaurant in Oakland, California. He tested the drink on two friends from Tahiti, who exclaimed, "mai tai-roa aé!" This means "out of this world—the best!" in Tahitian. Our version of the Mai Tai is the classic Trader Vic recipe and is the same recipe enjoyed at many of our favorite yacht clubs and on our boats during the summer season. We love it so much, we had an enamel mug created featuring the recipe and our favorite yacht club flags, which we offer at all our restaurants.

MAKES 1 COCKTAIL

1 ounce white rum
1 ounce dark rum
½ ounce triple sec
¼ ounce orgeat
¼ ounce simple syrup
½ ounce fresh lime juice
½ ounce dark rum floater
Garnish: lime wedge and Luxardo cherry

Add the white and dark rums, triple sec, orgeat, simple syrup, and lime juice to a shaker. Fill with crushed ice and shake vigorously. Pour the contents including the ice into a double old-fashioned glass. Float the dark rum (Meyer's or Gosling's black seal rum) on top. Garnish and serve.

CUCUMBER MOJITO

Havana, Cuba, is the birthplace of the mojito, although its exact origin is a subject of debate. It was known that the native people had remedies for various tropical illnesses, so a small boarding party went ashore on Cuba and came back with ingredients for an effective medicine. Our version of the classic mojito adds muddled cucumber for a refreshing and attractive cocktail. Enjoyed on hot summer days, the cucumber ribbon adds an exotic and fresh look.

MAKES 1 COCKTAIL

2 thick cucumber slices (peeled)
6 fresh mint leaves
2 ounces white rum
1 ounce fresh lime juice
¾ ounce agave syrup
Club soda, as needed
Garnish: Cucumber ribbon and mint sprig bouquet

Add the cucumber and mint leaves to a shaker and lightly muddle. Add the rum, lime juice, and agave syrup and fill with ice. Shake vigorously and pour the contents including the ice into a mason jar. Top with club soda and stir. Using a mandolin or sharp knife, cut strips lengthwise of cucumber 4 to 6 inches long, the width of the cucumber, and ⅛ inch thick, and place on bamboo skewer. Garnish and serve.

EL CUBANO

This drink is our cocktail to shake off the cobwebs from a late night since it contains sugar and caffeine and a little "hair of the dog." Unlike a Cuba Libre (rum and Coke), which can be sweet, this version is lighter and crisper and very refreshing. Named after its Cuban origin, it translates to "the Cuban."

MAKES 1 COCKTAIL

2 ounces dark rum
½ ounce Coca-Cola
1 ounce soda water
2 lime wedges, juiced
Garnish: Fresh lime wedge

Add the rum, cola, soda water, and lime juice to a double rocks glass filled with ice. Stir, garnish with a fresh lime wedge, and serve.

MARGARITAS

CLASSIC MARGARITA

The margarita is the national drink of Mexico and, as frequent visitors to the Baja Peninsula cities of Cabo San Lucas, La Paz, and Loreto, we have developed a true love of this cocktail. While there are conflicting stories of the origin of the margarita, we favor the one that it is named after actress Rita Hayworth (whose real name is Margarita Cansino) when she was performing in Tijuana in the 1940s. No matter the history of the drink, the margarita has become a staple in Southern California.

MAKES 1 COCKTAIL

1 lime wedge
Coarse salt, as needed
2 ounces blanco tequila
1 ounce triple sec
1 ounce fresh lime juice
Garnish: Lime wedge

Run a lime wedge around the rim of a double old-fashioned glass. Dip the rim in coarse salt and set aside.

Add the tequila, triple sec, and lime juice to a shaker. Fill with ice and shake vigorously. Pour the contents including the ice into the prepared glass. Garnish and serve.

COCONUT MARGARITA

The piña colada has a way of making the taste of rum disappear, so many a novice drinker has fallen victim to this rum-based drink. We decided it was better to use tequila, which stands up better to the taste of coconut so you can taste the alcohol. The tropical ingredients always make us smile since it brings back memories of Hawaiian vacations spent at the Grand Wailea or the Outrigger Canoe Club.

COCO MIX
MAKES ½ CUP

¼ cup Coco Lopez Coconut Cream
1 ounce fresh pineapple juice
1 ounce unsweetened coconut milk

COCONUT MARGARITA
MAKES 1 COCKTAIL

Toasted coconut flakes
2 ounces blanco tequila
½ ounce triple sec
½ ounce fresh lime juice
1 ounce Coco Mix + enough for rim
Garnish: Pineapple slice

To make the Coco Mix: Add the coconut cream, pineapple juice, and coconut milk to a glass jar. Mix well to combine, then seal and refrigerate until needed, up to 2 weeks.

Dampen the rim of a double old-fashioned glass. Dip the rim in the Coco Mix and then the toasted coconut flakes and set aside.

Add the tequila, triple sec, lime juice, and Coco Mix to a shaker. Fill with ice and shake vigorously. Pour the contents including the ice into the prepared glass. Garnish and serve.

PILIKIA MARGARITA

Named after our swordfish harpoon boat *Pilikia* (which means "trouble" in Hawaiian), the Pilikia is a twist on the classic margarita that uses agave syrup and orange bitters. While we have never gotten into trouble while drinking Pilikias, we have had a lot of fun shaking them up aboard *Pilikia* and sharing them with our family, friends, and guests.

MAKES 1 COCKTAIL

1 lime wedge
Coarse salt, as needed
2 ounces blanco tequila
½ ounce triple sec
1½ ounces fresh lime juice
½ ounce agave syrup
2 dashes orange bitters
Garnish: Lime wedge

Run a lime wedge around the rim of a double old-fashioned glass. Dip the rim in coarse salt and set aside.

Add the tequila, triple sec, lime juice, agave syrup, and bitters to a shaker. Fill with ice and shake vigorously. Pour the contents including the ice into the prepared glass. Garnish and serve.

SERRANO MARGARITA

The serrano is a hot chili pepper that adds a touch of "heat" to this take on the classic margarita. As the popularity of tequila has exploded in the last few years, mixologists have developed countless tequila-based drinks in the last few years. Our favorite is the Serrano, which opens the tastebuds to make any meal at Bluewater Grill more enjoyable.

MAKES 1 COCKTAIL

1 lime wedge
Tajín, as needed
1 or 2 thick slices serrano pepper
2 ounces blanco tequila
½ ounce triple sec
1½ ounces fresh lime juice
½ ounce agave syrup
¼ ounce fresh orange juice
Garnish: Lime wedge

Run a lime wedge around the rim of a double old-fashioned glass. Dip the rim in Tajín and set aside.

Add the serrano pepper to a shaker and lightly muddle. Add the tequila, triple sec, lime juice, agave syrup, and orange juice and fill with ice. Shake vigorously and pour the contents include the ice into the prepared glass. Garnish and serve.

WINE-BASED

RED SANGRIA

Sangria, a traditional Spanish beverage, is a refreshing mix of wine, fruit, and other flavorful additions. It's enjoyed globally for its vibrant, festive character. Our classic red sangria is made with red wine, typically a bold variety like Rioja or Tempranillo, and enhanced with sliced fruits like oranges, limes, and apples. It's often sweetened with a splash of orange juice and brandy and topped with soda water for extra zest.

Our white sangria is a lighter variation, using white wine such as Sauvignon Blanc, Pinot Grigio, or Spanish Verdejo to keep with the theme. We then add fruits like apples, peaches, berries, and grapes, to create a crisp and fruity flavor profile. Both versions can be customized or fortified with other liqueurs for added complexity. Served chilled at summer gatherings, sangria embodies conviviality and versatility, making it a perennial crowd-pleaser.

MAKES 1 QUART

1 (750 ml) bottle Spanish Rioja red wine
4 ounces fresh orange juice
¼ cup brandy
2 cups mixed fresh fruit (apples, peaches, berries, oranges, lemons)
4 ounces club soda or sparkling water
Garnish: Orange and lime wheel, apple slices

Fill a quart pitcher with the wine, orange juice, brandy, and fresh fruit. Let sit 8 to 12 hours.

To serve, fill a wineglass with ice. Add one orange wheel, lime wheel, and two slices of apple. Pour the sangria over the ice, top with 1 ounce club soda, and serve.

WHITE SANGRIA

MAKES 1 QUART

3 cups mixed slices of apples, peaches, strawberries, oranges, lemons, cucumber
¼ cup sugar
¼ cup brandy
¼ cup triple sec
1 (750 ml) bottle chilled Spanish Verdejo white wine
Club soda, optional

Add the fruit to a large bowl along with the sugar. Mix well and refrigerate overnight, tossing the fruit occasionally.

The next day, add the brandy and triple sec to the bowl with the fruit. Mix well and transfer all the contents to a large pitcher. Add the chilled wine and stir to combine. Refrigerate overnight.

To serve, fill a wineglass with ice. Add some of the soaked fruit into the glass, then pour the sangria over the ice. Top with club soda, if desired, and serve. Note: The sangria will keep up to 2 days in the refrigerator with the fruit; up to 1 week without the fruit.

VODKA SIPPERS

AMERICAN MULE

Our version of the Moscow Mule uses premium ginger beer and American vodka in place of the Russian variety that the drink originally contained when it was conceived in the 1940s. The drink originated in Los Angeles when Jack Morgan (owner of the Cock n' Bull on the Sunset Strip), and his pal John Martin, the original importer of Smirnoff Russian vodka, met Sophie Berezinski, a Russian immigrant who had a supply of copper mugs she could not sell. Sophie relentlessly traipsed across Los Angeles convincing restaurants and bars to sell the Moscow Mule using Smirnoff vodka and her copper mugs and an iconic cocktail was born. The copper mug conducts the ice-cold drink and frosts up, so it is cool and refreshing when dining on one of our patios during the hot Southern California summer.

MAKES 1 COCKTAIL

2 ounces premium vodka
½ ounce Amaro Averna
1 ounce fresh lime juice
Fever Tree Ginger Beer, as needed
Garnish: Lime wheel

Add the vodka, amaro, and lime juice to a copper mule mug. Fill with ice and top with ginger beer. Stir, garnish, and serve.

BLOODY MARY

The Bloody Mary is a classic cocktail celebrated for its bold, savory flavor and versatility. We like to make ours with vodka and our house-made Bloody Mary Mix. First created in the 1920s, the Bloody Mary's origins are debated, with ties to Paris and New York. Known as a popular brunch drink, its balance of flavors makes it a favorite hangover remedy and culinary delight.

MAKES 1 OR MORE COCKTAILS

BLOODY MARY MIX: MAKES 1¾ QUARTS

1 (46 ounce; 5 ¾ cups) can tomato juice
¾ cup prepared horseradish
½ cup fresh lemon juice (from 3 to 4 lemons)
½ cup Worcestershire sauce
2 teaspoons kosher salt
2 teaspoons fresh cracked black pepper
2 teaspoons Tabasco sauce
Premium vodka (2 ounces per serving)
Garnish: Lime wedges, olives, pickled beans, chilled prawns

Add the tomato juice, horseradish, lemon juice, Worcestershire sauce, salt, pepper, and Tabasco sauce to a bottle or container and refrigerate until needed. Shake well before using.

To serve, fill cocktail glass with ice and set aside. Note: Add a salt or celery salt rim, if desired.

Fill a cocktail shaker with ice. Add 2 ounces of vodka per serving along with 4 ounces of the Bloody Mary Mix. Shake for 10 seconds and strain into the prepared glass. Garnish and serve.

BUFFALO MILK

The Buffalo milk is a concoction made famous on Santa Catalina Island to commemorate the herd of American buffalo (bison) that was brought to Catalina in the 1920s for the filming of an adaptation of Zane Grey's book *Vanishing America*. Over the years, the herd has expanded and thinned leaving the island with about 150 permanent "residents" that remain as a tourist attraction. Our Buffalo milk is not the kind you might think of; rather, it is a creamy and delicious libation best enjoyed in Avalon on Catalina Island. It is not uncommon when hiking ashore to come across a bison, which can be very dangerous and must be given a wide berth.

MAKES 1 COCKTAIL

1 ounce premium vodka
½ ounce Kahlúa
½ ounce white crème de cacao
½ ounce banana liqueur
2 ounces whole milk
Garnish: 1 dollop whipped cream and freshly grated nutmeg

Add the vodka, Kahlúa, white crème de cacao, banana liqueur, and milk to a bar blender. Add a handful of ice and blend until smooth. Pour into a mason jar. Garnish and serve.

CALIFORNIA SHORES

CALIFORNIA SHORES

The California coastline, stretching over 800 miles, is a seafood lover's paradise. With the Pacific Ocean providing a bountiful array of fresh catches, enjoying seafood along the California shore is an experience that tantalizes the senses and captures the essence of coastal living.

With our five seaside locations nestled within the state, Bluewater Grill invites you to experience oceanfront dining at its best. Imagine sitting on a sundrenched patio overlooking the sea, the salty breeze ruffling your hair as you savor a hearty bowl of our San Francisco Cioppino. Each seafood-laden bite of fresh clams, mussels, shrimp, scallops, squid, crab, and succulent fish immediately transports you to the cool waters where they were harvested. California is renowned for its sustainable shellfish and species such as yellowtail and white sea bass, known for their unique flavor and freshness.

As you travel farther down the coast, our culinary offerings evolve, reflecting the diversity of the region. Indulge in succulent Dungeness crab, steamed to perfection and served either chilled with our house-made cocktail sauce and garlic aioli, or enjoy our crisp Seafood Louie Salad, loaded with mounds of mouthwatering crab, shrimp, and an array of garden-fresh vegetables, as you gaze out over the expansive and picturesque coastline.

Near the bottom of the California coastline, before it dips into Baja, the fusion of diverse cultures is reflected in our innovative seafood dishes. From locally harpooned swordfish, blackened and bursting with fresh flavors that's served with our Chipotle Rice and Roasted Corn and Avocado Relish to our Panko-Crusted Calamari Steak so tender it seems to melt in your mouth, the options are endless. The vibrant seafood scene ensures there is always something new to try, whether it's at our place, a gathering at your family home, or a casual beachside picnic with friends.

Venturing into southern California, our seafood scene continues to impress. Spiny lobsters are boiled briefly before being split, seasoned with butter, garlic, and spices, and then flat-grilled, offering a unique taste compared to their Atlantic counterparts. Served with warm tortillas, refried beans, and a simple squeeze of lime, their sweet and delicate meat is a true delight and brings back memories of surf trips to Puerto Nuevo, Mexico, on the Baja peninsula.

DUNGENESS CRAB

A traditional Christmas Eve dinner at our home includes Dungeness crab. The meal, which is more of a communal feast and hands-on experience, features freshly cooked crabs loaded with snowy white meat that is sweet, succulent, and pulled straight from the shell. We'll cook our crabs, just like we do at the restaurant, by either boiling or steaming, and then we'll serve them with melted butter and our homemade cocktail sauce and garlic aioli, or sometimes a bowl filled with our zesty Crab Louis Dressing. In Italian American communities, crab may be part of the "Feast of the Seven Fishes," a Christmas Eve celebration featuring multiple seafood dishes served alongside fresh-baked sourdough bread, crisp salads, and a bevy of pastas. For many families, like mine, crabbing during the holiday season is a time-honored tradition. We'll gather to catch, cook, and enjoy our bounty, making crabbing and the culinary experience a significant social and familial event.

FISHING FOR DUNGENESS CRAB

Recreational fishing for Dungeness crab has a rich history along the West Coast of the United States, particularly California, Oregon, and Washington, including Dungeness Spit, where the crab's name originates. Long before European settlers arrived in America, the indigenous peoples of the Pacific Northwest harvested Dungeness crab using handmade traps and other traditional methods. Crabbing was an important food source and cultural practice. As European settlers arrived in the nineteenth century, they adopted and adapted local crabbing techniques. The development of commercial fisheries during this period influenced recreational crabbing. By the early twentieth century, recreational crabbing was growing in popularity, particularly as coastal communities developed and transportation improved, making coastal areas more accessible for recreation. Initially, recreational crabbers used simple methods like baited lines and hoop nets. Over time, more sophisticated traps and pots became popular, allowing for efficient and effective crabbing. Today, we use a variety of gear, including ring nets and star traps, often baited with fish heads, chicken, or a punctured can of tuna that the seals can't steal. Recreational crabbing is a cherished tradition for our family on trips to Puget Sound and the Inside Passage.

CRAB AND SHRIMP LOUIE

Here's a West Coast classic renowned for its fresh flavors and satisfying textures. Featuring succulent Dungeness crabmeat atop a bed of crisp lettuce, this refreshing salad is adorned with ripe tomatoes, English cucumber, hard-boiled egg, and creamy avocado. It also features our house-made Louie dressing, which lends a delightful zing to each bite. Originating from the West Coast in the early twentieth century, Crab Louie began popping up at restaurants on the West Coast in the early 1900s, most notably at San Francisco's Hotel Francis and the Davenport Hotel in Washington in 1910. Today, this "King of All Salads" has evolved into a timeless favorite at Bluewater Grill, where it's celebrated for its simplicity and delectable combination of fresh ingredients. We were introduced to this salad on trips to Fisherman's Wharf with our parents and at the legendary Tadich Grill in downtown San Francisco.

SERVES 1 OR 2

LOUIE DRESSING
MAKES 2 CUPS

1 cup mayonnaise
3 tablespoons chili sauce
1 tablespoon sweet pickle relish
2 tablespoons peeled and finely diced yellow onion
2 tablespoons seeded and finely diced bell pepper
¼ cup finely diced celery
1 tablespoon finely diced fresh Italian flat-leaf parsley
1 tablespoon fresh lemon juice
1 garlic clove, peeled and minced
1 teaspoon Tabasco hot sauce
1 hard-boiled egg, peeled and chopped

LOUIE SALAD

3 ounces lettuce mix (mesclun, red leaf, green leaf, iceberg)
Louie Dressing
8 grape tomatoes, sliced in half
¼ cup (2 ounces) medium-diced English cucumber
1 hard-boiled egg, sliced
¼ avocado, thinly sliced
½ cup (4 ounces) fresh Dungeness crabmeat
Paprika, for garnish
1 green onion, cut 3 inches long, thinly sliced

PREPARE THE LOUIE DRESSING

Add the mayonnaise, chili sauce, relish, onion, bell pepper, celery, parsley, lemon juice, garlic, hot sauce, and egg in the bowl of a standup mixer with paddle attachment. Mix, while scraping the sides of the bowl as necessary, until incorporated. Refrigerate in a sealed container until ready to use, up to 4 weeks.

PREPARE THE SALAD

Place the lettuce mix in a large pasta bowl and top with the Louie Dressing. Arrange the tomato and cucumber in three separate areas. Add the sliced egg to one side. Arrange the avocado and crab on top of the dressing in the middle of the salad.

FINISHING THE DISH

Sprinkle a little paprika on top of the crab, garnish with the green onion, and serve.

BEVERAGE SUGGESTION

Since this dish originated in San Francisco, we recommend pairing it with a Chardonnay from nearby Napa Valley. Our favorite is Trefethen, from Oak Knoll.

DUNGENESS CRAB WITH HOMEMADE COCKTAIL SAUCE AND GARLIC AIOLI

Cocktail sauce, if you're not familiar, gained its name and notoriety from the classic shrimp cocktail made famous in 1967 by British celebrity chef Fanny Cradock. While seafood cocktails predate her recipe, she often receives credit for popularizing the name "cocktail sauce." To this day, oyster bars and seafood restaurants like Bluewater Grill still use cocktail sauce as a standard accompaniment to chilled shrimp, crab, raw oysters, and clams. The sauce sometimes omits horseradish and instead serves it on the side so guests can add their desired amount based on the level of "heat" they prefer. We use a brand of horseradish from Morehouse named Atomic Horseradish, which is famous for its extra hot and consistent heat level.

SERVES 4

DUNGENESS CRAB

4 (1½ pounds) live Dungeness crabs
Lemon wedges, for serving
Louie Dressing (page 48)
½ cup unsalted butter
1 tablespoon grated garlic (from 3 large cloves)
1 teaspoon kosher salt
1 teaspoon grated lemon zest, plus ¼ cup fresh lemon juice (from 1 or 2 large lemons)
2 tablespoons chopped fresh Italian flat-leaf parsley

COCKTAIL SAUCE
MAKES 2¼ CUPS

2 cups chili sauce
2 tablespoons minced yellow onion
1½ tablespoons minced celery
1 teaspoon Worcestershire sauce
2 tablespoons prepared horseradish
¾ teaspoon Tabasco sauce
2 tablespoons fresh lemon juice

GARLIC AIOLI
MAKES 2½ CUPS

¼ cup chopped fresh garlic
1 tablespoon fresh lemon juice
1 tablespoon kosher salt
¼ cup extra-virgin olive oil
¼ cup water
2 cups mayonnaise

PREPARE THE CRABS

Fill a large stockpot with 1 inch of water and set over high heat. When the water comes to a boil, add the crabs. Cover and steam until the shells turn bright orange, about 20 minutes.

MAKE THE SAUCES

To make the Cocktail Sauce: Add the chili sauce, onion, celery, Worcestershire sauce, horseradish, Tabasco sauce, and lemon juice to a mixing bowl. Mix well to combine, then refrigerate until ready to serve. The sauce will keep in the refrigerator in a sealed container for about 1 week.

To make the Garlic Aioli: Add the garlic, lemon juice, salt, olive oil, water, and mayonnaise to a blender and blend until smooth. Transfer to a bowl and refrigerate until ready to use.. The sauce will keep in the refrigerator in a sealed container for several days.

FINISHING THE DISH

If serving the crabs chilled, remove the crabs from the pot and immediately plunge into an ice bath. Let the crabs chill for 10 minutes then remove. Serve (1 crab per person) with sliced lemons and our Garlic Aioli, or try it with our Cocktail Sauce, and/or our Crab Louie Dressing. Suggested sides include warm San Francisco sourdough bread and a fresh garden salad with a light vinaigrette-based dressing.

If serving the crabs hot, do not plunge them into the ice bath, but set them aside until ready to serve. Add the butter, garlic, and salt to a small saucepan over medium-high heat. Cook, stirring occasionally, until the butter is melted and foaming, 3 to 5 minutes. Remove from the heat and stir in the lemon zest, lemon juice, and parsley. Serve (1 crab per person) with the lemon-garlic butter, lemon wedges, and the same sides suggested for the chilled crabs.

BEVERAGE SUGGESTION

Acrobat, Pinot Gris from Washington with its bright acidity and herbaceous notes, is a wonderful match for the sweetness of the Dungeness crab.

DIVING FOR SPINY LOBSTER

Recreational diving and hoop netting for the California spiny lobster is a popular activity along the Southern California coast. I have spent many nights aboard our boat *Solitaire*, night free diving the season opener or early October or hoop netting with friends and family at Catalina Island. The spiny lobster, known for its lack of claws and spiny exoskeleton, is highly prized for its sweet, succulent meat.

Spiny lobsters inhabit rocky reefs, kelp forests, and other underwater structures from central California to Baja California, Mexico. The recreational spiny lobster season in California typically runs from early October to mid-March, aligning with regulations designed to protect lobster populations during their breeding season.

Lobsters are nocturnal, making night diving the most effective method. Divers use underwater lights to spot and capture lobsters as they come out to forage. Divers use snorkels, fins, wetsuits, and scuba gear if diving deeper. A lobster gauge is essential to ensure that captured lobsters meet the legal size requirement (minimum carapace length of 3.25 inches). Divers catch lobsters by hand, using careful techniques to avoid damaging the lobster or the surrounding habitat. It requires skill to grab them swiftly, as they can quickly dart away.

Hoop nets are specially designed for capturing lobsters. They consist of a circular frame with netting that lays flat on the ocean floor and captures lobsters as they enter. Fresh fish, squid, or other seafood scraps are used as bait to attract lobsters into the net. Nets are typically set in rocky areas, kelp beds, or near reefs where lobsters are known to forage. Similar to diving, hoop netting is most effective at night. Nets are checked frequently to minimize bycatch and ensure lobsters do not escape.

Lobster diving and hoop netting are often social activities, with families and friends joining together for outings. This fosters a sense of community and shared tradition. Surf trips to Baja, like with my son or those featured in the film *Endless Summer*, invariably feature a stop at Puerto Nuevo for lobster and beer after surfing K-38 or a local surf break.

CALIFORNIA SPINY LOBSTER "PUERTO NUEVO STYLE"

Lobster served Puerto Nuevo Style is a beloved coastal dish that highlights California's fresh, succulent spiny crustacean. In this preparation, the lobster is split, then pan-fried or grilled, bringing out its rich, sweet flavors. Traditionally served alongside fluffy rice, refried beans, and warm flour tortillas, it allows guests to create their own flavorful bites by wrapping the lobster in the tortillas with beans and salsa. This simple yet hearty dish celebrates the natural taste of the spiny lobster, making it a must-try when visiting Puerto Nuevo, the Baja California coast, or Bluewater Grill.

SERVES 4

1 (12-ounce) bottle Mexican beer
1 tablespoon + 2 teaspoons kosher salt, divided
4 (1¼–1½ pounds) live California spiny lobsters
2 teaspoons Spanish paprika
1 teaspoon fresh cracked black pepper
1 cup Clarified Butter (page 72)

PREPARE THE LOBSTER

Fill a large stockpot with 1 inch of water, half the beer, and 1 tablespoon of salt over high heat. Drink the other half while cooking. When the pot comes to a boil, add the lobster. Cover and steam for 2 to 3 minutes. (Note: We are just parcooking them at this point.) Remove the lobster and set aside. When cool to the touch, split the lobsters in half lengthwise with a kitchen knife, and remove and discard the stomach and intestinal tract from the tail. Set the lobster aside.

Add the paprika, remaining 2 teaspoons salt, and black pepper to a small bowl and mix to combine. Season the lobster tails with the mixture.

FINISHING THE DISH

Add the Clarified Butter to a large cast-iron skillet and heat over medium heat. When the butter is sizzling, place the lobsters, cut-side down, into the skillet and pan-fry for 5 minutes on each side, or until the thickest part of the tail meat is tender and a "crust" has formed. Remove, drain on paper towels, and serve immediately or place the lobsters in a warm (200°F) oven until ready to serve with corn or flour tortillas, refried beans, Chipotle Rice (page 82), and lime wedges.

BEVERAGE SUGGESTION

Mexican beer, such as Tecate, Pacifico, or a microbrew Mexican-style lager served with salt and lime wedges.

GEMELLI PASTA WITH PESTO, SHRIMP, AND SCALLOPS

Gemelli pasta, with its unique twisted shape, pairs beautifully with shrimp and scallops, creating a dish that is both visually appealing and flavorful. The pasta's spiral design traps sauces and enhances the flavor with every bite. When cooked al dente, Gemelli provides the perfect texture to complement the tenderness of seafood like shrimp and scallops.

In this dish, the sweetness of the shrimp and the rich, buttery flavor of scallops contrast wonderfully with our savory pesto. Fresh mushrooms, asparagus, garlic, and white wine further elevate the flavors, adding brightness to the seafood while the natural brininess of the shrimp and scallops blend harmoniously with the pasta, making each forkful a delightful experience.

When you're looking for a perfect summer meal that's elegant enough for a special occasion, try this comforting yet refined dish.

SERVES 4

PESTO | MAKES ½ CUP

¼ cup toasted pine nuts
1 tablespoon fresh lemon juice
1 tablespoon fresh garlic cloves
¼ teaspoon fresh cracked black pepper
1 packed cup fresh basil leaves
¼ cup extra-virgin olive oil
2 tablespoons freshly grated Parmesan cheese

GEMELLI PASTA

2 tablespoons extra-virgin olive oil + ½ cup, divided
1 tablespoon sea salt
16 ounces dry Italian Gemelli pasta
1 cup cremini mushrooms
16 (16/20) raw shrimp, peeled & deveined, tail on (see page 60 for sizing)
12 fresh asparagus spears (about 1 pound), cut into 1-inch pieces on the bias
16 (30/40) scallops (see page 60 for sizing)
1½ tablespoon chopped garlic
½ cup Chablis or Sauvignon Blanc
3 cups heavy cream
1½ tablespoons sea salt and fresh cracked black pepper 50/50 mix
1 tablespoon chopped fresh Italian flat-leaf parsley

PREPARE THE PESTO

Add the pine nuts, lemon juice, garlic, and pepper to a food processor. Pulse until well chopped. Add the basil and pulse until combined. With food processor running, drizzle in the olive oil and pulse until combined. Add the cheese and pulse briefly to incorporate. Transfer to a small bowl and set aside until ready to use. Any leftovers can be stored in an airtight container and kept in the refrigerator up to 7 days.

PREPARE THE PASTA

Add 5 quarts of water to a large pot along with 1 tablespoon of sea salt and 1 tablespoon of olive oil. Bring to a boil over high heat. Add the pasta and cook, stirring occasionally, for 8 to 10 minutes, or until al dente. Drain and set aside.

PREPARE THE SAUCE

Add the remaining olive oil to a large sauté pan over medium-high heat. When the oil is shimmering, add the mushrooms and sauté, stirring occasionally, for 1 minute. Add the

shrimp and asparagus and cook for 1 minute. Add the scallops and garlic and cook for 30 seconds then deglaze the pan with the white wine. Once the wine is absorbed, about 2 minutes, add the cream, salt and pepper mix, and cook while stirring until the sauce is reduced by two thirds, about 5 minutes. Add the pesto to the pan and mix, and then add cooked pasta and toss to incorporate.

FINISHING THE DISH

Transfer the pasta to a large pasta bowl, top with the parsley, a sprinkle of Parmesan, and a grind of fresh pepper. Garnish with a basil leaf and serve.

BEVERAGE SUGGESTION

Italian Trebbiano Toscano from Antinori Villa Fassinio or a Li Veli Askos Verdeca from Puglia.

A NOTE ON SHRIMP SIZING

You've likely seen shrimp at your local grocery store with numbers like 51/60, 41/50, and 31/40. These numbers are important to determining the size and number of the shrimp that make up one pound. The slash between numbers is simply the range of shrimp in one pound. In the above examples, there would be 51 to 60 shrimp per pound (considered small shrimp), 41 to 50 shrimp per pound (medium), and 31 to 40 shrimp per pound (large). There's also jumbo (16/20) all the way up to super colossal (6/8). When you buy shrimp, a good rule of thumb is that the smaller the numbers, the bigger the shrimp.

A NOTE ON SCALLOP SIZING

When purchasing scallops, sizing is an important factor to consider, as it can impact both the cooking process and the overall dining experience. Scallops are typically sized by the number per pound, with a lower number indicating larger scallops and a higher number indicating smaller ones.

U10: This size means there are fewer than 10 scallops per pound. These are the largest and most prized, often used in high-end dishes where presentation and texture are important.

10/20: This range indicates there are between 10 and 20 scallops per pound. These are medium to large scallops, commonly used in a variety of dishes, offering a balance between size and cost.

20/30: This size range means there are between 20 and 30 scallops per pound. These are smaller than the above sizes but still suitable for many recipes. They are often used in recipes where scallops are not the main focus.

30/40: This indicates there are between 30 and 40 scallops per pound. These are smaller and more affordable, suitable for dishes where the scallops are mixed with other ingredients.

When choosing scallops, consider the intended preparation and presentation. Larger scallops are ideal for searing and showcasing as the main ingredient, while smaller scallops work well in dishes like stews or pastas.

PANKO CALAMARI STEAK WITH HOMEMADE TARTAR SAUCES

Fishing for Humboldt squid off Newport Beach from our boat is an exciting and messy adventure. These large, powerful creatures are known for their aggressive nature and quick movements, making them a thrilling catch, but when they come aboard prepare to get "inked." We wear our foul-weather gear, and it is pandemonium when a six-foot squid is in the cockpit. Cleaning squid is also one of the most difficult things to do and is like wrestling a greased watermelon. While fresh, locally caught squid is fantastic because everything tastes better when you catch it yourself, the frozen option is just as good with none of the work of catching and cleaning giant squid. Succulent calamari, tenderized and coated in our crispy breading, delivers a satisfying crunch with every bite. We find the breading, seasoned with a little salt and pepper, enhances the natural sweetness of the calamari while adding a savory dimension. We'll then pan-fry the squid to perfection, so the exterior achieves a golden-brown hue, locking in moisture and preserving the tenderness of the calamari within. Served with our house-made Tartar Sauce and Grilled Lemon Half, these are a must when you're ready to sink your teeth into a tender and crispy bite of seafood that's iconic to California waters.

SERVES 4

TARTAR SAUCE—NEW AGE
MAKES ¾ CUP

1 small yellow onion, peeled and finely minced
1 tablespoon white wine vinegar
½ cup mayonnaise
3 tablespoons unsweetened dill pickle relish
1 tablespoon capers, drained
1 tablespoon finely chopped fresh dill
1 tablespoon finely chopped fresh Italian flat-leaf parsley
1 tablespoon fresh lemon juice

TARTAR SAUCE—OLD SCHOOL
MAKES ¾ CUP

½ cup mayonnaise
¼ cup yellow mustard
½ cup pureed celery
1 small yellow onion, peeled and minced
¼ cup sweet pickle relish
1 tablespoon finely chopped fresh dill
1 tablespoon finely chopped fresh Italian flat-leaf parsley
1 tablespoon fresh lemon juice

GRILLED LEMON HALVES

4 lemons, cut in half

CALAMARI

4 (5–6 ounce) squid (calamari) steaks
1 cup all-purpose flour
1 tablespoon kosher salt
1 tablespoon freshly cracked black pepper
3 large eggs + 1 tablespoon water (egg wash)
2 cups panko breadcrumbs
½ cup canola oil
Chopped fresh Italian flat-leaf parsley, as needed, for garnish

PREPARE THE TARTAR SAUCE—NEW AGE

Soak the minced onion in the white wine vinegar for 15 minutes, then drain. Add the onion to a mixing bowl along with the mayonnaise, relish, capers, dill, parsley, and lemon juice. Mix until well incorporated. Place in a sealed container and refrigerate until needed, up to 1 week. Note: For a sweeter version, substitute sweet pickle relish and add ½ teaspoon of Dijon mustard.

PREPARE THE TARTAR SAUCE—OLD SCHOOL

Add the mayonnaise, mustard, celery, onion, relish, dill, parsley, and lemon juice to a mixing bowl. Mix until well incorporated. Place in a sealed container and refrigerate until needed, up to 2 weeks.

PREPARE THE GRILLED LEMON HALVES

Prepare an outdoor grill or cast-iron skillet over the stove to medium heat. Place the lemon halves, flesh-side down, on the grill or pan. Allow the lemons to caramelize on one side for 1 to 2 minutes. Remove and set aside.

PREPARE THE CALAMARI

Preheat the oven to 200°F.

Place one calamari steak on a cutting board and cover with plastic wrap. Using the smooth side of a kitchen mallet, pound the steak until about ⅛ inch thick. Repeat the process with the remaining steaks.

Next, set up a dredging station by filling one bowl with the flour. Season the flour with salt and pepper and mix to combine. Add the egg wash to a second bowl and the breadcrumbs to a third bowl.

Dredge the calamari steaks first in the seasoned flour, gently shaking off the excess flour. Then dredge in the egg wash, allowing the extra egg to drip back into the bowl. Then place in the breadcrumbs and use your fingers to help coat both sides of the calamari. Set the steaks aside.

Add the oil to a large, high-sided sauté pan over high heat. Heat the oil to 350°F. Use a candy thermometer to check the temperature. When the oil is ready, carefully add one steak to the oil and fry until the steak is golden brown, about 3 minutes. Transfer the fried steak to a paper towel–lined plate and place in the preheated oven to keep warm. Repeat with the remaining calamari steaks.

FINISHING THE DISH

When ready to serve, cut the calamari steaks in half on the bias and arrange in a shingled pattern on four large plates. Include a side of Tartar Sauce (whichever version you prefer) and Grilled Lemon Halves. Garnish with chopped parsley and serve. Suggested Sides: Coleslaw.

BEVERAGE SUGGESTION

We prefer a carbonated beverage like La Marca or Ruffino Prosecco to cut through the oil used when frying. The slight sweetness of a prosecco also cleanses the palate and enhances the subtle flavor of the squid.

SAUTÉED CALAMARI STEAK

Sautéed calamari steak is a tender and flavorful seafood dish that highlights the delicate taste of squid. We feel sautéed calamari steak is superior in taste and texture to abalone. At the restaurant, we lightly season the steaks with salt and pepper and sauté in oil to maintain their tenderness. A brief cooking time is crucial to avoid toughness, resulting in a juicy, tender steak with a slightly crisp exterior. We'll then serve the steaks with a lemon caper sauce and a squeeze of fresh lemon juice, making this dish a delicious, elegant meal. SEE PHOTO (PAGE 63, BOTTOM).

SERVES 4

4 (5–6 ounce) squid (calamari) steaks
1 cup all-purpose flour
1 tablespoon kosher salt
1 tablespoon freshly cracked black pepper
½ cup canola or safflower oil
Lemon Caper Beurre Blanc (page 76)
4 Grilled Lemon Halves (page 65)
Chopped fresh Italian flat-leaf parsley, as needed, for garnish

PREPARE THE CALAMARI

Preheat the oven to 200°F.

Place one calamari steak on a cutting board and cover with plastic wrap. Using the smooth side of a kitchen mallet, pound the steak until about ⅛ inch thick. Repeat the process with the remaining steaks.

Next, set up a dredging station by filling a large bowl with the flour, salt, and pepper and mix to combine.

Add the oil to a large, deep-sided sauté pan over high heat. Heat the oil to 350°F. Use a candy thermometer to check the temperature.

Dredge the calamari steaks in the seasoned flour, gently shaking off the excess flour. Carefully add one steak to the oil and fry until the steak is golden brown, about 3 minutes. Transfer the fried steak to a paper towel–lined plate and place in the preheated oven to keep warm. Repeat with the remaining calamari steaks.

FINISHING THE DISH

Cut the calamari steaks in half on the bias and arrange in a shingled pattern on four large plates. Top with Lemon Caper Beurre Blanc. Garnish with Grilled Lemon Halves and chopped parsley and serve. Suggested Sides: Scalloped potatoes and wilted fresh spinach.

BEVERAGE SUGGESTION

A nice New Zealand Sauvignon Blanc with hints of fruit-forward flavor and lemon-lime character pair well with this dish. We love any Marlborough County like Oyster Bay or Cloudy Bay.

SAN FRANCISCO CIOPPINO

Cioppino, an Italian word derived from Ligurian's "ciuppin" (meaning fish stew), is a warm, robust seafood dish originating from Fisherman's Wharf in San Francisco. Developed in the late 1800s, when fisherman would gather after a long day on the water and cook a communal meal using the day's catch, cioppino embodies simplicity and abundance reflecting the city's rich maritime heritage. Today, the Italian American stew still represents the city's fishing community and the abundant seafood available. At Bluewater Grill, we like to serve our hearty cioppino with its vibrant and flavorful medley of fresh fish, shellfish, tomatoes, and herbs with crunchy sourdough bread. Growing up, we took family trips to San Francisco and would spend the day at Fisherman's Wharf and Ghirardelli Square and ride the cable cars. These trips always included hot bowls of freshly prepared cioppino at Alioto's or Scoma's.

SERVES 4

CIOPPINO SAUCE
MAKES 3 QUARTS

2 tablespoons extra-virgin olive oil
1 cup diced yellow onion
2 tablespoons chopped garlic
½ cup diced green bell pepper
¼ cup diced celery
1 teaspoon minced fresh oregano
1 teaspoon crushed red pepper flakes
1 bay leaf
2 teaspoons kosher or sea salt
2 teaspoons fresh cracked black pepper
1 teaspoon sugar
1½ cups Pinot Grigio (preferably Italian)
2 tablespoons Pernod liquor
1 (29-ounce) can peeled San Marzano tomatoes, blended
2 tablespoons tomato paste
1½ cups water
2½ cups clam juice

CIOPPINO

20 live Manila clams, scrubbed
20 live black mussels, cleaned and debearded (page 162)
1 pound fresh fish, skinned and cut into 1-inch pieces (choose from "steak" cut fish, not thin fillets, such as ¼ pound salmon, halibut, sea bass, and/or mahi mahi)
12 (16/20) raw shrimp, peeled and deveined (see page 60 for sizing)
½ pound squid tubes and tentacles
8 (U15) sea scallops (see page 60 for sizing)
1 cup picked fresh Dungeness crabmeat
2 tablespoons chopped fresh Italian flat-leaf parsley

PREPARE THE CIOPPINO SAUCE

Add the oil to a large stockpot over medium-high heat. Heat until the oil is shimmering. Add the onion, garlic, bell pepper, and celery. Cook, stirring occasionally, until tender, about 5 minutes. Add the oregano, red pepper flakes, bay leaf, salt, pepper, and sugar. Stir to combine. Add the wine and Pernod Liqueur and continue to cook until reduced by half. Add the tomatoes, tomato paste, water, and clam juice. Stir to combine. Bring to a boil, then

reduce heat to low and simmer for 30 minutes. Remove from heat, discard the bay leaf, and set aside until ready to use. The sauce can also be transferred to an airtight container and placed in the refrigerator up to 5 days.

PREPARE THE CIOPPINO

Add 3 quarts of Cioppino Sauce to a large, deep-sided sauté pan and bring to a simmer over medium heat. Add the clams and mussels, cover, and cook until they start to open, 3 to 5 minutes. Add the fish and shrimp, cover again, and cook for 3 to 5 minutes, or until the fish is almost cooked through. Add the squid and cook, uncovered, for 1 minute. Add the scallops and cook, uncovered, for 1 minute. Remove from heat.

FINISHING THE DISH

Equally divide the clams, mussels, fish, shrimp, squid, and scallops into 4 individual bowls. Discard any unopen clams and mussels. Top each bowl with ¼ cup of Dungeness crabmeat and gently pour the hot Cioppino Sauce over the seafood, filling each bowl. Garnish with parsley and serve immediately with a side of warm San Francisco sourdough or rustic bread.

BEVERAGE SUGGESTION

To celebrate the Cioppino's Italian and Californian heritage, select a Querceto, Chianti Classico from Tuscany or Gary Farrel Russian River Pinor Noir.

PETRALE SOLE (OR SAUTÉED SAND DABS) MEUNIÈRE

"Flatfish" is a catchall name for many different species of fish that dwell flat on the ocean floor. All our favorites are technically flounder. The group includes halibut, plaice, dab—pretty much every flatfish in North America. On the California coast, these "flounders" include petrale sole, Dover sole, and the sand dab, while over on the East Coast the most frequently caught flatfish is the lemon sole. Growing up as a kid, I'd catch these lemon sole in the Seabrook Inlet or along the Jersey shore. When I moved out west, to California, I spent my weekend angling for sand dabs and petrale sole, particularly on Catalina Island. At Bluewater Grill, our favorite way to prepare these small flatfish is the classic French Sole Meunière made famous by Julia Child and which you'll find ahead, and Sole Doré, made famous at the historic restaurants at Fisherman's Wharf in San Francisco. Sole, sand dabs, and flounder are thin and delicate and possess a slightly nutty taste. Because they are so thin and cook so rapidly, the aromas from the lemon, butter, and wine pervade your senses while being sautéed under high heat to get a slightly crispy exterior.

SERVES 4

- **4 tablespoons unsalted butter (which will become Clarified Butter)**
- **4 (8–10-ounce) petrale sole or sand dab fillets, rinsed and patted dry**
- **Sea salt and fresh cracked black pepper, to taste**
- **½ cup all-purpose flour**
- **4 tablespoons softened unsalted butter**
- **3 tablespoons chopped fresh Italian flat-leaf parsley, divided**
- **½ cup capers, drained (only use if preparing sand dabs)**
- **1 lemon, half cut in 4 wedges; other half squeezed for 1 tablespoon juice.**

PREPARE THE CLARIFIED BUTTER

Clarified butter is easy to make once you understand the process. The method I use at home starts by unwrapping some butter (depending on how much I need) and placing it in my trusted Pyrex measuring cup. Place the butter in the microwave and cover with plastic wrap because sometime the butter can "pop," making a mess inside your microwave. Heat until the butter is just melted and liquid. Remove from the microwave and let the warm butter stand for several minutes until you see three distinct layers. The bottom layer is a milky substance, the center layer is a clear yellow color, and the top layer is clear with white salty foam. The center yellow layer is what we are after. To obtain this, the top layer must be poured off and discarded. Don't worry if you discard some of the yellow oil; it's important the top layer is completely removed. The next step is to slowly pour off the yellow oil into a container without any of the milky bottom layer contaminating it. Once this is done, discard the bottom layer, and your container with the yellow oil can now be called clarified butter. Keep in a warm place until ready to use.

PREPARE THE SOLE

Preheat the oven to the warming setting, or 200°F.

Season the sole or sand dabs on both sides with salt and pepper. Pour the flour on a plate and dredge each fillet to evenly coat, shaking off the excess flour.

Add 2 tablespoons of Clarified Butter to a large, nonstick skillet over medium-high heat. Add 2 fillets and cook until just done, about 2 minutes per side. Transfer the fish to a sheet pan and place in the oven. Cook the other 2 fillets and repeat the process. Keep the fish in the oven while preparing the sauce.

PREPARE THE BROWNED BUTTER SAUCE

In the same skillet used to prepare the fish over medium-high heat, add the softened unsalted butter. Melt until bubbling and stir in half of the chopped parsley and the fresh lemon juice. Whisk to combine. If preparing sand dabs, add the capers at this point. Remove from the heat and set aside.

FINISHING THE DISH

Arrange four warm dinner plates in a row on the kitchen counter. Evenly divide the warm fish fillets on each plate. Sprinkle with the remaining parsley and pour the Browned Butter Sauce over each fillet. Garnish with lemon wedges and serve. Suggested sides: Mashed potatoes, green beans, or roasted asparagus.

BEVERAGE SUGGESTION

To celebrate Julia Child, the author of *Mastering the Art of French Cooking*, select a Simonet-Febvre from Chablis, France.

SOLE DORÉ

Sole Doré is a classic preparation made with small flatfish like sand dabs or petrale sole, which are known for their delicate, sweet flavor and firm texture. Native to the Pacific Ocean, sand dabs and petrale sole are highly valued by chefs and seafood enthusiasts alike. The term *doré*, meaning "golden" in French, refers to the preparation style in which the fish is lightly dredged in flour and sautéed in butter dipped in egg wash, until it achieves a crisp, golden-brown crust. This cooking technique enhances the natural flavor of the fish, creating a subtle, nutty aroma from the browned butter. This dish pairs beautifully with seasonal vegetables or light starches like rice pilaf. Its simplicity allows the fish's freshness to shine.

SERVES 4

4 (8-ounce) petrale sole fillets, rinsed and patted dry
Sea salt and fresh cracked black pepper, to taste
2 cups all-purpose flour
4 large eggs, beaten
4 tablespoons softened unsalted butter

LEMON CAPER BEURRE BLANC

2 tablespoons cold unsalted butter
1 tablespoon capers, drained
2 lemons, cut 4 wedges and use the remaining to squeeze ½ cup juice
2 tablespoons chopped fresh Italian flat-leaf parsley, divided
Sea salt and fresh cracked black pepper, to taste

PREPARE THE SOLE

Preheat oven to the warming setting, or 200°F.

Season the sole on both sides with salt and pepper.

Set up a dredging station by adding the flour to a shallow dish or plate. Add the eggs to another bowl and beat until well mixed.

Dredge each fillet to evenly coat, shaking off the excess flour. Dip each fillet in the egg and then arrange in a baking dish. When finished coating the fillets, pour the remaining egg mixture on top of fillets in the dish and set aside.

Add the softened butter to a large nonstick skillet over medium-low heat. When the butter is melted, add the fillets in batches and cook until the fish is just done, about 3 minutes per side. Transfer the fish to a sheet pan and place in the oven. Cook the other 2 fillets and repeat the process. Keep the fish in the oven while preparing the sauce.

PREPARE LEMON CAPER BEURRE BLANC

In the same skillet used to prepare the fish, add the cold butter to the hot pan (with heat turned off) along with the capers, lemon juice, and half the parsley. Whisk until the butter has melted. Season with salt and pepper, if necessary. Set aside.

FINISHING THE DISH

Arrange four warm dinner plates in a row on the kitchen counter. Evenly divide the warm fillets of sole on each plate. Sprinkle with the remaining tablespoon of parsley and pour the Lemon Caper Beurre Blanc over each fillet. Garnish with lemon wedges and serve immediately.

BEVERAGE SUGGESTION

To appreciate the popularity of this dish, made famous in San Francisco, we prefer Cakebread Cellars, Carneros Chardonnay from Napa.

PILIKIA

HARPOONING SWORDFISH

Harpooning swordfish is a fishing method that involves targeting individual swordfish using a hand-thrown harpoon. This method is not only precise, but it is regarded as an environmentally friendly fishing method. By selectively targeting individual mature swordfish while avoiding bycatch of other marine species, there's less impact on our ecosystem. Swordfish landed by harpoon are also considered superior in quality. This is because they are immediately subdued upon capture, reducing stress and lactic acid buildup in their muscles, which can degrade the quality of their meat. Harpooning further minimizes physical damage to the fish compared to other angling methods like long-lining or netting in which swordfish may struggle and sustain injuries during capture. Harpoon fishing is highly regulated to ensure the method remains sustainable. Swordfish landed by harpoon generally fetch a higher market price. This premium is due to the higher quality and the sustainable nature of the method, which appeals to both environmentally conscious consumers and restauranteurs alike.

Harpooning swordfish remains a long-standing tradition in the Bluewater Grill family. Rick's father-in-law, A. C. "Fred" Duckett, owned and captained the legendary sword boat *Pilikia*, which fished the deep waters off southern California. Today, the *Pilikia* has been passed on to Rick and Cammi, who've been operating the boat since 1996 to provide us with fresh, sustainable swordfish.

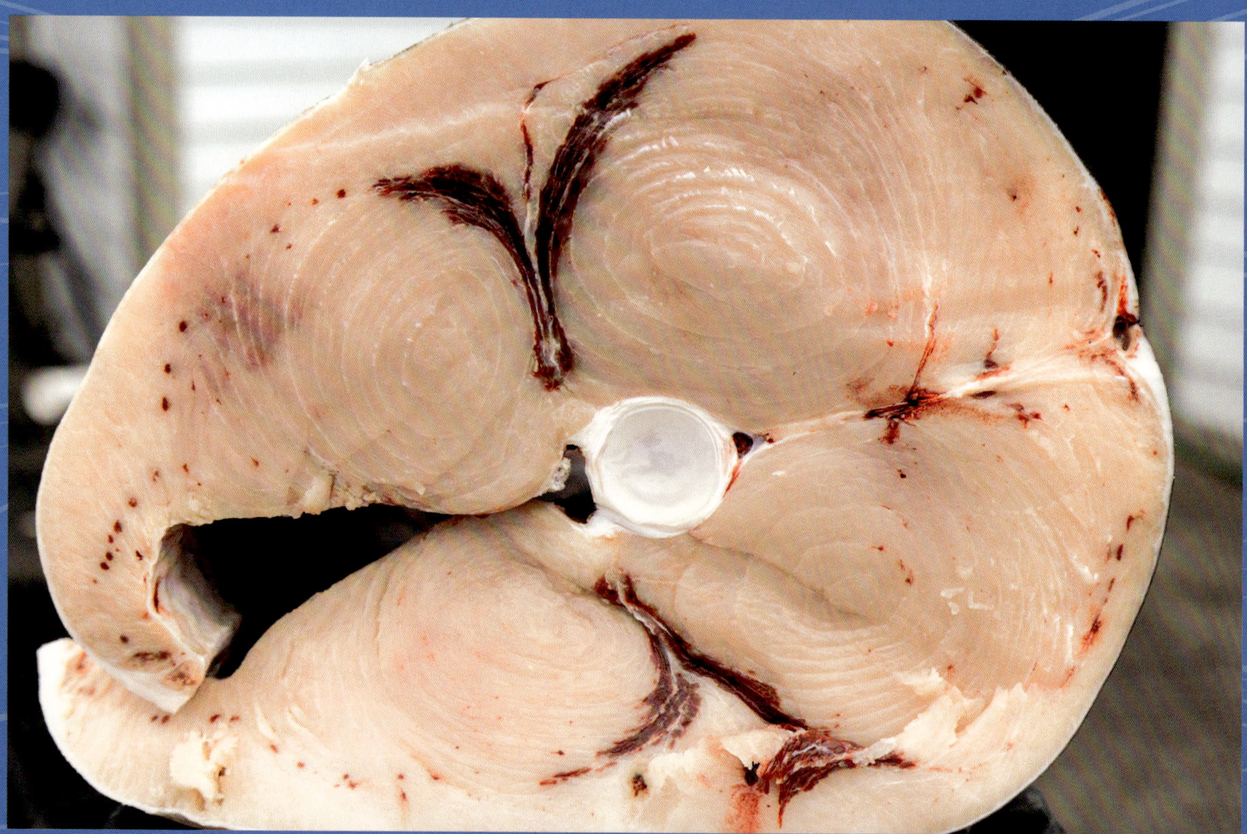

BLACKENED SWORDFISH WITH CHIPOTLE RICE

Enjoy this savory dish where meaty swordfish steaks are seasoned with a blend of smoky chipotle spices and seared to perfection. The blackening process creates a spicy, crispy crust, while the fish remains moist and tender inside. Accompanied by Chipotle Rice, Roasted Corn and Avocado Relish, and a garnish of both chive and tomato oil, this specialty of ours is a bold, savory option with just the right amount of heat.

SERVES 4

CHIPOTLE RICE
MAKES 6 CUPS

2 cups jasmine or white rice
3 cups water
1 tablespoon Better Than Bouillon Vegetable or Chicken Base
½ cup melted unsalted butter
¾ teaspoon white pepper
1 green bell pepper, medium dice
1 red bell pepper, medium dice
½ cup red onion, peeled and medium dice
2 tablespoons unsalted butter
½ cup chopped fresh cilantro + 2 tablespoons, divided
1 teaspoon chipotle powder
1 teaspoon ground cumin
1 teaspoon paprika
1 (10.5-ounce) can pinto beans, drained and rinsed
1 (10.5-ounce) can black beans, drained and rinsed
½ cup chopped fresh Roma tomatoes

ROASTED CORN AND AVOCADO RELISH
MAKES 1½ CUPS

1 ear white or yellow corn
2 tablespoons finely diced red onion
2 tablespoons finely diced red bell pepper
1 teaspoon minced garlic
1 teaspoon minced fresh, seeded jalapeño, charred on grill
¼ cup chopped fresh cilantro
1 tablespoon olive oil
1 tablespoon red wine vinegar
1 teaspoon kosher salt
½ avocado, small dice

CHIVE OIL
MAKES ABOUT ½ CUP

½ cup canola or safflower oil
2 green onions, green part only
¼ cup finely diced chives (or ½ bunch fresh Italian flat-leaf parsley, stems removed)
½ teaspoon chopped garlic
⅛ teaspoon kosher salt

TOMATO OIL
MAKES 1 CUP

½ cup extra-virgin olive oil
½ cup tomato paste
2 fresh thyme sprigs

BLACKENED SWORDFISH

½ cup Clarified Butter (page 72)
3 tablespoons blackening spice
4 (7–8 ounce) swordfish steaks (center cut, 1½ inches thick, bloodline removed)
Chopped fresh Italian flat-leaf parsley, as needed, for garnish

PREPARE THE CHIPOTLE RICE

Add the rice along with the water, the vegetable or chicken base, melted butter, and pepper to a large pot over high heat. Stir well to combine and until the base is dissolved, and then bring to a boil. Once boiling, reduce the heat to low and let cook for 15 minutes, or until the liquid is absorbed. Remove from the heat and let cool completely.

While the rice is cooling, add the bell peppers, onion, and butter to a saucepot over medium heat. Stir to combine and cook for 7 minutes, or until the vegetables are soft. Stir in the chopped cilantro, chipotle powder, cumin, and paprika. Add the cooled rice and mix until the rice and the vegetable spice mixture are well combined. Set aside.

Add the pinto beans and black beans in a saucepot over medium heat. Stir to combine the beans and heat for 5 minutes. Remove from the heat and stir in the tomatoes and remaining 2 tablespoons chopped cilantro. Add to the rice and vegetable mixture and stir until the beans are incorporated. Keep warm until ready to serve. Note: If the Chipotle Dirty Rice is made in advance, simply reheat with ¼ cup stock or water before serving.

PREPARE THE ROASTED CORN AND AVOCADO RELISH

Roast the ear of corn on an open gas cooktop flame or barbecue grill to slightly char the kernels, taking care to rotate the ear for even cooking. Remove the corn from the cob and add to a mixing bowl along with the onion, bell pepper, garlic, jalapeño, cilantro, oil, vinegar, and salt. Mix well until combined. Taste and adjust the seasoning if necessary. Transfer the relish to a sealed container and refrigerate until needed, or up to 7 days without avocado. When ready to use, add the avocado, mix thoroughly, and serve.

PREPARE THE CHIVE OIL

Add the oil, onions, parsley, garlic, and salt to a blender. Blend until smooth. Transfer the oil to a sealed container and refrigerate until needed, up to 2 weeks.

PREPARE THE TOMATO OIL

Add the oil, tomato paste, and thyme to a sauce pot. Mix well and place over low heat. Simmer for 1 hour, stirring occasionally to avoid burning. Remove from the heat and strain through chinois, cheesecloth, or fine sieve. Set aside until ready to use or store in an airtight container in the refrigerator up to 2 weeks.

PREPARE THE BLACKENED SWORDFISH

Set up a dredging station by filling a large plate with the Clarified Butter and another plate with the blackening spice. Dip each swordfish steak in the Clarified Butter then the blackening spice, making sure to evenly coat each side of the steaks. Set the steaks on a separate plate.

Heat a large cast-iron pan over medium-high heat. Add a seasoned steak (more if your pan allows) and cook until the blackening spice turns dark but not burned, about 5 minutes. Flip the fish, reduce the heat to medium, and continue to sear the fish for 5 to 8 minutes, or until the internal temperature of the fish reaches 130°F. Remove from the pan and set aside. Continue the process with the remaining swordfish steaks if necessary.

FINISHING THE DISH

Place 1 cup Chipotle Rice in the middle of four large plates. Place a swordfish steak on top of the rice along with 2 tablespoons of Roasted Corn and Avocado Relish. Drizzle 2 tablespoons of the Chive Oil over the top of each plate and dot ½ tablespoon of Tomato Oil around each plate. Garnish with parsley and serve.

BEVERAGE SUGGESTION

A dry Riesling from the United States is a perfect selection that will stand up to the bold flavors of the blackened swordfish. We recommend Kung Fu Girl or Dr. Loosen, Riesling from Washington.

ANGLING FOR WHITE SEA BASS

Recreational white sea bass fishing in southern California is a popular activity for anglers, like us, as well as spearfishermen, because of the quality of the catch. A member of the croaker family, white sea bass can grow quite large, some exceeding sixty pounds. They are valued for their firm, white meat and are considered a prized catch. The prime season for white sea bass fishing in southern California typically runs from late spring to early fall, peaking in the summer months. The exact timing can vary based on water temperatures and local conditions. Popular fishing spots include the coastal waters around the Channel Islands, Catalina Island, and along the coastline from Santa Barbara to San Diego. Kelp beds and rocky reefs are particularly good habitats for finding white sea bass. Using live bait, such as squid or sardines, is a common and effective method for targeting them. Anglers also use various artificial lures, including jigs and swimbaits, especially when fishing in deeper waters or around structure. We support the Balboa Angling Club, which conducts conservation efforts, including tagging programs, grow-out pens, and data collection to help manage and protect the white sea bass population. Because sea bass can be elusive in nature and prefer specific habitats, they do pose a challenge. Successful anglers often need to be patient, be knowledgeable about local conditions, and adaptable in their techniques. I can speak from experience when I say the reward of landing a large white sea bass makes the effort worthwhile, providing both a thrilling experience and a delicious meal. We serve white sea bass at Bluewater Grill in season from Southern California waters.

WHITE SEA BASS ADOBADA WITH GRILLED PINEAPPLE SALSA AND GREEN RICE

Here's a flavorful dish that combines tender white sea bass with the rich, smoky flavors of adobada, a traditional Mexican marinade. The adobada sauce is made with a blend of dried chiles, garlic, vinegar, and spices, which infuses the fish with a deep, tangy taste. White sea bass, known for its firm texture and mild flavor, pairs perfectly with the bold, spicy marinade. Grilled or pan-seared, this dish is served with Green Rice and Grilled Pineapple Salsa, making it a vibrant, mouthwatering meal that showcases the harmonious blend of fresh seafood and Mexican cuisine.

SERVES 4

GRILLED PINEAPPLE SALSA
MAKES 4 CUPS

1 fresh pineapple
½ cup diced red onion
2 tablespoons fresh lime juice
½ cup finely chopped cilantro
½ jalapeño, seeded and minced
1½ teaspoons kosher salt
½ teaspoon fresh cracked black pepper
1½ tablespoons extra-virgin olive oil

ADOBADA MARINADE
MAKES 2 CUPS

4 dried guajillo peppers, stemmed and seeded
¼ cup achiote paste
⅓ cup pineapple juice
¼ cup red wine vinegar
1 garlic clove, peeled and minced
1 teaspoon kosher salt
½ teaspoon ground cumin

GREEN RICE
MAKES 2½ CUPS

2 tablespoons olive oil
½ cup small diced yellow onion
1 garlic clove, peeled and minced
1 cup long-grain rice
1 cup vegetable stock
1 cup whole milk
½ cup chopped fresh cilantro
¼ cup chopped fresh spinach
½ teaspoon kosher salt
½ teaspoon fresh cracked black pepper

WHITE SEA BASS

4 (7-ounce) boneless, skinless white sea bass fillets
1 tablespoon kosher salt
1 tablespoon fresh cracked black pepper
2 tablespoons olive oil
4 cups cooked Green Rice
1 cup Grilled Pineapple Salsa
1 tablespoon fresh cilantro leaves
1 tablespoon red radishes, cut in ⅛ inch julienne strips
1 tablespoon green onion, cut into strips
½ cup Tomato Oil (page 82)
4 lime wedges

PREPARE THE GRILLED PINEAPPLE SALSA

Preheat an outdoor grill to medium-high heat. Trim the pineapple and remove the flesh from the core. Slice the pineapple flesh into ¼-inch slices. Place the slices on the preheated grill and grill until the slices are soft with charred grill marks. Remove the pineapple and dice into ¼-inch pieces, enough to fill 2 cups.

Add the pineapple, onion, lime juice, cilantro, jalapeño, salt, pepper, and olive oil to a mixing bowl. Mix until fully incorporated. Transfer the salsa to a sealed container and refrigerate until needed, up to 1 week.

PREPARE THE ADOBADA MARINADE

Add 2 cups of water to a saucepan along with the dried peppers over high heat. Bring to a boil, reduce heat to medium-low, and simmer for 5 minutes. Remove from the heat and drain the peppers. Add the peppers to a blender, along with the achiote paste, pineapple juice, vinegar, garlic, salt, and cumin, along with 2 tablespoons water. Blend until smooth and set aside until cooled.

PREPARE THE GREEN RICE

Add the oil to a stockpot over medium-high heat. When the oil is hot and shimmering, add the onion and sauté until translucent, about 2 minutes. Add the garlic and cook an additional minute. Add the rice and stock and cook 2 minutes.

Combine the milk, cilantro, and spinach in blender and puree. Add the pureed mixture to the pot and season with salt and pepper. Cover and bring to a boil. Reduce the heat to low and cook until all liquid is absorbed, about 15 minutes. Set aside.

PREPARE THE WHITE SEA BASS

Pour 1 cup of the cooled Adobada Marinade in the bottom of 9 × 9–inch Pyrex baking dish. Season the sea bass fillets with salt and pepper and place the fish on top of the marinade. Top the fillets with the remaining 1 cup of marinade. Cover and refrigerate overnight.

Add the olive oil to a large cast-iron skillet over medium-high heat. Heat until the oil is shimmering. Add the marinated sea bass fillets and cook until the internal temperature of the fish reaches 135°F, about 5 minutes per side. Remove from the heat and set aside.

FINISHING THE DISH

Place 1 cup of warm Green Rice in the center of four individual plates. Place one sea bass fillet on top of the rice. Top each fillet with ¼ cup of Grilled Pineapple Salsa. Top the salsa on each plate with ¼ tablespoon cilantro, radish, and green onion. Drizzle each plate with 2 tablespoons Tomato Oil and serve with lime wedges.

BEVERAGE SUGGESTION

Adobado sauce is a rich and smoky flavor so a creamy California Chardonnay stands up well to the bold flavor of the seasoning. We love Frank Family Napa Chardonnay from the Carneros region.

WHITE SEA BASS WITH THAI COCONUT CURRY

Southern California is a place where the ocean's bounty meets a vibrant tapestry of cultural influences. This recipe embodies that fusion, combining the delicate, flaky texture of locally caught white sea bass, a prized catch along our coastline, with the rich aromatic flavors inspired by the region's thriving Asian communities. Drawing on the traditions of Thai, Vietnamese, and Pacific Island cuisines, the creamy coconut milk and spices of this comforting and exotic dish perfectly complement the sea bass.

SERVES 4

THAI COCONUT CURRY

1 tablespoon vegetable oil
1 tablespoon unsalted butter
1 red bell pepper, sliced
4 garlic cloves, peeled and minced
1 tablespoon grated fresh ginger
1 shallot, peeled and finely chopped
½ cup vegetable broth
3 tablespoons mild red curry paste
2 teaspoon packed brown sugar
½ teaspoon turmeric
½ teaspoon ground cumin
½ teaspoon ground coriander
¼ tsp white pepper
2 tablespoons reduced-sodium soy sauce
1 tablespoon fish sauce
1 (14 ounce) can coconut milk
1 teaspoon fresh lime juice
1 tablespoon sriracha
1 handful torn Thai basil

WHITE SEA BASS

2 tablespoons olive oil
4 (7-ounce) boneless, skinless white sea bass fillets
1 tablespoon kosher salt
1 tablespoon fresh cracked black pepper
Thai basil, for garnish

PREPARE THE THAI COCONUT CURRY

Add the oil and butter to a large skillet over high. When heated, add the bell pepper. Sauté for 5 minutes, or until the peppers start to soften. Add the garlic, ginger, and shallot. Cook until soft and fragrant, about 2 minutes. Deglaze with the vegetable broth and simmer for 2 minutes while stirring and scraping up the brown bits on the bottom of the pan with a wooden spoon. Stir in the red curry paste. Add the brown sugar, turmeric, cumin, coriander, white pepper, soy sauce, and fish sauce. Cook for 1 minute, stirring frequently. Add the coconut milk and bring to a boil. Simmer for 5 minutes or until the sauce starts to thicken. Add the lime juice, sriracha, if using, and basil. Stir to combine. Simmer for no longer than 1 minute.

PREPARE THE SEA BASS

Add the olive oil to a large 10-inch sauté pan. Season both sides of the sea bass with salt and pepper and add the fish to the hot pan. Cook for 5 minutes, or until golden brown. Turn the fish over and add the Thai Coconut Curry. Reduce the heat to medium-low. Cook

an additional 5 minutes. Remove and transfer the fish and Thai Coconut Curry to individual serving plates. Garnish with fresh Thai basil and serve.

BEVERAGE SUGGESTION

We enjoy Marques de Riscal, Verdejo from Spain for this dish due to its tropical flavors of grapefruit, passion fruit, and melon.

PACIFIC NORTHWEST & THE ALEUTIAN CHAIN

PACIFIC NORTHWEST & THE ALEUTIAN CHAIN

Enjoying seafood in the Pacific Northwest and the Aleutian Chain offers a truly remarkable culinary experience, reflecting the natural abundance and deep cultural connection to the ocean. The Pacific Northwest, including Washington, Oregon, and British Columbia, is renowned for its fresh, sustainable seafood. Local fishermen pride themselves on harvesting some of the finest species, such as oysters, salmon, and crab. These waters are rich with nutrients, fostering an environment where marine life thrives, making the seafood exceptionally flavorful.

In this region, wild-caught salmon is king. Whether grilled on a cedar plank, served with a zesty chimichurri, or smoked, Pacific Northwest salmon is a staple. Restaurants, markets, and even home kitchens celebrate the seasonal runs of sockeye, Chinook, and coho salmon, offering dishes that capture the essence of the ocean. Oysters, clams, and mussels meanwhile are also featured prominently, harvested from the cold, pristine waters of the coast.

Moving up to the Aleutian Chain in Alaska, the seafood experience takes on an even more rugged, pristine character. These remote islands stretch into the Bering Sea, offering some of the world's finest king crab, halibut, and black cod. King crab, a luxurious delicacy prized for its sweet, tender meat, is a highlight of any seafood lover's trip to the region. The Aleutians are also home to massive halibut, which are sought after for their mild flavor and firm texture. In these northern waters, fishing isn't just a livelihood, but a way of life, deeply intertwined with the history and traditions of the Indigenous peoples.

Whether you're savoring wild-caught salmon in Seattle or indulging in fresh king crab in Alaska's Dutch Harbor, the Pacific Northwest and Aleutian Chain offer some of the finest seafood experiences in the world. Enjoy the following recipes, pulled from our favorite Bluewater Grill recipes from the region, so you can experience a bounty of cold-water seafood at home.

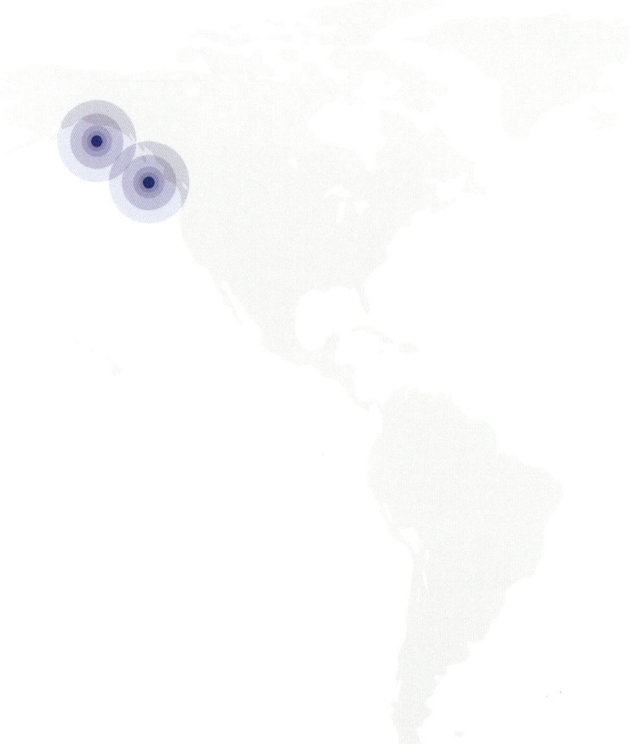

THE WONDERFUL WORLD OF OYSTERS

Oysters have been consumed by humans for thousands of years. Archaeological evidence suggests oysters were eaten by prehistoric humans, and they have been a staple in coastal diets across the world. In ancient Rome and Greece, oysters were considered a delicacy. Romans even developed early methods of aquaculture to ensure a steady supply. In North America, Native American tribes along the west and east coast of the United States harvested oysters, using them as a food source and trading commodity. European settlers in the Americas also adopted the practice of oyster harvesting. By the nineteenth century, oysters had become a common food in both Europe and America, often eaten raw or cooked in various dishes.

Due to overharvesting and pollution, natural oyster populations declined significantly by the late nineteenth and early twentieth centuries, leading to the rise of oyster farming (aquaculture). The Chinese are credited with some of the earliest forms of oyster farming, dating back to the Han dynasty (206 BC–220 AD). In the eighteenth century, modern oyster farming techniques were developed in France and have since spread worldwide. Today, oyster farming is a major industry, particularly in regions like North America, Europe, and Asia. A great resource book on the subject is *The Big Oyster* by Mark Kurlansky. The book explains in great detail the significance of oysters in America.

TASTE OF OYSTERS

Oysters have a unique and complex flavor profile that can vary significantly depending on their environment. Their taste is often described using the term *merroir*, similar to the *terroir* of wine, which refers to the influence of the local environment on the flavor. Merrior derives from the French word "*mer*" which means "sea" and "*terrior*" which means a region of land.

REGIONAL FLAVOR DIFFERENCES

West Coast Oysters (North America): Flavor: West Coast oysters are generally sweet and creamy with less intense brininess. They can also have fruity or melon-like notes, owing to the varied water temperatures and the abundance of algae. Examples include Kumamoto (California), Totten Inlet (Washington), and Fanny Bay (British Columbia).

East Coast Oysters (North America): Flavor: Typically, East Coast oysters are briny and have a crisp, clean flavor. They often exhibit a pronounced saltiness due to the cold waters and high salinity levels. Examples include Blue Point (New York), Wellfleet (Massachusetts), and Malpeque (Prince Edward Island).

European Oysters: Flavor: European oysters, such as the Belon from France, often have a strong, metallic, and almost mineral-like taste with a firm texture. They can also have a pronounced nuttiness. Examples: Belon (France), Colchester (United Kingdom), and Galway (Ireland).

Asian Oysters: Flavor: Asian oysters, like the Pacific oyster, tend to be sweet and creamy with a mineral finish. The flavor profile can vary significantly based on the specific water conditions. Examples: Pacific oysters (Japan, Korea).

FACTORS IMPACTING OYSTER FLAVOR OR MERRIOR

Water Salinity: Higher salinity levels typically result in brinier oysters, while lower salinity levels produce milder, sweeter flavors.

Water Temperature: Colder waters tend to make oysters firmer and brinier, whereas warmer waters can lead to a softer texture and sweeter taste.

Algae and Plankton: The type and amount of algae and plankton in the water affect the oyster's diet, influencing its flavor. Rich, diverse algae produce more complex, sweeter oysters.

Tides and Currents: Stronger currents can lead to firmer oysters due to increased exercise, while calm waters may result in softer textures.

Bottom Type: The seabed composition (sand, mud, rocks) where oysters grow can impart distinctive mineral notes to the oysters.

THE JOY OF EATING OYSTERS

Freshness: The freshest oysters have a clean, vibrant flavor and are often enjoyed raw to appreciate their pure taste.

Texture: The texture of oysters, ranging from firm to creamy, adds to the enjoyment, providing a variety of mouthfeel experiences.

Pairing: Oysters can be paired with a variety of condiments (lemon, mignonette, cocktail sauce) and beverages (champagne, white wine, stout), enhancing their natural flavors.

Cultural Experience: Eating oysters can be a communal and celebratory experience, often associated with seaside dining and special occasions.

Versatility: Oysters can be enjoyed in various preparations—raw, grilled, baked, fried—each method bringing out different aspects of their flavor.

The nuanced flavors and varied textures, combined with the influence of their environment and the joy of different preparations and pairings, make oysters a beloved delicacy worldwide.

HOW TO SHUCK AN OYSTER

Shucking an oyster refers to the process of opening its shell to access the meat inside. Proper technique is crucial to avoid injury and to keep the oyster intact.

Necessary Tools

Oyster knife: A short, sturdy knife with a blunt tip.
Oyster glove or kitchen towel: For protecting your hand from the knife.

THE STEPS

Preparation: Clean the oysters under cold running water to remove any dirt or debris. Place an oyster flat-side up on a stable surface, using a towel to hold it in place if necessary.

Find the Hinge: Locate the hinge at the narrow end of the oyster. This is where you will insert the knife.

Insert the Knife: Hold the oyster firmly with the towel or wear a protective glove. Insert the tip of the oyster knife into the hinge and gently twist until you feel the shell begin to pop open. Be careful to keep your hand clear of the blade.

Open the Shell: Once the hinge is pried open, slide the knife along the top shell to sever the muscle that holds the shell closed. Remove the top shell and discard it. Visually inspect the oyster to make sure it is alive and fresh. Smell to make sure. Dispose of any oysters that are not pristine.

Detach the Oyster: Slide the knife under the oyster to cut the bottom muscle, freeing the oyster from the shell. Be careful to preserve as much of the oyster's liquid (known as liquor) as possible, as it enhances the flavor.

Serve: The oyster is now ready to be served raw, typically on the half shell.

Shucking oysters requires practice and care, but it is a rewarding skill that allows you to enjoy this seafood delicacy at its freshest.

OYSTERS ON THE HALF SHELL WITH MIGNONETTE

Oysters on the half shell embody a maritime delicacy, an oceanic delight served atop a chilled bed of ice. Each oyster tells a story of its aquatic habitat, echoing the tides and currents from which it emerged. Prized for their briny essence and velvety texture, oysters offer an array of flavors, ranging from buttery and sweet to mineral-rich and tangy. Their ritualistic consumption involves a deft shuck, revealing the glistening white flesh within, awaiting a squeeze of lemon, or homemade Cocktail Sauce. We also like to add a splash of our Mignonette, a traditional accompaniment to raw shellfish. Mignonette helps neutralize the seafood's briny flavor thanks to the acidity of vinegar, the sweetness of the shallot, and the heat of the black pepper. The Mignonette also allows the merroir of the oyster or clam (such as salinity, diet, and origin) to shine through, much the way terroir imparts flavor to wine.

SERVES 6 (4 OYSTERS EACH)

MIGNONETTE
MAKES 1 CUP

1 cup red wine vinegar
1 tablespoon minced shallot
½ teaspoon fresh cracked black pepper

OYSTERS

24 fresh oysters, shucked on the half shell (page 103)
Crushed ice, for serving
Seaweed, optional, for garnish
½ cup Mignonette
½ cup Cocktail Sauce (page 50)
¼ cup extra hot horseradish
6 fresh Italian flat-leaf parsley sprigs, for garnish
6 lemon wedges

PREPARE THE MIGNONETTE

Add the vinegar, shallot, and pepper to a bowl. Whisk until combined. Transfer to a sealed container and refrigerate until ready to use, up to 3 weeks.

PREPARE THE OYSTERS

Shuck the oysters (see page 103), making sure not to leave shell fragments, mud, or other debris on the oyster itself.

FINISHING THE DISH

Fill the bottom of a shellfish or shallow pan with crushed ice. Arrange the seaweed, if using, in the center of the ice. Arrange the shucked oysters on top of the ice, leaving the center of the ice open. Place the Mignonette, Cocktail Sauce, and horseradish in small containers and arrange in the center of the pan. Garnish with the parsley and lemons and serve with cocktail forks.

BEVERAGE SUGGESTION

We love West Coast oysters farmed in Washington or British Columbia, so it is only natural to pair with a local wine. The Pinot Gris produced by Acrobat is crisp and clean and was awarded Best Wine to Pair with Oysters by Wine Enthusiast, and we agree.

ROASTED OYSTERS—THREE WAYS

In 1607, when English settlers landed on the shores of the Chesapeake Bay, they discovered Native Americans savoring a favorite tradition of cooking oysters over a firepit. As the country developed this tradition, it continued in any area that was host to an oyster bed. Today, we cook our roasted oysters over a barbecue grill or under the broiler to achieve a crispy finish. Our favorite roasted oysters use three different and distinctive toppings, but you can experiment with any mixture of your favorite spices, sauces, beer, or wine. A wonderful way to start a party is to gather around a barbecue, roast oysters with different toppings, and eat them right off the grill while sipping a cold beer or crisp Sauvignon Blanc.

SERVES 4 (4 OYSTERS EACH)

THAI GREEN CURRY SAUCE
MAKES 1½ CUPS

1 tablespoon olive oil
½ yellow onion, peeled and chopped
1 red bell pepper, chopped
2 garlic cloves, peeled and chopped
1 tablespoon finely minced fresh ginger
¼ cup Thai green curry paste
2 tablespoons packed dark brown sugar
1 tablespoon fish sauce
7 ounces canned coconut milk
¼ cup chicken stock

MOTOYAKI SAUCE
MAKES ¾ CUP

½ cup Japanese mayonnaise (Kewpie)
½ tablespoon fresh lemon juice
½ teaspoon sugar
½ tablespoon mirin
1 tablespoon miso paste (Shiro Miso)

ROASTED GARLIC

1 head garlic
1 tablespoon olive oil
Kosher salt and fresh cracked black pepper, to taste

GARLIC PARSLEY BUTTER
MAKES ⅔ CUP

1 stick (½ cup) unsalted butter
2 cloves Roasted Garlic, minced
2 tablespoons minced shallot
¼ cup chopped fresh Italian flat-leaf parsley
1 lemon, zested (about 1½ teaspoons)
¼ teaspoon kosher salt
¼ teaspoon fresh cracked black pepper

OYSTERS

16 fresh oysters, shucked on the half shell (page 103)
6 fresh Italian flat-leaf parsley sprigs, for garnish
6 lime wedges
6 lemon wedges

PREPARE THE THAI GREEN CURRY SAUCE

Add the oil to a sauté pan over medium-high heat. When heated and the oil is shimmering, add the onion and peppers, and sauté until soft, about 5 minutes. Add the garlic and ginger and cook for 30 seconds. Add the curry paste, brown sugar, and fish sauce and stir to coat all the vegetables. Add the coconut milk and chicken stock and bring to a simmer. Reduce the liquid by half, stirring occasionally, until the sauce thickens, about 15 minutes.

Remove from the heat and transfer to a food processor. Process until smooth. Taste and adjust with salt and pepper, as needed. Set aside until ready to serve.

PREPARE THE MOTOYAKI SAUCE

Add the mayonnaise, lemon juice, sugar, mirin, and miso paste in a mixing bowl. Mix until well combined. Set aside until ready to serve.

PREPARE THE ROASTED GARLIC

Preheat the oven to 350°F. Cut ¼ inch off the top of the garlic bulb. Drizzle the bulb with olive oil and season with salt and pepper. Place the bulb, root-side down, on a baking sheet and roast in the oven for 30 minutes. Remove and let cool, then squeeze out the flesh of the cloves. Set aside and mince as needed.

PREPARE THE GARLIC PARSLEY BUTTER

Add the butter, Roasted Garlic, shallot, parsley, lemon zest, salt, and pepper to a food processor. Blend until well incorporated. Set aside until ready to use.

PREPARE THE OYSTERS AND FINISHING THE DISH

Preheat an outdoor grill to high heat or the oven set to broil.

Place the shucked oysters on a large sheet pan. Top the oysters with either the Thai Green Curry Sauce, Motoyaki Sauce, or the Garlic Parsley Butter.

Place on the grill or under the broiler and roast until the oysters have just started to shrink, about 7 minutes. (Note: The time will vary depending on the size of the oysters so watch them closely.) Remove, garnish with the parsley, and serve immediately with lime and lemon wedges.

BEVERAGE SUGGESTION

We love to stand around the barbecue and roast appetizers as a socially interactive experience. The best thing to drink is a shared bottle of Sauvignon Blanc with notes of grapefruit and lemongrass. Our favorite is Silverado from Napa.

Growing up in New England, I didn't have much exposure to king crab. I first learned about the species from my college roommate. He worked on an Alaskan crab processing boat in the early eighties that cleaned, cooked, and froze the crab at sea. During this time, El Niño conditions contributed to an explosion in the crab population, creating a crab gold rush and increasing the demand for king crab, particularly in Asia. King crab fisherman became millionaires in one season, which later inspired the book *Working on the Edge* by Spike Walker, who spent nine seasons as a crewman aboard some of the most successful crab boats in the Alaskan fleet. I remember reading his book about laboring in the brutal outer reaches of the Bering Sea. It makes you truly appreciate king crab when you know fisherman like Spike encountered 110-mile-an-hour winds, rode out some of the worst storms in Alaska's history, worked nonstop for seventy-four hours without sleep, participated in record catches of king crab, saw ships sink, helped rescue their crews, and had close friends die at sea. Today, that crabbing alure and element of danger continues with the long-running series *Deadliest Catch* on Discovery Channel.

The first time I experienced king crab at the table was inside Alaska's Sitka Hotel in 1985. I can still remember the intense crab flavor and the sweet taste combined with the firm rewarding chunks. I feel terrible admitting it, since I'm from the East Coast, but king crab is right up there with Maine lobster as my favorite seafood. At Bluewater Grill, we like serving king crab simply steamed with melted butter and lemon. The best size king crab legs to purchase are the 9/12s (9 to 12 legs per 10-pound case). Since the crab has already been cooked and frozen at sea, you just need to defrost and heat the legs before serving.

DIFFERENT SPECIES OF KING CRAB

There are several species of king crab, each known for its large size and succulent meat. Each species has its own unique flavor and texture, making them all popular in different culinary contexts. The most common species include:

Red King Crab: This is the most prized and commercially important species. It's known for its sweet, tender meat and large size. Red king crabs are found primarily in the Bering Sea and the waters surrounding Alaska.

Blue King Crab: Slightly smaller than the red king crab, the blue king crab has a milder flavor. It's typically found near St. Matthew Island and the Pribilof Islands in Alaska.

Golden (or Brown) King Crab: This species is smaller and has a slightly different flavor profile compared to the red and blue king crabs. It's usually found in deeper waters, particularly in the Aleutian Islands, and has a pricklier shell compared to the red and blue king crab.

Scarlet (or Deep-Sea) King Crab: Found in deep-sea environments, this species is less common and not typically fished commercially. Its meat is also considered less desirable compared to the red, blue, and golden king crabs.

STEAMED KING CRAB LEGS

Steaming king crab legs is a simple and effective way to enjoy their sweet, delicate meat. Here's how you do it:

SERVES 3–6

6 king crab legs (about 1 pound each)
1 cup melted salted butter
2 lemons, cut in quarters

Fill a large pot with about 2 inches of water. Place a steamer basket or a colander inside the pot, making sure it sits above the water level. Bring the water to a boil over high heat. Once the water is boiling, place the king crab legs in the steamer basket or colander. If the legs are too large, you can bend them at the joints or cut them to fit. Cover the pot with a lid and steam the crab legs for 5 to 7 minutes. Since king crab legs are already precooked, you're essentially just reheating them. You'll know they're ready when they're hot all the way through. Carefully remove the crab legs from the steamer using a pair of tongs.

FINISHING THE DISH

Serve them immediately with melted butter and lemon wedges. (Note: If you prefer, you can add some white wine, garlic, or herbs to the steaming water for extra flavor. Just be careful not to overcook the crab legs, as they can become tough.)

BEVERAGE SUGGESTION

Eating king crab is a wonderfully self-indulgent thing so what better thing to do than splurge on a bottle of Chardonnay? We recommend a buttery and bold Chardonnay to cut through the butter used when dipping chunks of crab. Cakebread or Pahlmeyer are our favorites.

WILD PACIFIC SALMON

Wild Pacific salmon are renowned for their rich flavor, firm texture, and vibrant color, making them a prized catch for seafood lovers. These salmon are born in freshwater rivers and streams along the Pacific coast and migrate to the ocean, where they grow and mature before returning to their birthplace to spawn. There are five main species of wild Pacific salmon, each with distinctive characteristics. Each species plays a crucial role in both the ecosystem and the fishing industry, offering a range of flavors and culinary possibilities.

Chinook (King) Salmon: These are the largest and most prized, known for their high oil content and rich, buttery flavor.

Coho (Silver) Salmon: These are smaller than the king salmon, with a firm texture and a milder taste, often sought after for their versatility in cooking.

Sockeye (Red) Salmon: These are famous for their deep red flesh and bold flavor, making them ideal for smoking and grilling.

Pink (Humpback) Salmon: These are the most abundant, with a lighter, more delicate flavor and softer texture, often used in canned or processed salmon products.

Chum (Dog or Keta) Salmon: These have a lower oil content, making their flesh less rich but still flavorful, often used for drying or smoking.

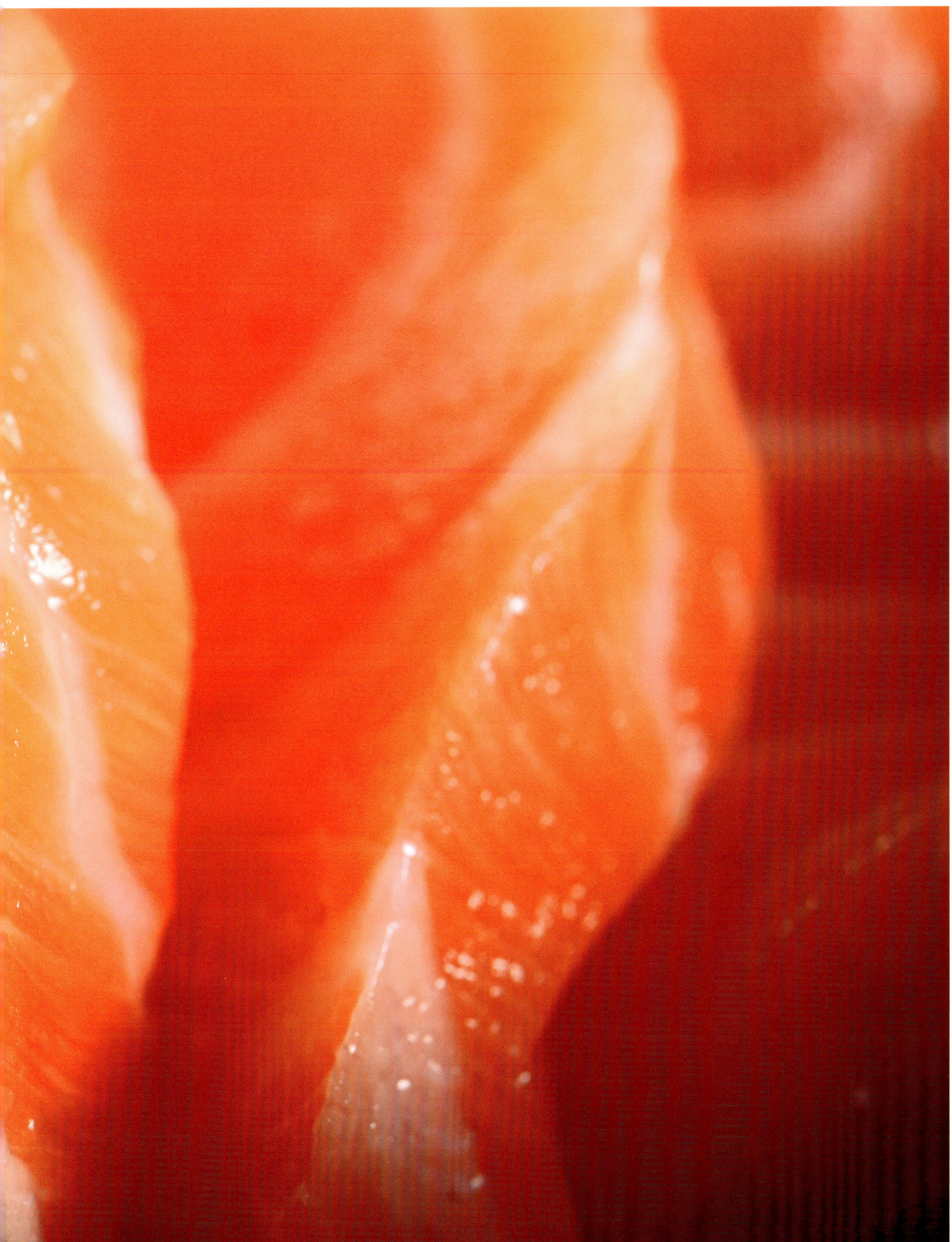

SALMON GRAVLAX

The nostalgia of my mother's gravlax goes beyond the mere culinary delight of this traditional Nordic dish. It's a sensory and emotional experience that weaves together memories, family traditions, and the comfort of home. Many people like me remember standing by their mom's side, watching and learning as she prepared the gravlax, absorbing tips and techniques that would later be passed down. Personally, I remember sitting around our family table, enjoying gravlax during a festive meal while sharing stories and laughter. These moments become ingrained in my memory. Gravlax also connects me to my cultural roots, providing a tangible link to my ancestry and the culinary traditions of my heritage. Recalling the first time I tasted my mom's gravlax as a child, and how my palate evolved to appreciate its complex flavors, as well as the stories my mom shared with me about her own experiences making gravlax adds another layer of familial and historical context.

When I make gravlax myself, using my mom's recipe, I'm not just cooking; I'm preserving a piece of family history and creating new memories for the next generation. The nostalgia of my mom's gravlax is a rich tapestry of sensory experiences, emotional connections, and cherished traditions. It's more than a dish; it's a symbol of love, heritage, and the enduring bonds of family.

We encourage you to make gravlax with your family. From selecting the freshest salmon to preparing the cure, each step of the process can be a shared activity that creates strong family bonds and lasting memories.

The distinctive aroma of dill, the briny scent of the sea, and the subtle fragrance of spices bring back vivid memories of my mother's kitchen. Meanwhile, the delicate balance of salty, sweet, and aromatic flavors, paired with the silky texture of the salmon, evokes a comforting familiarity. In addition, the sight of the vibrant, orange-pink salmon, garnished with fresh dill, is a visual cue that takes me back to family meals. Knowing that my mother put time and effort into preparing the gravlax, carefully curing the salmon over days, reflects her love and dedication. For me, the taste of my mom's gravlax evokes feelings of comfort and security, reminding me of the warmth and safety of home. Preparing gravlax the way my mother does is a way to honor her legacy and keep her memory alive, creating a sense of continuity and connection to my heritage.

MOTHER'S SALMON GRAVLAX

MAKES 2 POUNDS

1 teaspoon white pepper
1 cup rough chopped fresh dill (about 1 large bunch)
¾ cup kosher salt
¾ cup sugar
2 pounds fresh, wild-caught salmon fillets, bones removed with skin on

Add the pepper, dill, salt, and sugar to a large mixing bowl. Mix well to combine. Add the salmon and coat all sides with the mixture. Transfer the salmon to a baking sheet or other flat tray and cover with plastic wrap. Refrigerate for 48 hours. Remove and rinse the salmon under cold water to remove any excess salt. Pat dry. Slice very thin (about ⅛ inch) and serve.

SMOKED SALMON

Like my mother's gravlax, homemade smoked salmon is another delicacy that combines

family tradition with rich flavor and personal touches, turning fresh salmon into a gourmet treat. The process begins with selecting the highest-quality salmon, typically a fillet with a good fat content for optimal flavor. The salmon is then cured in a mixture of salt, sugar, and spices, sometimes with the addition of herbs or citrus zest for added complexity. This curing process, which can take several hours to a couple of days, draws out moisture and enhances the salmon's natural flavors.

After curing, the salmon is rinsed and patted dry, ready for smoking. The smoking process can be done using various methods, including cold smoking for a more delicate, silky texture, or hot smoking for a firmer, flakier finish. Wood chips, such as alder, apple, or hickory, are often used to impart a smoky, aromatic flavor that complements the salmon's natural richness. The use of a Traeger or electric smoker with wood pellets is a great way to smoke salmon. Heat the smoker to 180°F and smoke approximately 3 hours, until the salmon reaches an internal temperature of 135°F.

Here's a classic smoked salmon recipe that I make both at home and at the restaurant using a simple brining and smoking process. This recipe works well with a variety of salmon, particularly Chinook, coho, and sockeye.

CLASSIC SMOKED SALMON
MAKES 2 POUNDS

1 cup kosher salt
3 cups packed dark brown sugar
1 tablespoon fresh cracked black pepper
1 tablespoon chopped yellow onion
2 tablespoons fresh minced garlic
1 teaspoon dried dill, optional, for additional flavor
2 quarts water
1 cup apple juice or white wine, optional, for additional flavor
2 pounds fresh, wild-caught salmon fillets, bones removed with skin on
Apple, cherry, or alder wood chips or pellets

PREPARE THE BRINE

Add the salt, brown sugar, pepper, onion, garlic, and dried dill, if using, to a large mixing bowl. Mix well to combine. Add 2 quarts water and the apple juice (or wine). Stir until the salt and sugar are fully dissolved.

BRINE THE SALMON

Add the salmon fillets to the brine, making sure the fillets are fully submerged. If necessary, weigh them down with a plate. Cover the bowl and refrigerate for 6 to 8 hours. (Note: For a stronger flavor, you can brine the salmon overnight or for up to 12 hours.) Remove the salmon fillets from the brine and rinse thoroughly under cold water to remove any excess salt. Pat dry, then place the salmon on a wire rack set over a baking sheet. Refrigerate for at least 2 hours or until a thin, tacky layer (pellicle) forms on the surface. This step is crucial for the smoke to adhere properly.

PREPARE THE SMOKER

Soak the wood chips in water for at least 30 minutes, then drain. This helps produce more smoke. This step is not necessary if using pellets.

Preheat an outdoor smoker to 180°F. If using a charcoal smoker, maintain a consistent temperature by adding charcoal and wood chips as needed.

SMOKE THE SALMON

When the smoker is at temperature, place the salmon fillets on the smoker grates, skin-side down. Add the soaked wood chips to the smoker. Smoke the salmon for 3 hours, depending on the thickness of the fillets and your desired level of smokiness. The internal temperature of the salmon should reach 135°F. Once the salmon is smoked, remove from the smoker and let cool to room temperature. Serve immediately or refrigerate. Smoked salmon can be stored in an airtight container in the refrigerator for up to 1 week or frozen for longer storage.

Serve with crackers, cream cheese, capers, and fresh dill.

Other serving options: Top bagels with cream cheese, smoked salmon, red onion, and capers for a classic breakfast or brunch. Or incorporate smoked salmon into salads, scrambled eggs, quiches, or pasta dishes for added flavor.

BEVERAGE SUGGESTION

An off-dry Riesling like Chateau St. Michelle "Eroica" or Kung Fu Girl is the perfect wine to complement smoked fish.

CEDAR PLANK SALMON WITH MAPLE DIJON GLAZE

Cedar plank salmon is a method of cooking fish, particularly salmon, that involves grilling the fish on a cedarwood plank. This technique imparts a unique, smoky flavor to the fish while keeping it moist and tender. The origins of cedar plank cooking can be traced back to Native American tribes of the Pacific Northwest. These tribes used this method to cook salmon and other fish over open flames, often at community gatherings. By placing the fish on planks of cedarwood, they were able to infuse the fish with the wood's natural flavors, adding a distinctive taste that became a hallmark of their cuisine. Using planks to cook salmon is traditionally done when cooking an entire salmon. At Bluewater Grill, we hired a retired woodworker to mill a 4 × 8-inch plank we could use to cook a single piece of fish. We served the fish on the plank on the plate, which adds a rich cedar aroma along with the maple glaze. These planks are now available at specialty food stores and on Amazon as Cedar Grilling Planks.

SERVES 4

MAPLE DIJON GLAZE
MAKES 1 CUP

1 cup maple syrup
1 tablespoon grated fresh ginger
1 tablespoon fresh lemon juice
1 tablespoon light soy sauce
½ teaspoon minced fresh garlic
1 tablespoon Dijon mustard

CEDAR SALMON BRINE

2 quarts water
½ cup packed dark brown sugar
5 tablespoons kosher salt

SALMON

4 (8-ounce) fresh wild salmon steaks, bones removed, skin on
½ cup Maple Dijon Glaze, divided
½ tablespoon kosher salt
½ tablespoon fresh cracked black pepper
4 Grilled Lemon Halves (page 65)

SOAK THE CEDAR PLANK

Begin by soaking one large untreated cedar plank (enough to hold the 4 fillets) in water for at least 12 hours. You can also soak four individual planks, one for each fillet. Soaking in water helps prevent the wood from catching fire on the grill and ensures it produces smoke, which adds flavor to the fish.

PREPARE THE MAPLE DIJON GLAZE

Add the maple syrup, ginger, lemon juice, soy sauce, and garlic to a small saucepan over medium-high heat. Stir to incorporate and bring to a boil. Once boiling, reduce the heat to low and simmer for 20 minutes, whisking occasionally. Remove from the heat and whisk in the mustard. Transfer the glaze to an ice bath to cool. Set aside until ready to use or store in an airtight container in the refrigerator up to 2 weeks.

PREPARE THE CEDAR SALMON BRINE

Add ½ gallon (2 quarts) warm water along with the brown sugar and salt to a large bowl. Whisk together until the sugar and salt are dissolved. Set aside.

PREPARE AND GRILL THE SALMON

Place the salmon in the brine, cover with plastic wrap, and refrigerate for 12 hours. Remove and place the fillets skin-side up on top of the presoaked cedar plank(s).

Prepare an outdoor grill to medium-high heat (350°F to 400°F). When the grill is at temperature, add the salmon and cedar plank(s) to the grill for 2 minutes to heat one side of the plank. Remove the fillets from the plank, turn the plank over so the hot side is up, and return the fillets, skin-side down, on top of the hot side of the plank. Brush the tops of the fillets with half of the Maple Dijon Glaze. Cover the grill and cook the salmon for 10 minutes, or until the internal temperature of the fillets reaches 130°F to 135°F. Remove from the grill.

FINISHING THE DISH

Place the salmon on the plank in the center of a large serving platter or four individual plates. Serving the fish directly on the plank adds to the presentation. Top the fish with the remaining Maple Dijon Glaze, garnish with the grilled lemon halves, and serve.

BEVERAGE SUGGESTION

The Willamette Valley in Oregon is famous for its Pinot Noir and Pinot Gris. We particularly enjoy Four Graces, Pinot Noir, from the Willamette Valley.

SALMON WITH CHIMICHURRI

There are various legends about the origins of chimichurri. The most accepted version believes the classic accompaniment of Argentinean steaks and empanadas was created by Irish immigrants who used Worcestershire sauce, which created a more flavorful condiment with locally available ingredients. Others believe the Basques or English introduced chimichurri to the table. Regardless of the origins, chimichurri is an uncooked condiment that has ubiquitous variations, and the recipe is different depending on who you ask and where you happen to be since it's used throughout Argentina, Paraguay, and Uruguay. The following recipe is our preferred version, especially for this salmon dish. Some cooks prefer to substitute red wine vinegar for the lemon juice, but we feel the citrus brings a level of freshness that complements the fish.

SERVES 4

CHIMICHURRI
MAKES 2 CUPS

¼ cup minced fresh Italian flat-leaf parsley
¼ cup minced fresh cilantro
4 tablespoons minced fresh oregano
2 tablespoons minced fresh garlic
⅜ cup (6 tablespoons) fresh lemon juice
¼ teaspoon cayenne pepper, or to taste
1 cup extra-virgin olive oil
¼ teaspoon kosher salt
¼ teaspoon fresh cracked black pepper

SALMON

1 teaspoon olive oil
4 (8-ounce) fresh wild salmon steaks, bones removed, skin on
Kosher salt and fresh cracked black pepper, to taste
1 tablespoon chopped fresh Italian flat-leaf parsley, with 4 sprigs reserved

PREPARE THE CHIMICHURRI

Add the parsley, cilantro, oregano, garlic, lemon juice, cayenne, olive oil, and salt and pepper to a medium-sized mixing bowl. Mix well until combined. Transfer half of the mixture to a blender and puree until smooth. Add the pureed mixture back to the bowl and whisk together until combined. Set aside until ready to serve or refrigerate in an airtight container up to 7 to 14 days.

PREPARE THE SALMON

Add the olive oil to a large skillet over medium-high heat. Season both sides of the salmon fillets generously with salt and pepper. When the skillet is hot and oil is shimmering, add the fillets, skin-side down. Cook for 4 minutes, or until the skin is crispy. Turn the fillets over and cook for another 3 to 4 minutes, or until the fish is cooked through and reaches an internal temperature of 130°F to 135°F. Remove the fish.

FINISHING THE DISH

Place about ¼ cup of the Chimichurri in the center of four individual serving plates. Place a salmon fillet, skin-side up, on top. Garnish with the parsley along with 1 sprig per plate and serve.

BEVERAGE SUGGESTION

We prefer an oak-aged Finca Flichman Argentinean chardonnay to stand up to the acidity in the Chimichurri.

SALMON WITH MUSHROOMS, SPINACH, AND RED CHILI CHIMICHURRI

Wild salmon with sautéed mushrooms, spinach, and chimichurri is one of our more vibrant, healthy dishes that balances rich flavors and fresh ingredients. The wild salmon, known for its firm texture and deep flavor, is pan-seared or grilled to perfection, bringing out its natural oils and slightly smoky taste. Paired with sautéed mushrooms and spinach, the dish gains an earthy, hearty depth. The mushrooms add umami and a satisfying bite, while the spinach offers a fresh, slightly bitter contrast that complements the richness of the fish. Meanwhile, the Red Chili Chimichurri, a zesty Argentine sauce, brings the dish together with its bright spicy notes. The sauce's acidity cuts through the richness of the salmon and mushrooms, creating a balanced flavor profile. This dish is a perfect example of how simple, fresh ingredients can be transformed into a delicious and nutritious meal.

SERVES 4

RED CHILI CHIMICHURRI
MAKES 1 CUP

½ cup extra-virgin olive oil
2 tablespoons red wine vinegar
½ cup finely chopped fresh Italian flat-leaf parsley
4 garlic cloves, peeled and finely chopped
¾ teaspoon dried oregano
1 teaspoon sea salt
½ teaspoon crushed red pepper flakes

SALMON

4 (7–8-ounce) salmon fillets, skin on, pin bones removed
½ tablespoon sea salt
½ tablespoon fresh cracked black pepper
½ cup extra-virgin olive oil, divided
¼ cup cremini mushrooms
⅓ cup fresh spinach
4 Grilled Lemon Halves (page 65)

PREPARE THE CHIMICHURRI

Add the oil, vinegar, parsley, garlic, oregano, salt, and pepper flakes to a mixing bowl. Mix well until combined. Let stand for 2 hours at room temperature before serving. Set aside.

PREPARE THE SALMON

Season the salmon fillets with salt and pepper and set aside.

Add ¼ cup olive oil to a hot sauté pan over medium-high heat. When heated, add the mushrooms and sauté for 1 minute. Add the spinach and sauté until slightly wilted. Set aside and keep warm.

Add the remaining ¼ cup olive oil to a separate pan over medium-high heat. When heated, add the salmon fillets and cook skin side first until crispy, about 6 minutes. Flip and cook an additional 6 minutes, or until internal temperature reaches 135°F for medium rare. At the restaurant, we prefer a slightly opaque center to our fish, If you like your fish cooked through, add 2 minutes per side for medium.

FINISHING THE DISH

Arrange the mushrooms and spinach in the center of individual serving plates. Place a salmon fillet off-center over the mushrooms and spinach. Top with the Red Chili Chimichurri, garnish with a grilled lemon half, and serve.

BEVERAGE SUGGESTION

In the spirit of chimichurri, we like to pair a Malbec from Argentina like Don Miguel.

FISHING FOR ALASKAN HALIBUT

Catching Alaskan halibut on our boat in Alaska is an incredible experience filled with many memorable moments: The cool, crisp air and the breathtaking scenery of Alaska's rugged coastline as you set out on the pristine waters. The thrill of the chase as you wait patiently, feeling the anticipation build with every tug on the line, is unforgettable. The moment you hook a halibut, the battle begins, requiring strength and determination to reel in these powerful fish.

While most of the fish we catch are in the thirty-to-sixty-pound range, stories of catching a "barn door" halibut are particularly thrilling. *Barn door* refers to exceptionally large halibut, typically over one hundred pounds, with some even reaching three hundred to four hundred pounds. The current world record is 515 pounds. These massive fish are known for their strength and size, making them a coveted catch in Alaskan waters. The sheer size of these fish would take your breath away. It's a true "barn door," and an impressive testament to the rich marine life of Alaskan waters.

Landing any halibut requires skill and teamwork, adding to the shared excitement. Once on the boat, the sense of achievement is immense. This experience is not just about the catch but also about the challenge, the thrill, and the memory of conquering one of the ocean's giants.

The camaraderie with friends or family is epic as you share the experience, swapping stories and enjoying the serenity of nature. Back at anchor, the joy of preparing and enjoying fresh halibut while recalling the day's adventures adds another layer to the nostalgia. These memories of fishing in Alaska are etched in our minds as some of the most special and rewarding times spent outdoors.

ORANGE AND WALNUT–CRUSTED HALIBUT WITH SCALLOPED POTATOES

This recipe presents a harmonious blend of flavors and textures featuring one of the most prized fish in Alaska—the Pacific Halibut. At the restaurant, we combine the delicate sweetness of fresh Alaskan halibut with the tangy zest of orange and the earthy richness of walnuts. The crust that forms adds a vibrant citrusy aroma while the crushed nuts provide a crunchy coating, enhancing the halibut's texture. When pan-seared, the halibut's moisture is retained while the crust forms a golden, flavorful exterior. Top the halibut with our Lemon Caper Beurre Blanc and pair it with our Scalloped Potatoes and Grilled Asparagus for a memorable and indulgent seaside experience.

SERVES 4

SCALLOPED POTATOES
SERVES 6 (4 OUNCE) PORTIONS

¾ cup water
1 cup heavy cream
1 teaspoon Better Than Bouillon Chicken Base
2 teaspoons chopped fresh thyme
1 teaspoon kosher salt
1 teaspoon fresh cracked black pepper
1½ pounds russet potatoes, peeled and thinly sliced ⅛ inch thick
¼ cup freshly grated Parmesan cheese

ORANGE AND WALNUT CRUST

¾ cup walnuts
¼ cup panko breadcrumbs
¼ cup finely chopped fresh Italian flat-leaf parsley
2 tablespoons finely chopped fresh basil
2 tablespoons finely chopped fresh chives
¼ teaspoon kosher salt
¼ teaspoon fresh cracked black pepper

ROASTED ASPARAGUS

24 fresh asparagus spears
Olive oil, as needed
Kosher salt and fresh cracked black pepper, to taste

HALIBUT

1 cup all-purpose flour, seasoned with kosher salt and fresh cracked black pepper
3 eggs, beaten + 1 tablespoon water (egg wash)
4 (8-ounce) fresh Alaskan halibut skinless fillets
2 tablespoons extra-virgin olive oil
Kosher salt and fresh cracked black pepper, to taste
Lemon Caper Beurre Blanc (page 76)

PREPARE THE SCALLOPED POTATOES

Preheat the oven to 350°F.

Add ¾ cup water to a medium saucepot over medium-high heat along with the cream, chicken base, thyme, salt, and pepper. Whisk until combined and the chicken base is dissolved. Bring to a simmer then remove from the heat. Set aside.

Layer the potato slices in a 9 × 9 baking dish and pour the chicken base mixture over the top. Sprinkle the cheese over the top of the potatoes. Cover the dish with foil and bake for 50 minutes, or until the potatoes are fork-tender. Remove and let sit for 10 minutes before serving.

Silverado
VINEYARDS
2022
MILLER RANCH
SAUVIGNON BLANC
YOUNTVILLE · NAPA VALLEY
ESTATE GROWN

PREPARE THE ORANGE AND WALNUT CRUST

Add the walnuts to a food processor and process until coarsely chopped. Add the walnuts to a mixing bowl along with the breadcrumbs, parsley, basil, chives, salt, and pepper. Mix well and set aside until ready to use.

PREPARE THE ROASTED ASPARAGUS

Preheat the oven to 375°F. Arrange the asparagus spears on a baking sheet. Drizzle with olive oil and season with salt and pepper. Roast until crisp, taking care not to overcook. Remove and keep warm.

PREPARE THE HALIBUT

Set up a dredging station by adding the seasoned flour to a shallow dish or plate. Add the eggs and water to another bowl and beat until well mixed. Place the Orange and Walnut Crust on another plate.

Begin by breading the halibut. Dredge each piece first in the seasoned flour, gently shaking off the excess. Next dip into the egg wash, fully submerging each piece and letting the excess run back into the bowl. Then press each piece of halibut into the Orange and Walnut Crust, making sure to coat each side. Set aside.

Add the oil to a large deep-sided sauté pan over medium-high heat. When the oil is shimmering, add the halibut. Cook for about 5 minutes per side, or until the internal temperature of the fish reaches 135°F. Remove from the heat.

FINISHING THE DISH

Add 1 cup of Scalloped Potatoes on the side of four individual serving plates and arrange 6 stalks of Roasted Asparagus next to the potatoes. Place the halibut in the center of the plate, top with a couple tablespoons of Lemon Caper Beurre Blanc, and serve.

BEVERAGE SUGGESTION

Halibut has a delicate flavor so we don't like to overwhelm the palate. A Sauvignon Blanc or Sancerre will cut though the Lemon Caper Beurre Blanc and enhance the halibut flavor. We love the Silverado Napa Sauvignon Blanc.

B&G

MISO-GLAZED SABLEFISH (BLACK COD)

Sablefish, also known as black cod or butterfish, is rich and buttery and an excellent pairing with our savory-sweet and well-balanced miso glaze. Miso, if you're not familiar, is a traditional Japanese seasoning produced by fermenting soybeans with salt and "koji," a form of culinary fungus. Miso is high in protein and rich in vitamins and minerals and played an important role in feudal Japan. Miso is still widely used in traditional and modern cooking in Japan. When making this delicious dish at home, it's important to marinate the fish long enough so the miso flavors penetrate deeply into the fish before being sautéed to perfection. I first discovered this fish as an alternate to Chilean sea bass, which we feel is overfished and do not serve. Mick Jagger talked about it after having dinner at the Slanted Door in San Francsico. I later came to know the owner, Charles Phan, the inventor of modern Vietnamese cuisine.

SERVES 4

MISO MARINADE
MAKES 2 CUPS

½ cup mirin
1 cup sake
½ cup sugar
1 cup white miso paste

SABLEFISH

4 (7–8-ounce) sablefish fillets (skin-on)
¾ cup Miso Marinade
¼ cup extra-virgin olive oil
3 cups Coconut Ginger Rice (page 280)
2 cups Sautéed Green Beans (page 280)
¼ cup unagi sushi sauce, for garnish
Julienne green onion, cilantro leaves, and daikon sprouts, as needed, for garnish

PREPARE THE MISO MARINADE

Add the mirin and sake to a saucepan over medium-high heat. Bring to a boil, then turn off the heat. Add the sugar and mix until dissolved. Set aside to cool. When cool, add the miso paste and mix until fully dissolved and incorporated. Store covered in the refrigerator until ready to use.

PREPARE THE SABLEFISH

Place the sablefish fillets in a large ziptop bag and add the Miso Marinade. Toss gently to coat the fish evenly. Place the bag in the refrigerator for 2 hours.

Add oil to a large sauté pan or flat grill over medium heat. When the oil is hot, add the marinated sablefish. Cook skin-side down for 6 minutes. Flip and cook for an additional 6 minutes, or to an internal temperature of 140°F.

FINISHING THE DISH

Place four plates on the counter and equally divide the rice and beans in the center of each plate. Add one sablefish fillet on top of the rice and beans. Drizzle a circle of unagi sushi sauce around the plated food and garnish with the green onion, cilantro leaves, and daikon sprouts.

BEVERAGE SUGGESTION

We like to pair Trimbach French Pinot Noir from Alsace with Sablefish. The wine's crisp acidity will cut through the richness of the miso and allows the delicate fish to shine without being overshadowed by the wine.

MIDWEST LAKES & RIVERBANKS

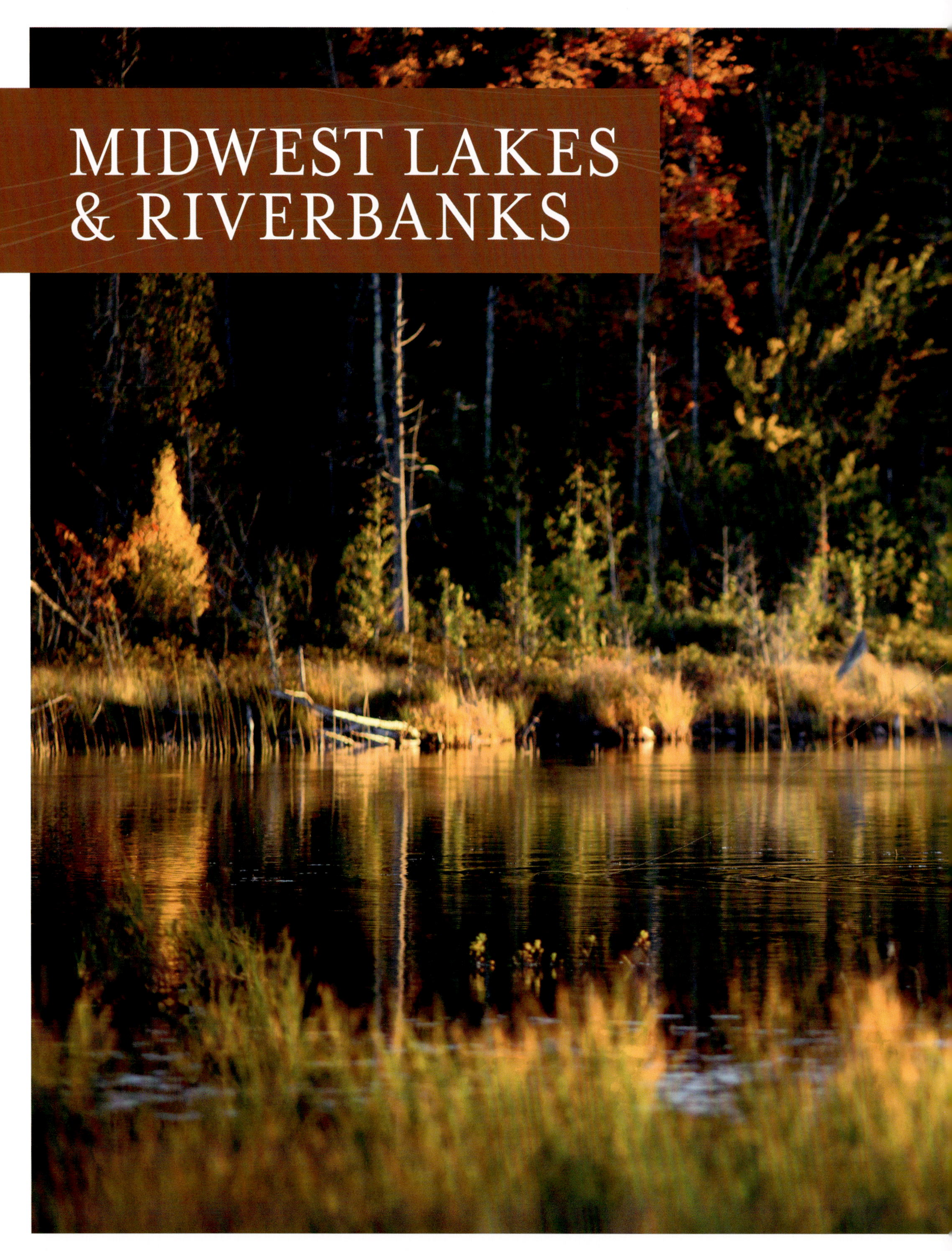

MIDWEST LAKES & RIVERBANKS

Dining on fresh seafood in the Midwest, particularly along the lakes and riverbanks, is a unique and rustic experience, with a focus on freshwater fish such as trout, smelt, walleye, and whitefish. While this area may not have ocean access, its numerous lakes and rivers, especially the Great Lakes, are teeming with flavorful and diverse fish species that have been central to local cuisine for generations.

Countless friends tell stories of fishing during summer vacations at the family lake camp and enjoying sautéed or deep-fried walleye, attending a "smelt fry" at the local volunteer fire department fundraiser or pan-fried trout.

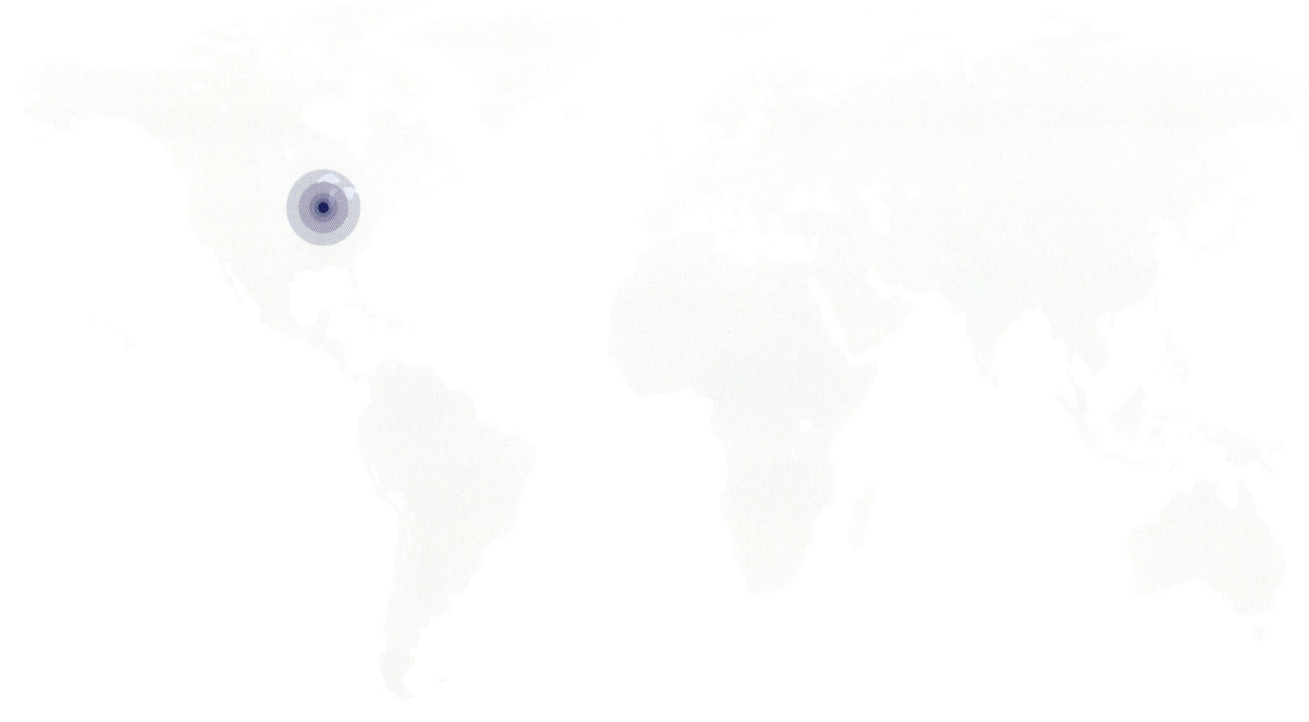

A WORD ABOUT IDAHO TROUT

Idaho is the state that farms the most trout in our country. Thanks to its ideal conditions, Idaho-raised trout offers a taste of the pristine waters of the Rocky Mountains, where the fish are raised in cold, clear streams, ensuring their superior quality and flavor. The most prominent species raised in Idaho's favorable climate is the rainbow trout, prized for its mild flavor, tender flesh, and adaptability to various cooking methods. Idaho also farms populations of cutthroat, brook, and brown trout, but the rainbow remains the most common and commercially available species associated with Idaho.

When purchasing trout at your local market (likely Idaho rainbows), look for fillets that are firm and have a vibrant color, indicating freshness. They should have a mild, clean smell of fresh water.

Cooking trout, as you'll find with our popular recipe that follows, is simple and versatile; it can be grilled, baked, or pan-fried to bring out its natural flavors. For a classic preparation, season the fillets with salt, pepper, and a squeeze of lemon before cooking. The delicate, flaky texture of trout pairs beautifully with a variety of sides, from roasted vegetables to a fresh salad.

When you eat trout, you're savoring a fish that reflects the purity of its environment. It's not only delicious but also a healthy choice, rich in omega-3 fatty acids. Whether you're an avid angler or a gourmet enthusiast, Idaho trout brings the taste of the wild to your plate.

TROUT AMANDINE

This is a classic French dish featuring fresh rainbow trout coated in our popular Almond-Panko mixture, pan-fried to a golden crisp, and adorned with our delicious and zesty Lemon Caper Beurre Blanc. The citrus provides a wonderful contrast to the nutty flavor of the almond crust. For the crust, feel free to substitute cashews, macadamia, walnut, pistachio, or combine several different kinds. We love these nutty crusts because they seal in the moisture of the fish while developing a nutty aroma due to the "toasting" of the nuts when pan-fried. Fish prepared in this manner can be complemented by a topping of various sauces like the Lemon Caper Beurre Blanc featured in this recipe. The next time you're in the mood for a timeless gem, try this dish. You'll be pleased with its simplicity in preparation and its sophisticated flavors.

SERVES 4

ALMOND PANKO CRUST
MAKES 4 CUPS

3¼ cup sliced, blanched almonds
½ cup panko breadcrumbs
1 tablespoon chopped fresh Italian flat-leaf parsley
⅛ teaspoon kosher salt
⅛ teaspoon fresh cracked black pepper

TROUT

1 cup all-purpose flour
1 tablespoon kosher salt
1 tablespoon freshly cracked black pepper
3 large eggs + 1 tablespoon water (egg wash)
1 cup Almond Panko
4 (8-ounce) boneless trout, skin on
2 tablespoons olive oil
Sautéed Green Beans (page 280)
Scalloped Potatoes (page 126)
2 tablespoons Lemon Caper Beurre Blanc (page 76)
4 Grilled Lemon Halves (page 65)

PREPARE THE ALMOND PANKO CRUST

Add the almonds to a food processor and pulse until coarsely chopped. Add the breadcrumbs, parsley, salt, and pepper and pulse until blended. Transfer to a sealed container and refrigerate until ready to use, up to 4 weeks.

PREPARE THE TROUT

Set up a dredging station by filling one bowl with the flour. Season the flour with salt and pepper and mix to combine. Add the egg wash to a second bowl, and the Almond Panko mixture to a third bowl.

Dredge the trout first in the seasoned flour, gently shaking off the excess flour. Then dredge in the egg wash, allowing the extra egg to drip back into the bowl. Then place in the Almond Panko mixture and use your fingers to help coat both sides of the trout. Set aside.

Add the oil to a large deep-sided sauté pan over medium-high heat. When heated, add the breaded trout in the pan. Reduce the heat to medium-low and cook for 6 minutes, or until golden brown. Carefully turn the fish over and cook another 6 minutes, or until golden brown. Remove from the heat.

FINISHING THE DISH

Place some Sautéed Green Beans and Scalloped Potatoes in the center of each serving plate. Top with the trout. Spoon the Lemon Caper Beurre Blanc over the fish, garnish with the grilled lemon half, and serve.

BEVERAGE SUGGESTION

A wine with good acidity to balance the rich butter sauce like a French Chablis or Sancerre. We enjoy Michel Redde Sancerre from the Loire Valley.

PANKO-CRUSTED WALLEYE

Walleye, often referred to as the crown jewel of Midwest fish, is a firm, white-fleshed fish that we also like to cook because of its mild flavor and versatility. Our walleye is panko-crusted and served with fresh sautéed spinach and our decadent Scalloped Potatoes. It's a popular dish in many lakeside kitchens. "Snowbirds," or Midwesterners fleeing the frigid winters who spend time in the Southwest, love the fact we offer walleye, as it's a nostalgic reminder of their Midwest home, which is blanketed in snow.

SERVES 4

1 cup all-purpose flour
1 tablespoon kosher salt
1 tablespoon freshly cracked black pepper
3 large eggs
¼ cup whole milk
1 cup panko breadcrumbs
4 (8-ounce) boneless walleye fillets, skin on
½ cup olive oil
4 Grilled Lemon Halves (page 65)

PREPARE THE SEASONED FLOUR

Add the flour to a large bowl and season with salt and pepper. Mix to combine.

PREPARE THE WALLEYE

Set up a dredging station by placing the bowl with the seasoned flour on the counter. Add the eggs and milk to a second bowl and beat until well mixed. Place the bowl next to the flour. Add the panko breadcrumbs to a third bowl and place next to the bowl with the eggs and milk.

Dredge the walleye first in the seasoned flour, gently shaking off the excess flour. Then dredge in the egg wash, allowing the extra egg to drip back into the bowl. Finally, place the walleye in the panko breadcrumbs and use your fingers to help coat both sides of the fish. Set aside.

Add the oil to a large, deep-sided sauté pan over medium-high heat. When heated and the oil is shimmering, add the walleye to the pan. (Note: You will likely need to cook the fish in batches.) Reduce the heat to medium-low and cook for 6 minutes, or until golden brown. Carefully turn the fish over and cook another 6 minutes, or until golden brown. Remove from the heat.

FINISHING THE DISH

Place some sautéed spinach and Scalloped Potatoes (optional) in the center of each serving plate, top with the walleye, and serve with ramekins of tartar sauce and/or lemon halves.

BEVERAGE SUGGESTION

When in Rome, we recommend Alexis Baily Vineyard, Minnesota's first winery. Seyval Blanca is clean, bright, and crisp. The Seyval variety can survive the brutal Minnesota winters and is used in this award-winning wine.

SMELT FRY WITH GARLIC AIOLI

Smelt, a smaller fish found in abundance in the Great Lakes, is best enjoyed fried. Popular at fish fries, particularly in the spring when they are in season, we'll lightly batter and deep-fry the smelt, creating a crispy, satisfying dish served with our Garlic Aioli. Their mild flavor and crunchy texture make this fish a local favorite during smelt runs, celebrated in many Midwest communities. Our Midwestern and European guests at Bluewater practically come to tears when they eat our deep-fried smelt or "fries with eyes," as we like to call them.

A smelt fry is a popular community gathering in the Midwest where fried smelt is served, often as part of a fundraising event for the local fire department, festival, or gathering. Smelt fries are often held in the spring when the smelt are "running" and are plentiful. If you're not familiar, smelt are small, silvery fish found in both fresh and saltwater. They're a popular delicacy, particularly in regions bordering the Great Lakes and coastal areas. Smelt are typically caught in large numbers during their spawning season, when they move into shallow waters. Smelt fries are a wonderful way for people to enjoy fresh local seafood and to celebrate the coming of summer as the memory of the long, cold winter fades. SEE PHOTO (PAGE 141, TOP LEFT).

SERVES 4–6

1 cup all-purpose flour
½ teaspoon sea salt + more for seasoning, divided
½ teaspoon fresh cracked black pepper
1 cup vegetable oil, for frying
1 pound whole lake smelt or headed and gutted smelt (30–40 fish)
2 lemons, cut in half
1 teaspoon finely chopped fresh oregano
Lemon wedge, for serving
Garlic Aioli (page 50), for serving

PREPARE THE SMELT

Set up a dredging station by filling a bowl with the flour. Season the flour with ½ teaspoon of the salt and pepper and mix to combine.

Add the oil to a large, deep-sided sauté pan over high heat. The oil should fill the pan at least 2 inches. Heat the oil to 350°F. Use a candy thermometer to check the temperature.

Dredge the smelt in the seasoned flour, gently shaking off the excess flour. Add the smelt to the pan. (Note: You will likely need to cook the smelt in batches.) Fry, turning occasionally, until golden brown and crispy, about 5 minutes. Remove from the heat and transfer the smelt to a paper towel–lined plate to drain.

FINISHING THE DISH

Arrange the smelt in a bowl, squeeze the lemon halves over the smelt, and toss. Add the oregano and toss. Add a little more sea salt, or to taste, and toss. Serve the smelt with a lemon wedge and a side of Garlic Aioli.

BEVERAGE SUGGESTION

Since smelt fries are ubiquitous in Minnesota, it's only fitting this dish get paired with a Minnesota-brewed beer like Summit Twins Pils, an unfiltered, full-body German-style pilsner.

LAKE SUPERIOR WHITEFISH WITH MOUSSELINE SAUCE

Lake Superior whitefish is a prized catch from the cold, clear waters of the Great Lakes. Known for its delicate, mild flavor, and tender, flaky texture, this freshwater fish has been a staple in the diets of the region's Indigenous peoples. It's also popular in traditional Jewish cuisine as it is an abundant kosher fish. The whitefish thrives in the depths of Lake Superior, feeding on a diet of small invertebrates and plankton, which contributes to its clean, slightly sweet taste.

Preparing and serving Lake Superior whitefish is a culinary delight, whether it's smoked, baked, grilled, or fried. The fish is versatile and pairs well with a variety of seasonings and sides, making it a favorite in regional cuisine. Smoked whitefish, in particular, is a local specialty, often enjoyed on its own or used in spreads and dips. The fish is also celebrated for its nutritional benefits, being high in protein and omega-3 fatty acids while low in mercury. For those who savor the taste of fresh, locally sourced fish, Lake Superior whitefish offers an authentic and flavorful experience.

SERVES 4

MOUSSELINE SAUCE
MAKES 1¼ CUP

4 large egg yolks
2 teaspoons kosher salt
½ teaspoon white pepper
3 tablespoons water
1 cup Clarified Butter (page 72)
1 tablespoon fresh lemon juice
½ cup heavy cream

WHITEFISH

1 cup all-purpose flour
1 tablespoon kosher salt
1 tablespoon freshly cracked black pepper
½ cup olive oil
4 (8-ounce) boneless whitefish fillets, skin on
½ cup Mousseline Sauce

PREPARE THE MOUSSELINE SAUCE

Add the egg yolks in a bain-marie over low heat and season with salt and pepper. Add the water to the egg yolks. Vigorously beat the eggs, using a small whisk, making figure 8–shaped movements. Notes: Every motion of the whisk should be such that you can see the bottom. In addition, during the cooking process, if you notice the egg yolks are too thick, you can add a little water. Cooking should be done at a temperature of approximately 300°F to obtain a hollandaise-like sauce. When the preparation has the consistency of cream, remove from the heat and gradually whisk in the Clarified Butter. Add the lemon juice and keep warm. Next, beat the heavy cream until you obtain a whipped cream, using an electric whisk if desired. Gently add the whipped cream to the sauce and combine gently with a rubber spatula. Adjust the seasoning with salt and pepper if necessary. Keep warm on low heat until ready to serve.

PREPARE THE SEASONED FLOUR

Add the flour to a large bowl and season with salt and pepper. Mix to combine.

PREPARE THE WHITEFISH

Dredge the whitefish in the seasoned flour, gently shaking off the excess flour. Set aside.

Add the oil to a large deep-sided sauté pan over medium-high heat. When heated, add the whitefish to the pan. (Note: You will likely need to cook the fish in batches.) Reduce the heat to medium-low and cook for 6 minutes, or until golden brown. Carefully turn the fish over and cook another 6 minutes, or until golden brown. Remove from the heat.

FINISHING THE DISH

Place some sautéed spinach and mushrooms in the center of each serving plate. Top with the whitefish. Spoon the Mousseline Sauce over the fish and serve.

BEVERAGE SUGGESTION

We recommend a Gruner Veltliner from Bernhard Ott, Austria, with whitefish due to its citrus and mineral flavors.

ATLANTIC & MID-ATLANTIC SEABOARD

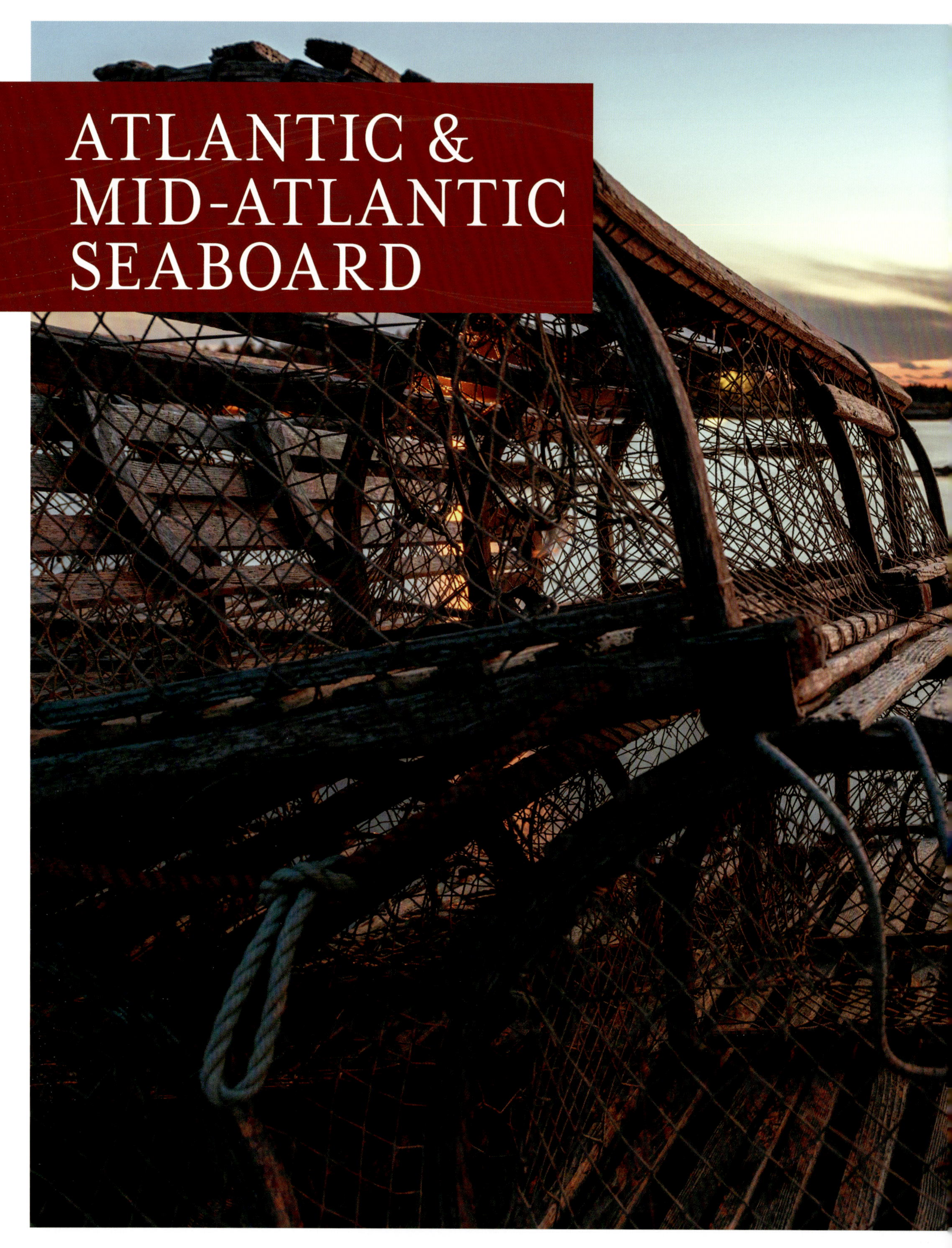

ATLANTIC & MID-ATLANTIC SEABOARD

The Atlantic Coast and Mid-Atlantic Seaboard, in my opinion, offers some of the most delicious and diverse seafood experiences in the United States. Stretching from Maine to Virginia, this coastal region is renowned for its fresh catch and the culinary traditions that showcase the best of the ocean's bounty. Whether you're visiting a seaside shack or cooking at a waterfront home, the seafood here is nothing short of exceptional.

One of the highlights of the Atlantic Coast is its shellfish. Maine lobsters are famous worldwide for their sweet, tender meat, while the oysters of Virginia's Chesapeake Bay—perfect for our Oysters Stew—are revered for their briny, slightly sweet flavor. Maryland is synonymous with blue crabs, particularly during the summer months when crab feasts are a tradition. We like to feature blue crabs in such dishes as our Maryland-Style Crab Cake and our Sautéed Soft-Shell Crab with Lemon Caper Beurre Blanc. Farther north, New England is home to the iconic clam chowder, a rich, creamy soup brimming with tender clams, potatoes, and onions. In Rhode Island, clam cakes and clear broth chowders offer a lighter, yet equally flavorful, alternative. In addition to clams, scallops are a delicacy found along the coast, and we'll sear them to perfection and present them with a variety of delicious sides like our Goat Cheese Grits.

The Mid-Atlantic Seaboard also offers a unique twist on coastal cuisine. Fried fish sandwiches, crab cakes, and shrimp are staples in beach towns from Delaware to North Carolina. The waters of this region are teeming with bluefish, striped bass, and haddock, making for great fishing and dining opportunities, as you'll experience in this adventurous chapter.

I believe what makes seafood along the Atlantic Coast so special is its freshness. Many markets and restaurants source their seafood locally, ensuring that what ends up on our plate was caught only hours before. Paired with coastal views, salty breezes, and the warmth of the sun, enjoying seafood in this region is more than just a meal—it's an unforgettable experience that connects us to the sea itself.

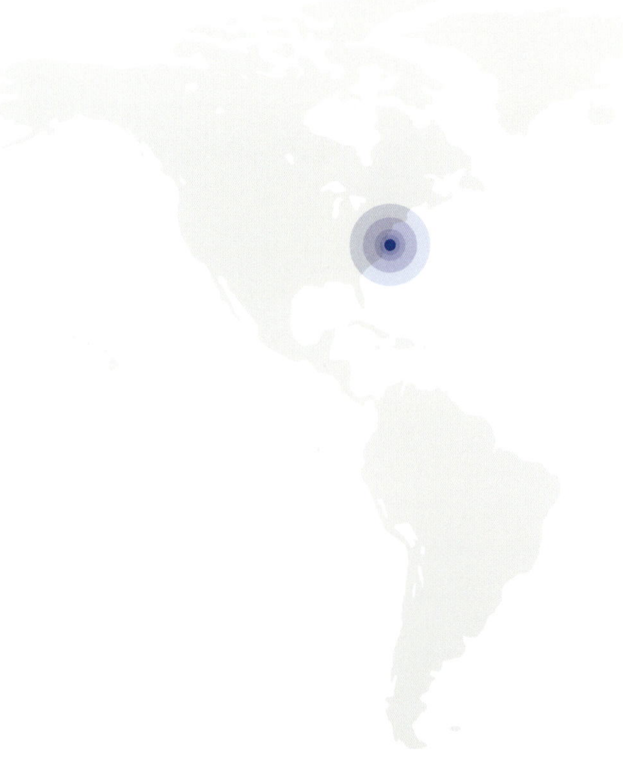

STEAMED CLAMS

Steamed clams are regional favorites across the world. In this section, we present two variations we serve in our restaurants with chunks of our famous crusty sourdough bread for dunking.

Growing up in New England, "real" steamers are small, soft-shell clams harvested in coastal estuaries, from the Arctic to North Carolina, the most famous being Ipswich. When I was little, I'd go clam digging in the mudflats using long-tined, short-handled clam rakes. I also used clam hods—wooden baskets with a handle and wire bottom for washing the mud off the harvested clams.

The classic method of cooking steamers is to steam them in a small amount of water and serve with a cup of clam broth (the seawater released from the clams during steaming), and melted butter. You remove the membrane covering the foot of the clam by pulling it down like a sock, rinse the clam in the cup of clam broth, and finish by dunking the clam in melted butter. A sip of the clam broth brings back a flood of memories of summers spent in New England at the "shore."

Because East Coast clams are not readily available—and because only experienced "East Coasters" know how to properly eat them—we use Manila clams for our steamer pots at the restaurant. We find the best hard-shell clams to be Manilas, which are farm-raised on the West Coast.

IPSWICH STEAMER CLAMS

Only "East Coasters" are allowed to order these since these delicious clams take technique and experience to consume. We might even check your birth certificate to make sure you were born in New England or the surrounding area.

SERVES 2–4

1½ pounds live steamer (soft-shell) clams
½ cup melted butter
Fresh Italian flat-leaf parsley sprig, for garnish

PREPARE THE CLAMS

Add 1 cup of water to a medium-sized pot over high heat and bring to a boil. When boiling, add the clams. Cover the pot and cook until the clams open, about 8 minutes. Remove from the heat and discard any unopen clams.

FINISHING THE DISH

Transfer the clams to a serving bowl and garnish with a sprig of parsley. Pour the liquid from the pot (clam broth) into individual cups. Serve the clams alongside the clam broth and melted butter. To properly eat an East Coast steamer, remove the membrane from the clam's foot and discard. Holding the clam with your fingers, dip into the clam broth, then the butter, and enjoy.

BEVERAGE SUGGESTION

A nice cold Sam Adams Boston Lager—the original Boston beer company named after Founding Father Samuel Adams.

PROVENÇALE-STYLE STEAMED CLAMS

SERVES 2

1½ pounds live Manila clams, scrubbed
¾ cup dry white wine (Chablis or Sauvignon Blanc)
¼ cup clam juice
¼ cup water
1 tablespoon unsalted butter
1½ tablespoons chopped fresh garlic
Fresh Italian flat-leaf parsley, chopped, for garnish
1 Grilled Lemon Half (page 65), for garnish

PREPARE THE CLAMS

Add the clams, wine, clam juice, ¼ cup water, butter, and garlic. Cover and cook until the clams open, about 8 minutes. Remove from the heat and discard any unopen clams.

FINISHING THE DISH

Garnish the pot with chopped parsley and serve alongside a bowl for the shells. Include cocktail forks, spoons, and a grilled lemon half.

BEVERAGE SUGGESTION

A Trimbach Pinot Blanc from France is an excellent pairing. The wine is high in acidity with citrus notes, which helps to cut through the butter, garlic, and hearty brine to enhance the clam flavor.

CLAM CHOWDERS

New England and Manhattan clam chowders are two iconic American soups with distinct histories and flavors that reflect their regional roots. We serve both at the restaurant.

New England clam chowder originated in the northeastern United States, particularly in New England, during the early eighteenth century. Brought by French, British, and Nova Scotian settlers, this chowder is a thick, creamy soup made from a base of milk or cream, potatoes, onions, and clams. The chowder's rich and hearty taste is enhanced using bacon or salt pork, which adds a smoky depth. The chowder's velvety texture and delicate brininess from the clams make it a comforting classic, which we enjoy serving to our guests with oyster crackers, Tabasco sauce, and hot sourdough bread and butter.

Manhattan clam chowder, on the other hand, has a more vibrant history and flavor profile. Emerging in the nineteenth century, particularly in New York City, the chowder is believed to have been influenced by Portuguese and Italian immigrants. Unlike its creamy cousin, Manhattan clam chowder is tomato-based, giving the soup a bright, tangy flavor. The broth is thinner and more robust, with a blend of vegetables like carrots, celery, and onions, and a slight kick from spices like thyme and celery seed. This chowder's taste is more complex and refreshing, a reflection of the diverse, urban environment where it was born.

Both chowders are beloved, yet they represent the culinary diversity and cultural influences of their respective regions. At the restaurant, we also serve a local's favorite that we call the "Ying and Yang" It's a bowl filled with half New England Clam Chowder (white) and half Manhattan Clam Chowder (red). This not only reflects the Chinese symbol for balance and harmony, but the chowder combination illustrates how light and dark are interconnected, as each side contains a part of the other, symbolizing unity within duality.

NEW ENGLAND CLAM CHOWDER

Chowder was originally brought to New England from Europe over 250 years ago and is mentioned in literature of the day in 1760. Originally made with fish and salt pork, New Englanders changed the recipe to use plentiful local ingredients like clams and potatoes.

MAKES 2 QUARTS OR 6 (10-OUNCE) BOWLS

4 slices diced bacon
3 tablespoons unsalted butter
1½ cups yellow onion, peeled and chopped in ¼-inch pieces
3 celery stalks, diced in ⅛-inch pieces
2 garlic cloves, peeled and minced
⅓ cup all-purpose flour
2 cups clam juice
1 cup half-and-half
4 cups peeled and cubed (¼- to ½-inch pieces) russet potato
1½ teaspoons sea salt
½ teaspoon fresh cracked black pepper
1 cup heavy cream
3 (10-ounce) cans clams, chopped, and drained, juice reserved
2 tablespoons chopped fresh Italian flat-leaf parsley, for garnish
Oyster crackers, Tabasco sauce, and hot sourdough bread and butter, for serving

Add the bacon to a Dutch oven over medium heat. Cook until the bacon is crisp and the fat has rendered. Remove the bacon and transfer to a paper towel to drain. Add the butter to the bacon fat along with the onion and celery. Sauté for 4 minutes. Add the garlic and cook for 1 minute. Sprinkle in the flour and cook while stirring constantly for 2 minutes. Gradually stir in the clam juice and half-and-half and whisk until smooth. Return to a simmer, stirring frequently, scraping any bits of flour stuck to the bottom or sides of the pan. Add the potatoes, salt, and pepper. Cover and reduce the heat to medium-low. Stir occasionally until the potatoes are slightly softened, about 15 minutes. Add the cream, clams, and reserved clam juice, and simmer for 10 minutes, or until slightly thickened. Remove from the heat.

FINISHING THE DISH

When ready to serve, warm the chowder over low heat (about 160°F). Portion into cups or bowls, taking care to stir the chowder well before ladling to get even distribution of ingredients. Garnish with the chopped bacon and parsley. Serve with oyster crackers, Tabasco sauce, and hot sourdough bread and butter, if desired.

BEVERAGE SUGGESTION

A light, sweet prosecco or Riesling will cut through the rich cream and buttery consistency of the chowder. In keeping with the East Coast location, we prefer Herman J. Wiemer Dry Reisling from the Seneca Lake region of upstate New York.

MANHATTAN CLAM CHOWDER

Chowder has evolved over the years as a cream-based stew in New England. In the 1800s, the first tomato-based chowders were served at Delmonico's in New York. This was influenced by the Portuguese fisherman who assembled stews with tomatoes, onions, and pork.

SERVES 4 TO 6

2 slices diced bacon
1 tablespoon extra-virgin olive oil
2 medium carrots, cubed in ¼-inch pieces
2 celery stalks, diced in ⅛-inch pieces
1 cup yellow onion, peeled and chopped in ¼-inch pieces
1 garlic clove, peeled and minced
½ teaspoon dried thyme
¼ teaspoon celery seed
1 (12-ounce) can crushed tomatoes
1⅔ cups clam juice
4 cups peeled and cubed (½-inch pieces) russet potato
3 (10-ounce) cans clams, chopped, and drained juice reserved
1½ teaspoons sea salt
½ teaspoon fresh cracked black pepper
Tabasco sauce, to taste
2 tablespoons chopped fresh Italian flat-leaf parsley, for garnish
Oyster crackers, Tabasco sauce, and hot sourdough bread and butter, for serving

Add the bacon to a Dutch oven over medium heat. Cook until the bacon is crisp, and the fat has rendered. Remove the bacon and transfer to a paper towel to drain. Add the olive oil along with the carrots, celery, and onion to the bacon fat. Sauté for 4 minutes, stirring occasionally. Add the garlic and cook for 1 minute. Add the reserved bacon, along with the thyme, celery seed, tomatoes, and clam juice. Stir to combine and bring to a simmer. Add the potatoes and cover for 20 to 30 minutes, or until the potatoes are cooked but not mushy. Add the clams and reserved clam juice and return to a simmer. Add the salt, pepper, and Tabasco sauce. Cover and reduce the heat to medium-low, stirring occasionally, for 10 minutes. Remove from the heat.

FINISHING THE DISH

When ready to serve, warm the chowder over low heat (about 160°F). Portion into cups or bowls, taking care to stir the chowder well before ladling to get even distribution of ingredients. Garnish with the parsley. Serve with oyster crackers, Tabasco sauce, and hot sourdough bread and butter, if desired.

BEVERAGE SUGGESTION

A nice crisp rosé from Provence pairs well since the freshness and minerality highlight the seafood notes and tomato acidity. We prefer Sables d'Azur Rose from Provence in France.

OYSTER STEW

As a young boy, I traveled regularly to New York City with my parents. We always made a point to stop at the Grand Central Station Oyster Bar for a hearty bowl of oyster stew. Later, when I worked at Forty-Second and Sixth Avenue as an adult, I also made it a habit to order the stew from the legendary establishment, located in the lower level of the Grand Central terminal.

Opened in 1913, the Grand Central Station Oyster Bar has become a quintessential part of New York's culinary and cultural history. The restaurant is renowned for its fresh seafood, particularly oysters, and its unique ambiance, which evokes a sense of nostalgia for many visitors. The restaurant's interior is famous for its vaulted ceilings and intricate tile work designed by Rafael Guastavino, a Spanish architect known for his innovative use of tiles and vaults. The beautiful arched ceilings create an iconic look that has remained unchanged for more than a century.

Walking into the Grand Central Oyster Bar is like stepping back in time. The combination of the bustling environment, the clinking of oyster shells, and the aroma of fresh seafood evokes a bygone era of elegance and charm. The menu has remained true to its roots, offering a wide selection of oysters from both coasts, as well as other seafood classics like clam chowder, lobster, and crab cakes. The traditional dishes and the emphasis on fresh, high-quality ingredients have earned the restaurant a loyal following.

One of the Oyster Bar's most famous dishes is the Oyster Pan Roast (a.k.a. Oyster Stew). The stew is creamy and savory with oysters, butter, cream, and a secret blend of spices and cooked to perfection in the restaurant's original steam kettles and served with toast. This is the inspiration for our oyster stew, which we serve at our restaurant.

Oyster stew, incidentally, has a rich history that reflects both regional and cultural influences. It is especially prominent in American cuisine, particularly along the East Coast and in the Southern states. The dish is traditionally associated with special occasions and holidays, such as Christmas Eve. In the American South, oyster stew became popular in the southern United States due to the abundance of oysters along the coastlines. It was served as a luxurious dish during the winter months when oysters were in peak season. There is a theory that Irish immigrants brought the tradition of oyster stew to America. In Ireland, Catholics were prohibited from eating meat on Christmas Eve, leading to the consumption of fish and shellfish. Upon arriving in America, many Irish immigrants adapted this tradition to include oyster stew. Later, during colonial times, oysters were incredibly plentiful and cheap, making them a staple food source. Early American settlers frequently consumed oysters, leading to the development of various oyster-based dishes, including stews.

When making oyster stew at home, make sure to use the freshest oysters possible for the best flavor. Many seafood markets sell shucked oysters by the pint with their liquor included, but I advise that you purchase live oysters and shuck them while reserving the liquor. This will deliver the freshest oysters. In addition, when adding the milk and cream, make sure you're cooking the stew over low to medium-low heat to prevent curdling. Lastly, feel free to play around with the depth and flavor of the stew. For example, try adding a splash of sherry, some garlic, or even a pinch of cayenne pepper for an elevated taste. **SEE PHOTO (PAGE 162, UPPER RIGHT).**

TRADITIONAL OYSTER STEW

SERVES 2 TO 4

4 tablespoons unsalted butter
1 small yellow onion, peeled and finely chopped
2 celery stalks, finely chopped
2 dozen medium oysters, shucked with their liquor reserved (page 103), about 2 cups
2 cups whole milk
2 cups heavy cream
Sea salt and fresh cracked black pepper, to taste
Paprika, for garnish
Chopped fresh Italian flat-leaf parsley, for garnish
Oyster crackers or crusty bread, for serving
Worcestershire sauce, for serving
Tabasco sauce, for serving

Add the butter to a large pot or Dutch oven over medium heat. When the butter is melted, add the onion and celery, and cook until soft and translucent, 5 to 7 minutes. Add the reserved oyster liquor, whole milk, and heavy cream. Stir well with a whisk to combine. Reduce the heat to medium-low and heat the mixture gently, being careful not to let it boil, as this can cause the milk and cream to curdle. Once the milk and cream mixture is hot (but not boiling), add the oysters. Cook for 3 to 5 minutes, or until the oysters start to curl at the edges and are just cooked through. Be careful not to overcook the oysters, as they can become tough. Season the stew with salt and pepper, to taste.

FINISHING THE DISH

Portion the stew into cups or bowls, taking care to stir the stew well before ladling to get even distribution of ingredients. Garnish with paprika and parsley. Serve with oyster crackers, Worcestershire sauce, and Tabasco sauce for individual flavor preferences.

BEVERAGE SUGGESTION

Our best-selling wine is Oyster Bay Sauvignon Blanc from Marlborough County, New Zealand. The wine explodes with a fruit-forward bouquet and complements the creaminess of the stew.

SEAFOOD STEW

This hearty stew is a comforting and flavorful dish that showcases the bounty of the Atlantic Ocean. Packed with a variety of seafood and complemented by a rich, aromatic broth, this stew is perfect for a cozy dinner, and one we serve often at the restaurant during the cold winter months. Feel free to mix and match your favorite seafood. Sometimes we'll add lobster, crab, or calamari. What's important is using the freshest seafood possible for the best flavor. As I'm sure you know, fresh seafood should have a clean, ocean-like smell without any strong odors. If you have some extra shrimp shells or fish bones from prepping the seafood for this recipe, you can use them to make a quick fish stock for a fresher and richer flavor. SEE PHOTO (PAGE 161, BOTTOM).

SERVES 4 TO 6

2 tablespoons olive oil
1 large yellow onion, peeled and finely chopped
2 garlic cloves, peeled and minced
2 celery stalks, finely chopped
1 large carrot, peeled and diced
1 red bell pepper, diced
1 (14.5-ounce) can diced tomatoes
4 cups fish stock (or chicken stock)
1 cup dry white wine
1 teaspoon dried thyme
1 teaspoon dried oregano
1 bay leaf
Sea salt and fresh cracked black pepper, to taste
1 pound russet potatoes, peeled and diced
1 pound firm whitefish (cod or haddock), cut into bite-size pieces
1 pound shrimp 16/20, peeled and deveined (see page 60 for sizing)
1 pound sea scallops, 31/35, (see page 60 for sizing)
1 dozen littleneck clams, scrubbed
1 dozen mussels, scrubbed and debearded (page 162)
¼ cup chopped fresh Italian flat-leaf parsley
1 lemon, juiced
Crusty bread, for serving

Add the oil to a large pot or Dutch oven over medium heat. When heated, add the onion and cook until softened and translucent, about 5 minutes. Add the garlic, celery, carrot, and bell pepper. Cook for 5 to 7 minutes, or until the vegetables begin to soften. Stir in the tomatoes, fish stock, and wine along with the thyme, oregano, bay leaf, salt, and pepper. Bring the mixture to a boil, then reduce the heat to low and let simmer for 15 minutes. Add the potatoes, cover, and simmer until the potatoes are tender, 10 to 12 minutes. Add the fish and cook, uncovered, for 3 minutes. Add the shrimp and scallops and cook for 3 minutes. Finally, add the clams and mussels. Cover the pot again and cook until the clams and mussels have opened, 5 to 7 minutes. Discard any clams or mussels that do not open. Stir in the parsley and lemon juice. Taste and adjust seasoning with salt and pepper, if needed.

FINISHING THE DISH

Portion into cups or bowls, taking care to stir the stew well before ladling to get even distribution of ingredients. Serve with hot crusty bread.

BEVERAGE SUGGESTION

A Beaujolais, like Louis Jadot Beaujolais Villages from France, has a light fruity finish that pairs well with the tomato base in this recipe.

ATLANTIC MUSSELS

Atlantic black mussels, also known as Mytilus edulis, are a species of bivalve mollusk commonly found along the North Atlantic coast, particularly in colder waters ranging from the Arctic down to North Carolina in the United States. These mussels are characterized by their small to medium size, typically measuring 2 to 4 inches, and their smooth, dark blue to black shells, which contrast with their tender off-white to orange flesh inside.

Atlantic black mussels are a sustainable seafood choice, as they are farmed extensively using environmentally friendly methods such as suspended aquaculture. This involves growing the mussels on ropes in clean, nutrient-rich waters, which not only ensures a high-quality product but also contributes to the health of the marine ecosystem by filtering water as they feed on plankton.

In the kitchen, Atlantic black mussels are prized for their sweet, slightly briny flavor and versatility. They are often steamed and served in a variety of broths, ranging from simple garlic and white wine sauces to more complex preparations like Thai coconut curry or Spanish chorizo. Their delicate texture and ability to absorb surrounding flavors make them a favorite in many cuisines, providing a delicious and nutritious seafood option that's low in fat and high in protein.

DEBEARDING A MUSSEL

Debearding mussels is a simple process. The "beard" refers to the fibrous threads (byssal threads) that mussels use to attach themselves to surfaces. Here's how to remove it:

Rinse the Mussels: Place the mussels in a colander and rinse them under cold running water to remove any dirt or debris.

Inspect the Mussels: Look for any open mussels and tap them gently. If they close, they're still alive and safe to cook. Discard any that remain open or have broken shells.

Locate the Beard: Hold the mussel firmly in one hand. The beard looks like a small bundle of brownish or greenish threads sticking out of the side of the shell.

Remove the Beard: Grip the beard with your fingers or a clean kitchen towel. Pull it toward the hinge (the narrower end of the mussel shell). The beard should come out with a firm tug.

Repeat and Store: Continue with the rest of the mussels. After debearding, you can cook the mussels immediately or store them in the refrigerator (preferably covered with a damp cloth) for up to 1 day.

TIPS: Debeard mussels as close to cooking time as possible since removing the beard can cause the mussels to weaken and die.

Mussels can sometimes be stubborn, so using a pair of kitchen tweezers can help with more challenging beards.

Once debearded, the mussels are ready to be cooked using the following recipes.

STEAMED MUSSELS WITH SPANISH CHORIZO

Here's a vibrant and flavorful dish that combines the briny sweetness of fresh mussels with the smoky, spicy richness of chorizo. It's also a popular dish we serve at the restaurant. The mussels are steamed in a broth made from white wine, garlic, onions, and tomatoes that absorbs the paprika and garlic notes of the chorizo, creating a robust and aromatic sauce. As the mussels open, they release their natural juices into the broth, enhancing its depth of flavor. The chorizo adds a satisfying meaty texture and a hint of heat that contrasts beautifully with the delicate mussels. Served with crusty bread to soak up the flavorful broth, this dish is a celebration of Spanish culinary tradition, blending seafood and charcuterie in a way that's both comforting and sophisticated, making it perfect for a casual yet indulgent meal. SEE PHOTO (PAGE 165, BOTTOM).

SERVES 2 AS AN APPETIZER

GARLIC BUTTER
MAKES ½ CUP

1 stick salted butter
3 garlic cloves, peeled and smashed
Finely chopped fresh curly parsley, for garnish

MUSSELS AND CHORIZO

1 tablespoon extra-virgin olive oil
½ cup small diced yellow onion
2½ ounces Spanish chorizo, small dice
½ cup grape tomatoes, sliced in half
3 garlic cloves, peeled and chopped
½ pound black mussels, scrubbed and debearded (page 162)
½ cup dry white wine
Chopped fresh cilantro, for garnish
1 grilled baguette, sliced

PREPARE THE GARLIC BUTTER

Add the butter, garlic, and parsley to a saucepan over medium heat. Cook, stirring often, until the butter is completely melted. Keep warm until ready to use.

PREPARE THE MUSSELS

Add the oil to a large sauté pan over high heat. When heated, add the onion, and cook for 2 minutes. Add the chorizo, tomatoes, and garlic, and cook until the chorizo and garlic just start to brown, about 3 minutes. Add the mussels, wine, and 2 tablespoons of the Garlic Butter. Cover until the mussels open, about 8 minutes. (Note: Shake the pan to allow the mussels to release their muscle connectors, which often makes them open quicker.) Remove the pan from the heat and discard any unopened mussels.

FINISHING THE DISH

Transfer the mussels and broth into a large bowl. Garnish with cilantro and serve hot with grilled baguette slices, shellfish forks, and a shell bowl.

BEVERAGE SUGGESTION

We enjoy Abadia de San Campio Albarino from Spain to pair with this Spanish-inspired dish.

STEAMED MUSSELS WITH THAI RED CURRY

Steamed mussels with Thai red curry is a dish that bursts with exotic flavors and vibrant colors. At the restaurant, we enjoy cooking mussels, especially when they're steamed in a fragrant broth made with Thai red curry paste, coconut milk, and a blend of aromatic ingredients like garlic and ginger. The curry paste infuses the dish with a complex mix of heat, sweetness, and spice, while the coconut milk adds a rich, creamy texture that mellows the intensity of the curry. The result is a delicious blend of sweet, spicy, and savory elements that complement the natural sweetness of the mussels. Garnished with fresh cilantro and a squeeze of lime, this dish offers a tantalizing balance of flavors and is best enjoyed with some crusty bread to soak up the delicious curry. SEE PHOTO (PAGE 165, TOP).

SERVES 4

1 tablespoon extra-virgin olive oil
½ yellow onion, peeled and chopped
1 red bell pepper, chopped
2 garlic cloves, chopped
1 tablespoon finely minced ginger
4 tablespoons Thai Red Curry paste
2 tablespoons packed dark brown sugar
1 tablespoon fish sauce
1 (14-ounce) can coconut milk
2 tablespoons finely chopped fresh cilantro, divided
½ cup chicken broth
2 pounds black mussels, scrubbed and debearded (page 162)
8 lime wedges, for garnish
Crusty bread, for serving

Add the olive oil to a large sauté pan over medium-high heat. When heated, add the onions and pepper and cook until soft, about 3 minutes. Add the garlic and ginger and cook for 30 seconds. Add the curry paste, brown sugar, and fish sauce and stir to coat all the vegetables. Add the coconut milk, half of the cilantro, and chicken broth and bring to a simmer. Reduce slightly until the sauce thickens, about 10 minutes. Add the mussels and steam until the shells open, about 8 minutes. (Note: Shake the pan to allow the mussels to release their muscle connectors, which often makes them open quicker.) Remove the pan from the heat and discard any unopened mussels.

FINISHING THE DISH

Transfer the mussels and broth into a large bowl. Garnish with lime wedges and the remaining cilantro and serve with crusty bread, shellfish forks, and a shell bowl.

BEVERAGE SUGGESTION

A Gewurztraminer with its fruit-forward off-dry flavor profile pairs well with the sweet and spicy Thai curry. Our favorite is from Chateau St. Michelle in Washington's Columbia Valley.

STEAMED MUSSELS WITH THAI GREEN CURRY

Like our steamed mussels with Thai red curry, this version features Thai green curry and is another delicious shellfish dish that's relatively fast to prepare while relying on simple and readily available ingredients. The vibrant colors of the Thai curry, along with the glossy shells of the mussels and fresh green herbs, make for an attractive and appetizing presentation. This recipe, like the previous, combines traditional Thai ingredients and techniques with a globally loved seafood, creating a fusion that can appeal to a wide audience. Try it and you'll discover a dish that stands out for its rich, complex flavors, nutritional benefits, and the engaging experience it provides. It's another great example of how simple ingredients can come together to create something truly special, which is why we enjoy serving it often at the restaurant. SEE PHOTO (PAGE 164, TOP).

SERVES 4

- 1 tablespoon extra-virgin olive oil
- 3 lemongrass stalks, trimmed, crushed, and cut in 3-inch segments
- 5 Makrut lime leaves, crushed
- 1 tablespoon chopped fresh garlic
- 2 shallots, peeled and finely chopped
- 2 tablespoons chopped fresh ginger
- 1 tablespoon Thai Green Curry Paste
- 1 (14-ounce) can coconut cream
- 1½ tablespoons fish sauce + more when finishing the dish
- ½ tablespoon sugar
- 2 pounds black mussels, scrubbed and debearded (page 162)
- ¼ cup chopped Thai basil, reserve some for garnish
- 8 lime wedges

Add the olive oil to a large sauté pan over medium-high heat. When heated, add the lemongrass and lime leaves and cook for 2 minutes. Stir in the garlic, shallots, and ginger and cook for 1 minute. Stir in the curry paste, coconut cream, fish sauce, and sugar and bring to a boil. Then add the mussels and lower heat to medium and cook for 5 minutes, or until all mussels open. (Note: Shake the pan to allow the mussels to release their muscle connectors, which often makes them open quicker.) Remove the pan from the heat and discard any unopened mussels.

FINISHING THE DISH

Divide the mussels into four bowls. Add the Thai basil and additional fish sauce, to taste. Pour the pan sauce over the mussels and toss in each bowl to coat evenly. Garnish with extra basil and lime wedges. Serve with shellfish forks and a shell bowl.

BEVERAGE SUGGESTION

A Gewurztraminer with its fruit-forward off-dry flavor profile pairs well with the sweet and spicy Thai curry. We recommend one from Chateau St. Michelle in Washington's Columbia Valley.

DAY BOAT SCALLOPS

Atlantic Day Boat scallops are a premium type of sea scallop, prized for their freshness, flavor, and sustainable harvesting methods. These scallops are caught by small, independent fishing vessels that venture out to sea and return with their catch within twenty-four hours, ensuring the scallops are exceptionally fresh when they reach the market.

Harvested primarily along the Atlantic coast of the United States, particularly in New England, day boat scallops are larger and sweeter than bay scallops. They are typically harvested using dredges, though some fishermen use more sustainable methods like hand-harvesting by divers. This careful approach not only preserves the delicate marine environment but also results in scallops that are fresher and of higher quality than those caught by larger commercial fleets, which may spend days or weeks at sea before returning with their catch.

Day boat scallops are "dry," meaning they haven't been treated with preservatives or chemicals, which is common with other scallops to retain water weight. This results in a pure, concentrated flavor and a better sear when cooked. They are a favorite among chefs and seafood enthusiasts like us, while valued for their delicate, sweet taste and tender texture, making them a highlight in many savory dishes.

ADAMS
BOSTON
LAGER

SEARED SCALLOPS WITH BACON AND ROASTED JALAPEÑO AIOLI

Day boat scallops are fragile and must be handled with care. Due to the fragile nature of this product, they continue to cook after they are removed from the heat so don't cook them through beforehand. SEE PHOTO (PAGE 173, BOTTOM).

SERVES 1

2 tablespoons 90/10 olive oil/canola blend
3 (U10) fresh day boat scallops (see page 60 for sizing)
Sea salt and fresh cracked black pepper, to taste
¼ cup Roasted Jalapeño Aioli (page 174)
½ ounce Tomato Oil (page 82)
1 teaspoon chopped fresh cilantro
1 ounce cooked and chopped bacon

ROASTED JALAPEÑO AIOLI
MAKES ABOUT 1 CUP

2 jalapeños
1 cup mayonnaise
1 garlic clove, peeled and minced
1 tablespoon fresh lime juice
½ teaspoon kosher salt

PREPARE THE ROASTED JALAPENO AIOLI

Preheat the oven or a broiler to high heat. Place the jalapeños on a baking sheet and roast until the skins are blistered and charred, about 10 minutes, turning occasionally. Transfer the jalapeños to a bowl and cover with plastic wrap for 5 minutes to steam. Peel off the skins, discarding the stems and seeds for a milder flavor, or leave some seeds in for extra heat. Finely chop the roasted jalapeños, then add them to a blender or food processor with the mayonnaise, garlic, lime juice, and salt. Blend until smooth and creamy. Taste and adjust seasoning as needed. Store in an airtight container in the refrigerator for up to 5 days.

PREPARE THE SCALLOPS

Add the oil to a medium sauté pan over high heat. While the pan is heating, season the scallops with salt and pepper. When the oil is shimmering, add the scallops and sear until golden brown on one side, about 60 seconds. Turn the scallops over and sear the other side for 20 seconds. Remove from the pan and drain on paper towels.

FINISHING THE DISH

Arrange the Roasted Jalapeño Aioli and Tomato Oil in a zigzag pattern to a plate. Sprinkle the cilantro down the middle. Place the scallops in the center on top of cilantro with the heavily seared side up. Garnish with the bacon and serve.

BEVERAGE SUGGESTION

A light Chardonnay is a great match for the sweetness of the seared scallops. Our favorite is Joseph Drouhin, Macon-Villages from France.

SEARED SCALLOPS WITH GOAT CHEESE GRITS

Seared sea scallops with goat cheese grits and sautéed asparagus and corn are a delightful combination of flavors and textures. The scallops are rich, tender, and slightly sweet, with a golden crust that adds a satisfying crispness. Meanwhile, the goat cheese grits provide a creamy, tangy contrast, their smooth texture balancing the scallops' seared exterior, while the sautéed asparagus brings a subtle bitterness. The corn adds a pop of sweetness, both complementing the dish with a fresh, vegetal note. Together, these elements create a harmonious bite at the Bluewater Grill that's both indulgent and vibrant, each ingredient enhancing the others beautifully. SEE PHOTO (PAGE 173, TOP).

SERVES 4

GOAT CHEESE GRITS
MAKES 2 CUPS

4 cups chicken broth
1 garlic clove, peeled and minced
¾ cup old-fashioned grits
4 tablespoons unsalted butter
1½ tablespoons heavy cream
Salt and fresh cracked black pepper, as needed, to taste
1 cup goat cheese

ASPARAGUS AND CORN MIXTURE
MAKES 2½ CUPS

¼ cup 90/10 olive oil/canola blend
2 cups trimmed fresh asparagus cut into 1-inch pieces on the bias
2 ears fresh corn, kernels cut off the cob
2 tablespoons unsalted butter

SEARED SCALLOPS

16 (U10) sea scallops (see page 60 for sizing)
Sea salt and fresh cracked black pepper, as needed
2 tablespoons canola or safflower oil
½ cup Chive Oil, for garnish (page 82)
1 lemon, zested, for garnish

PREPARE THE GOAT CHEESE GRITS

Add the chicken broth to a medium saucepan over high heat and bring to a boil. When boiling, reduce the heat to medium. Add the garlic, then slowly stir in the grits. Stir frequently while cooking until the grits are tender, about 20 minutes. Remove from the heat and stir in the butter and cream and season with salt and pepper. Stir in the goat cheese and set aside until ready to serve.

PREPARE THE ASPARAGUS AND CORN MIXTURE

Add the oil to a sauté pan over high heat. When heated, add the asparagus and corn and sauté until the asparagus is tender, but not overcooked, about 5 minutes. Remove from heat, add the butter, and set aside. Toss when butter has melted to evenly coat the asparagus.

PREPARE THE SCALLOPS

Dry the scallops with paper towels and season with salt and pepper. Set aside.

Add the oil to a sauté pan over high heat. When heated, add the scallops to the pan and sear, without moving the scallops, until the underside is well caramelized, about 2 minutes. Carefully turn the scallops over and continue to sear. Work in steps until all the scallops are caramelized on the outside opaque/translucent in the middle, about 1 more minute. Remove the scallops from the heat and transfer to a paper towel–lined plate until ready to serve.

FINISHING THE DISH

Arrange four plates on the counter and evenly divide the Goat Cheese Grits. Evenly divide the Asparagus and Corn Mixture on top of the grits. Arrange four seared scallops on top of the vegetables and grits on each plate. Garnish plate with Chive Oil and sprinkle lemon zest over scallops and serve.

BEVERAGE SUGGESTION

A medium Chardonnay is a great match for the sweetness of the seared scallops and the herbal asparagus and roasted corn mixture. We prefer Cambria Estate Chardonnay from Santa Maria in central California.

PONZU SCALLOPS WITH WASABI AIOLI

Ponzu scallops are a heartfelt menu item at Bluewater, representing our lost friends and colleagues. Our original executive chef, Brian Hirsty, created this dish from raw Peruvian farm-raised scallops, which we discovered at the Boston Seafood Show. They quickly became a fan favorite and remain a signature item at our restaurant. My wife, Julie Ann, calls them "Sea Bon-Bons" since they are sweet like a bonbon yet savory from the pickled ginger and masago. We like to send an order of Ponzu scallops to friends and family as a treat when they dine at Bluewater.

SERVES 2

WASABI AIOLI

1 ounce wasabi powder
1–2 ounces water
¼ cup mayonnaise

PONZU SCALLOPS

6 live scallops in the shell
¼ teaspoon Ponzu (page 284)
¼ teaspoon Wasabi Aioli
½ teaspoon minced pickled ginger
½ teaspoon masago (Japanese fish roe)
Decorative seafood, for garnish, optional

PREPARE THE WASABI AIOLI

Add the wasabi powder and 1 or 2 ounces of water to a bowl and whisk to make a paste. Whisk in ¼ cup mayonnaise until smooth and fully incorporated. Set aside until ready to use, or store in an airtight container in the refrigerator for up to 7 days.

PREPARE THE PONZU SCALLOPS

Shuck each scallop, discarding the top shell and loosening the scallop meat from the bottom shell. Arrange on a decorative plate filled with crushed ice. Top each scallop with an equal amount of Ponzu Sauce, Wasabi Aioli, pickled ginger, and masago. Garnish with decorative seafood, if desired, and serve.

BEVERAGE SUGGESTION

A crisp Chardonnay is a great match for the sweetness and saltiness of the raw scallops. We enjoy Chalk Hill from Sonoma California.

STEAMED MAINE LOBSTER

Steamed lobster is a New England classic— a symbol of the area's rich maritime heritage.

The tradition of cooking lobster dates back to Native American tribes who were known to cook lobsters over hot rocks or by steaming them in pits covered with seaweed. The practice of steaming lobster as we know it today became popular in the nineteenth century when lobster was abundant and considered a cheap food for the working class.

As lobster became more widely appreciated, particularly by affluent diners in the twentieth century, the method of steaming the crustacean became a preferred cooking technique. Steaming preserves the tender, sweet flavor of the lobster meat, which is often served with melted butter and lemon. Today, steamed lobster is celebrated as a luxurious delicacy, often featured in upscale restaurants and at seaside clambakes, where its preparation is as much a ritual as it is a meal. This simple yet elegant dish continues to capture the essence of coastal American cuisine.

For steaming lobster, a steaming pot is essential and a specialized piece of cookware designed specifically for steaming lobsters and other shellfish. It typically consists of a large, deep pot with a tight-fitting lid and a removable steamer basket or rack. The pot is usually made from stainless steel or aluminum, which allows for quick and even heating. When purchasing a lobster pot, if you don't have one already, look for these features:

FEATURES OF A LOBSTER STEAMING POT

Large Capacity

The pot should be large enough to accommodate multiple lobsters or large shellfish. The large capacity ensures enough space for the lobsters to be cooked evenly without being overcrowded.

Steamer Basket or Rack

A removable basket or rack sits should sit inside the pot, keeping the lobsters elevated above the boiling water. This design allows the steam to circulate around the lobsters, ensuring they cook evenly.

Tight-Fitting Lid

The pot should have a tight-fitting lid to trap steam inside. The lid also helps maintain the steam pressure and temperature, which is essential for cooking the lobsters quickly and thoroughly.

Material

The pot should be made from black and white speckled enameled stainless steel or aluminum for durability and efficient heat conduction. These materials ensure the pot heats up quickly and retains heat well, making the steaming process more efficient.

HOW TO STEAM LOBSTERS

Steaming Lobsters is the process of cooking lobsters by exposing them to steam rather than boiling water. Steaming also preserves the natural flavors and textures of the lobster better than boiling. It also makes it easier to handle the lobsters after cooking.

Begin by filling the lobster steaming pot with water. Add enough water to the bottom of the pot while ensuring the water doesn't touch the steamer basket or rack. (Note: If you're not using the basket or rack, fill the bottom of the pot with 2 inches of water.) Next, place the pot on the stove over high heat and bring the water to a boil. When the water is boiling, add the live lobsters. Place them into the steamer basket or on the rack, making sure they are not stacked too tightly.

Cover the pot with the tight-fitting lid and steam the lobsters. The cooking time (see below) varies depending on the size of the lobsters. The lobsters are done steaming when their shells turn bright red, and the meat is opaque and firm. An internal temperature of 145°F (63°C) indicates they are fully cooked.

LOBSTER STEAMING TIMES

Times are based on the average weight of each lobster NOT the total weight to cook. The time starts when the lobsters are added to the pot and the steam starts to form.

For example, if you are steaming 3 (2½-pound) lobsters, your cooking time will be approximately 18 to 20 minutes.

LIVE LOBSTER

1-pound:	8 to 10 minutes
1¼ pounds:	10 to 12 minutes
1½ pounds:	12 to 14 minutes
1¾ pounds:	14 to 16 minutes
2 pounds:	16 to 18 minutes
2½ pounds:	18 to 20 minutes
3 pounds:	20 to 25 minutes
5 pounds:	35 to 40 minutes

After the lobster is finished steaming, carefully remove the lobster from the pot using tongs or a slotted spoon and serve immediately.

LOBSTER ROLL (MAINE AND CONNECTICUT STYLES)

The lobster roll controversy on whether it should be served hot or cold is rooted in regional pride, culinary traditions, and personal preferences. Some people have strong personal memories and attachments to a particular style of lobster roll, often based on what they grew up eating or their first memorable experience with the dish. For many New Englanders, for example, the style of lobster roll they prefer is a matter of regional and cultural identity. It's not just about taste; it's about representing their local traditions and culinary heritage. The lobster roll debate often becomes heated because people are passionate about their food and regional specialties. It's similar to other food controversies like New York versus Chicago pizza or vinegar-based versus tomato-based barbecue. Chefs and food enthusiasts enjoy debating and experimenting with traditional dishes, leading to variations and adaptations that can stir controversy among purists.

MAINE-STYLE (COLD) LOBSTER ROLL

The traditional preparation of a Maine lobster roll is fresh lobster meat mixed with mayonnaise, lemon juice, and sometimes celery or herbs, and served cold. This style is deeply ingrained in the culinary heritage of Maine, where lobster fishing is a significant industry. The addition of mayonnaise and other ingredients reflects a tradition of lobster salads and cold seafood dishes and is often associated with summer picnics, coastal diners, and seafood shacks along the Maine coastline. Spending summers in Maine, my mother would prepare special Tupperware containers with deviled eggs and cold lobster rolls to bring with us on our boat, *Sun Song*, for a day cruise or to go "gunkholing" on a local island in Blue Hill Bay. She would also make "crab rolls" in the same fashion as the lobster roll using sweet Maine crab that were a bycatch of lobster fishing. I would greedily eat one of each without any guilt. SEE PHOTO (PAGE 172, BOTTOM).

MAKES 1 ROLL

NOTE: You can also make this roll with a 50/50 lobster-crab mixture (Clobster Roll) or 100% crabmeat (Crab Roll).

LOBSTER MAYONNAISE
MAKES ABOUT 1 CUP

1 cup mayonnaise
¼ cup finely diced celery
1 lemon, zested
1 teaspoon finely minced shallot
½ teaspoon sea salt
½ teaspoon fresh cracked black pepper

LOBSTER ROLL

6 ounces steamed fresh lobster meat (page 180), chilled
2 tablespoons Lobster Mayonnaise
Sea salt and fresh cracked black pepper, to taste
1 brioche roll
2 tablespoons unsalted butter
Chopped fresh Italian flat-leaf parsley, for garnish
Accompaniments: Pickle spear, lemon wedge, potato chips

PREPARE THE LOBSTER MAYONNAISE

Add the mayonnaise, celery, lemon zest, shallot, and salt and pepper to a mixing bowl. Mix well to combine and set aside.

PREPARE THE LOBSTER ROLL AND FINISHING THE DISH

Add the lobster meat and Lobster Mayonnaise to a mixing bowl and season with salt and pepper. Gently toss to combine. Set aside.

Slice the roll about three quarters of the way down and toast on both sides using a flat grill or sauté pan with butter over medium heat until golden-brown. Remove from the heat and stuff the roll with the lobster mixture. Garnish with parsley and serve with a pickle spear, lemon, or potato chips.

BEVERAGE SUGGESTION

Since we would usually eat lobster rolls on our boat or at a "dockside" restaurant like Beal's Lobster Pier in Southwest Harbor, Maine, I recommend a local microbrew like Atlantic Brewing Company pilsener.

CONNECTICUT-STYLE (HOT) LOBSTER ROLL

The hot lobster roll, in which fresh lobster meat is warmed in butter and served in a toasted bun, is said to have originated in Connecticut. This style emphasizes simplicity and the natural flavor of the lobster, which resonates with the straightforward, no-frills approach to seafood typical in Connecticut. SEE PHOTO (PAGE 172, TOP).

MAKES 1 ROLL

NOTE: You can also make this roll with a 50/50 lobster-crab mixture or 100% crabmeat.

LOBSTER ROLL

6 ounces steamed fresh lobster meat (page 180), chilled
2 tablespoons warm melted butter
1 brioche roll
2 tablespoons unsalted butter
Sea salt and fresh cracked black pepper, to taste
Chopped fresh Italian flat-leaf parsley, for garnish
Accompaniments (optional): Pickle spear, Grilled Lemon Half (page 65), potato chips

Add the lobster meat to the warm melted butter, making sure the meat is well submerged in the butter. Soak until the lobster meat is warm. (Note: You don't want to further cook the lobster meat so make sure the melted butter is not overly hot.)

While the lobster is soaking, prepare the roll. Slice the roll about three quarters of the way down and toast on both sides using a flat grill or sauté pan with butter over medium heat until golden-brown. Remove from the heat and stuff the roll with the lobster meat. Season with salt and pepper, garnish with parsley, and serve with a pickle, lemon, or potato chips.

BEVERAGE SUGGESTION

Since the Connecticut-style lobster roll is served hot and dredged in butter, a crisp acidic wine like Sauvignon Blanc or Chablis complements this well and cuts through the butterfat to let the lobster flavor shine through. We love Oyster Bay Sauvignon Blanc from New Zealand.

THE L

HOUSE

NEW ENGLAND LOBSTER BAKE

A classic New England clam or lobster bake is a time-honored tradition that captures the essence of the region's coastal culture. This communal feast has roots in Native American cooking practices, where seafood, particularly clams, was cooked using hot stones covered with seaweed. The modern clambake evolved in the nineteenth century, combining these indigenous techniques with the bounty of the Atlantic, especially lobster.

A traditional clam or lobster bake is often held on a beach, where the fresh sea air and ocean views enhance the experience. The preparation begins with digging a shallow pit in the sand, which is then filled with hot stones. A layer of wet seaweed is placed over the stones, creating a steamy environment. Lobsters, clams, mussels, corn on the cob, and sometimes potatoes and sausages are added, each layer separated by more seaweed. The bake is then covered and left to steam, allowing the flavors of the sea to infuse the ingredients.

After an hour or so, the feast is ready. Diners gather around, often with melted butter and lemon wedges on hand, to enjoy the succulent lobster, briny clams, and sweet corn. The New England lobster bake is more than just a meal; it's a celebration of community, tradition, and the region's maritime heritage.

Naturally, at the Bluewater Grill, we cannot dig a pit in the sand and invite our guests down to the beach, so we've replicated the classic lobster bake in the kitchen. You can easily make this at home, particularly in your backyard or on your deck with a lobster pot and a propane tank.

SERVES 8

- 3 pounds new red potatoes
- 2 pounds live New England soft-shell or Manila clams, scrubbed
- 2 pounds live Prince Edward Island black mussels, scrubbed and debearded (page 162)
- 2 cups white wine
- ¼ cup kosher or sea salt
- 4 pounds Maine rockweed, optional
- 6–8 (1¼–½ pound) live Maine lobsters
- 1 pound kielbasa sausage (or hot dogs)
- 8 ears fresh corn
- 1 stick (½ cup) unsalted butter
- 2 cups melted butter
- 2 lemons, cut in wedges
- Minced fresh Italian flat-leaf parsley, for garnish

PARBOIL THE POTATOES

Add the potatoes to a medium-sized pot and fill with salted water until the potatoes are covered. Place over high heat and bring to a boil. Once boiling, reduce the heat to medium and simmer for 5 minutes. Remove from the heat, drain the potatoes, and set aside.

PREPARE THE CLAMS AND MUSSELS

Lay a double layer of cheesecloth about 15 inches square on a work surface. Arrange half of the clams on the cloth. (Note: Discard any clams that are gaping and do not close when tapped.) Fold the cheesecloth to form a flat, somewhat loose bundle. Tie the ends with kitchen string. Repeat with the

remaining clams and mussels. (Note: The cheesecloth bags are not critical, and the shellfish can just be layered with the potatoes, but it does make them easier to serve when in the bags.) Set aside.

PREPARE THE LOBSTER BAKE

Insert the steamer basket or rack in a lobster steaming pot (page 180) and fill with the wine, salt, and a little water, if necessary. Add enough wine to fill 2 inches of the pot (or use water to make up the difference). Using a backyard gas burner or stovetop, cover the pot and bring to a boil over high heat. Once boiling, turn off the heat. If using the rockweed, arrange a thin layer to the steamer rack at this time. Set the lobsters on top of the rockweed, and then cover lobsters with a layer of rockweed. For the next layer, arrange the parboiled potatoes along with the bundles of clams and mussels. Cover with another layer of rockweed. Add the kielbasa on top of the rockweed. Cover and bring to a boil over high heat. Once boiling, cook for 8 minutes. After 8 minutes, remove the kielbasa and replace with the ears of corn. Resume cooking for another 8 minutes. While waiting for the lobsters and shellfish to finish, enjoy the kielbasa by cutting into slices and serving with your favorite toppings. If using hot dogs, place in hot dog buns, dress, and serve.

After 16 minutes, check the lobsters and shellfish for doneness. The lobsters should be bright red, and all the shellfish should have opened.

FINISHING THE DISH

Using a pair of tongs, remove everything from the pot, discard the rockweed, and pile the food on a large platter. Butter the ears of corn with the stick of butter. (Note: You can also break or cut the corn into smaller cobs.) Snip open the bundles of clams and mussels with scissors and discard any shellfish that failed to open. Divide the melted butter into ramekins for each person. Garnish the platter with lemon wedges and chopped parsley and serve along with tools for cracking the lobster shells and plenty of napkins.

BEVERAGE SUGGESTION

Clambakes are fun family-style parties where you eat as the different items come out of the pot. We recommend a selection of lighter beers like Sam Adams Golden Pilsener from Boston and a French Chablis or Sancerre to offset the butter used to dunk the clams and lobster which allows the succulent flavor of the seafood to shine through.

BAKED STUFFED LOBSTER WITH CRAB AND SHRIMP

Baked Stuffed Lobster is a decadent New England adaptation of lobster thermidor, which originated in France when the dish was first served to Napoleon. The New England version leaves the succulent meat in the shell and is stuffed with a rich, buttery, and flavorful Ritz-cracker-crab-and-shrimp stuffing. It's then baked to perfection, in which the process infuses the stuffing with the lobster's natural juices, resulting in a delicious combination of textures and tastes. This gourmet delight was made famous by Anthony "Tony" Athanas, a legendary Greek restaurateur at his famous Pier 4 on the Boston waterfront in the early sixties. My brother Joseph, incidentally, worked at several of Tony's restaurants. Joseph met his wife, Dorothy, a native of Salem, Massachusetts, at Tony's Hawthorne by the Sea on the North Shore. Pier 4 later became the highest-grossing restaurant in the United States in the 1980s.

SERVES 1

- Sea salt, as needed
- 1¼ pounds live Maine lobster
- 4 ounces Lobster Stuffing
- 1½ ounces Clarified Butter (page 72)
- Melted butter and lemon wedges, as needed, for garnish

LOBSTER STUFFING

Serves 6

- ½ pound crushed Ritz crackers (or use panko breadcrumbs)
- ½ cup Clarified Butter (page 72)
- ¾ cup lump crabmeat
- ¾ cup bay shrimp
- 2 tablespoons chopped fresh Italian flat-leaf parsley
- ¼ cup sherry wine
- ½ cup chicken stock
- 1 teaspoon kosher salt
- ¼ teaspoon fresh cracked black pepper

PREPARE THE LOBSTER

Fill a large pot with water. (Note: Allow three quarts of water per 1½ pounds of lobster.) The lobster should be completely submerged when added. Add ¼ cup sea salt for each gallon of water. (4 quarts = 1 gallon.) This adds significant flavor to the lobster. Bring the saltwater to a rolling boil. Add the live lobster using a pair of tongs. Do not cover. Boil for 3 minutes.

Remove the lobster from the water and place on cutting board. Allow to cool to the touch. When cool, flip the lobster on its back and use a sharp kitchen knife to cut the belly from its head down to the tail. Be careful not to cut all the way through the shell. Next, remove the brain sac and intestinal line. Crack the claws with the back of the knife or use a pair of crackers. Gently break open the body shell to flatten the lobster and open up the tail and body cavity.

PREPARE THE LOBSTER STUFFING

Add the crushed crackers along with the Clarified Butter, crabmeat, shrimp, parsley, sherry,

GUINNESS
DRAUGHT
STOUT

chicken stock, salt, and pepper to a mixing bowl. Gently combine. (Note: This stuffing makes enough for six lobsters so adjust the recipe so there aren't any leftovers to accommodate the number of lobsters you need to stuff.)

FINISHING THE DISH

Preheat the oven to 350°F.

Place the lobster on a sheet tray. Lightly mound the Lobster Stuffing inside the cavity and tail; do not pack down. Place the lobster in the preheated oven and bake for 10 to 12 minutes, or until the lobster is cooked through and the stuffing is golden brown. Transfer to a large plate and serve with melted butter and lemon wedges.

BEVERAGE SUGGESTION

We love a hearty stout like Guinness to complement this dish, but for those who are not stout drinkers, we recommend an okay, buttery Chardonnay like Chalk Hill from Sonoma. The fruit-forward wine stands up well to the rich flavor of the lobster, crab, shrimp, and stuffing.

CRABBING FOR BLUE CLAWS

Growing up on the East Coast as a child, my family and I spent many of our summers in Stone Harbor New Jersey at "the shore." One of my fondest memories was tying crab traps to the back of my bike and riding out to one of my favorite spots to go "crabbing." Crabbing using menhaden for bait is a popular method for catching blue crabs, particularly in coastal estuaries.

Menhaden, also known as moss bunker, is highly effective because of its oily and aromatic nature, which attracts the crabs. I used box traps shaped like cubes with the bunker tied in the middle. The four sides of the trap had "doors" that would open when I threw the trap and lay flat on the bottom. I'd let the traps "soak" for 20 to 30 minutes. While the crabs were navigating their way to the bait, I'd spend my time skipping rocks and drinking soda pop.

When the time was up, I'd "pull" the traps. I'd slowly bring in the line until I could feel a slight tension, which was the weight of the trap. Then I'd quickly yank the line so the trap doors would fold up and shut, trapping the crabs inside. I'd then haul the trap ashore to see what we caught. Sure enough, I often caught a fair amount of crab while throwing back any bycatch like starfish, small puffer fish, or undersized crab. The "keepers" would get tossed into a bucket with fresh seawater to be cooked later. Indeed, my childhood memories of crabbing were an enjoyable and rewarding activity that combined outdoor adventure with the satisfaction of catching and cooking my own fresh seafood.

MARYLAND-STYLE CRAB CAKES

My father was a graduate of the Naval Academy in Annapolis, Maryland, where he met my mother and where crab cakes reign supreme. Maryland crab cakes—a variety of fishcake—are a culinary icon renowned for their simplicity and exquisite flavor and are enjoyed by seafood enthusiasts worldwide. These succulent cakes—a hallmark of Maryland's cuisine—are traditionally made with Blue Claw crabmeat from Chesapeake Bay and mixed with minimal fillers. Marylanders often argue about the amount of breadcrumb, if any, incorporated into any crab cake recipe. At the restaurant, we opt for a happy medium since it is our feeling a crab cake should have a little breadcrumb and a little binder so the cake can retain its "fishcake" credibility while still allowing the sweet, tender crabmeat to shine through. When making them at home, you can add or remove the breadcrumb to your liking. Just make sure to adjust the yield so you get the right number of cakes in the end.

MAKES 12 (2-OUNCE) CRAB CAKES

1 egg
¼ cup mayonnaise
¼ cup Clarified Butter (page 72)
¼ cup chopped fresh Italian flat-leaf parsley
1 teaspoon Dijon mustard
2 tablespoons Old Bay Seasoning
½ teaspoon Worcestershire sauce
1½ pounds picked fresh crabmeat (Blue, Dungeness, or Jonah)
1 cup panko breadcrumbs
2 tablespoons canola or safflower oil
3 tablespoons Tartar Sauce, for serving (page 62)

PREPARE THE CRAB CAKES

Add the egg, mayonnaise, Clarified Butter, parsley, mustard, Old Bay, and Worcestershire sauce. Mix well to combine. Gently fold in the crabmeat and breadcrumbs. Form into 2-ounce patties using a plastic-wrapped ring mold or your hands. Set aside.

Add the oil to a sauté pan over medium-high heat. When heated and the oil is shimmering, add the crab cakes and cook until golden brown on each side and hot in the center, about 4 minutes per side. (Note: Cook in batches to avoid crowding the pan.)

FINISHING THE DISH

Place 2 crab cakes on each serving plate. Serve warm with Tartar Sauce.

BEVERAGE SUGGESTION

A medium-oaked Chardonnay is a great match for the sweetness of the crab. We prefer Edna Valley from San Luis Obispo, California.

SOFT-SHELL CRAB

Soft-shell crabs are basically blue claw crabs that have molted or shed their "exoskeleton" so they can grow into a bigger shell. Blue claws spend most of their lifecycle with a hard shell but will molt up to twenty times over their lifespan. During the brief period between shedding their old, smaller hard shell and developing a larger hard shell, the crabs are most vulnerable in their soft-shell stage, making them a culinary delight. They have a rich, buttery sweetness and tender flaky meat. Since the crabs can be eaten shell and all, the soft-shell adds a pleasant crunchy texture. The preferred cooking methods for enjoying soft-shell crabs are pan-sautéed with a panko coating, which is the first recipe we're featuring, or they can be dusted in flour and served with a Lemon Caper Beurre Blanc, our second highlighted dish.

CLEAN THE CRABS BEFORE BEGINNING

Once you have your fresh soft-shell crabs, it's important to prep them before cooking. Here's how to do it:

Using kitchen shears, remove the eyes and mouth from front of the crab (approximately 1 inch on the leading front edge of the shell). Lift the carapace from the rear, discarding the "flap" on the underneath of the crab and remove the lungs from both sides on the inside. Rinse the center cavity of the crab under cold running water and replace the carapace. Pat the crab dry, inside and out, and set aside.

PANKO-BREADED SOFT-SHELL CRAB

SERVES 1 (2 CRABS)

½ cup all-purpose flour
½ tablespoon sea salt
½ tablespoon fresh cracked black pepper
2 large eggs
¼ cup whole milk
1 cup panko breadcrumbs
2 soft-shell crabs, cleaned (page 198)
Sea salt and fresh cracked black pepper, to taste
1 cup canola or safflower oil
1 lemon half, for serving

PREPARE THE DREDGING STATION

Fill a bowl with the flour. Season the flour with salt and pepper and mix to combine. Add the eggs and milk to a second bowl and beat until well combined. Add the breadcrumbs to a third bowl.

PREPARE THE SOFT-SHELL CRABS

Lightly season the two crabs with salt and pepper. Then dredge each one in the seasoned flour, gently shaking off the excess flour. Next, dredge the crabs in the egg wash, allowing the extra egg to drip back into the bowl. Then place the crabs in the breadcrumbs and use your fingers to coat all sides, including inside and out. Set the crabs aside.

Add the oil to a large, high-sided sauté pan over medium heat. Heat the oil to 350°F. Use a candy thermometer to check the temperature. When the oil is ready, carefully add the crabs to the oil and fry on both sides until golden brown, 6 to 8 minutes. Transfer the crabs to a paper towel–lined plate to drain.

FINISHING THE DISH

Arrange the two crabs on a plate, garnish with the lemon half, and serve.

BEVERAGE SUGGESTION

We love to drink Oyster Bay New Zealand Sauvignon Blanc with soft-shell crab; the fruit-forward palate offsets the crispy panko batter.

SAUTÉED SOFT-SHELL CRAB WITH LEMON CAPER BEURRE BLANC

SEE PHOTO (PAGE 201, BOTTOM).

SERVES 1 (2 CRABS)

1 cup all-purpose flour
1 tablespoon sea salt
1 tablespoon fresh cracked black pepper
2 soft-shell crabs, cleaned (page 198)
Sea salt and fresh cracked black pepper, to taste
2 tablespoons Clarified Butter (page 72)
1 tablespoon capers, drained
½ cup Lemon Caper Beurre Blanc (page 76)
Chopped fresh Italian flat-leaf parsley, for garnish
1 lemon half, for garnish

PREPARE THE SEASONED FLOUR

Fill a bowl with the flour. Season with salt and pepper and mix to combine.

PREPARE THE SOFT-SHELL CRABS

Lightly season the crabs on all sides, including inside and out, with salt and pepper. Dredge each crab in the seasoning flour to evenly coat, shaking off the excess flour.

Add 2 tablespoons of Clarified Butter to a large, nonstick skillet over medium heat. Add the crabs and cook on both sides until golden brown, 6 to 8 minutes.

FINISHING THE DISH

Remove the skillet from the heat and add the Lemon Caper Beurre Blanc. Gently toss the crabs in the sauce until the sauce is warm. Transfer to a plate, garnish the parsley and the lemon half, and serve.

BEVERAGE SUGGESTION

A Chardonnay with good acidity is a great match for the sweetness of the crab and will cut through the Lemon Caper Beurre Blanc. We enjoy William Hill Chardonnay from Napa California.

BLUEFISH—A CAPE COD TRADITION

Fishing for bluefish on Nantucket Sound is an electrifying experience, capturing the essence of sportfishing excitement. I remember angling trips with my high school friends Fred and Chuck as we headed out into Nantucket Sound from Nauset. It wasn't long until we saw the signs of a feeding frenzy: Gulls and terns dive-bombing a large bait ball from above while a school of bluefish attacked from below. It was a thrill to see—and a clear sign the bluefish were on the hunt. The air was filled with the birds' cries, and the surface was alive with activity. The water began to boil with the frantic movements of baitfish trying to escape the predatory bluefish below.

As we drew nearer, the scene intensified. The water churned with fleeing baitfish, creating ripples and splashes. Our heart raced in anticipation, knowing we were about to engage with one of the ocean's most aggressive hunters. We quickly grabbed our rods, equipped with a strong line and a lure that mimicked a baitfish—perhaps a topwater popper or shiny metal spoon. With swift, confident motions, we cast our lures into the heart of the frenzy. The lures hit the water with one splash each, instantly blending into the chaotic scene. Almost immediately, powerful strikes send a jolt through our rods. The bluefish, known for their ferocity, had taken our bait. The lines tightened, the reels hummed, and our rods bent sharply under the weight of the fish. The bluefish took off with incredible speed, stripping our lines from our reels. The battle began, with each fish making powerful runs and sudden direction changes, testing our skill and equipment.

Bluefish are notorious fighters, often leaping out of the water in acrobatic displays. Each jump and head shake challenging, requiring quick reflexes and a steady hand to keep the fish hooked. The fight is a test of endurance. We reeled in our lines, only for the bluefish to take off again, repeating the cycle until they began to tire. As the bluefish exhausted itself, we took turns carefully guiding our fish closer to the boat. The vibrant blue-green hues of the bodies glistened in the sunlight, and we were mindful of the care needed to land the fish and avoid their sharp teeth. Catching these fish is memorable and rewarding and seared in my memory as a joy of my early adult life spending summers on Cape Cod.

Because bluefish have a high oil content and pronounced flavor, make sure to purchase the highest-quality bluefish available. If catching your own, ensure the fish is quickly bled upon capture, gutted, and placed immediately on ice.

BAKED ATLANTIC BLUEFISH WITH GREEN RICE AND BEEFSTEAK TOMATOES

SERVES 4

HERB SEASONING

1 teaspoon minced fresh tarragon
1 teaspoon minced fresh Italian flat-leaf parsley
1 teaspoon minced fresh chives
1 teaspoon Old Bay Seasoning
2 garlic cloves, peeled and minced
2 tablespoons softened unsalted butter
1 lemon, juiced
2 tablespoons dry white wine

BLUEFISH

4 (8-ounce) fresh skinless bluefish fillets
½ tablespoon sea salt
½ tablespoon fresh cracked black pepper
1 lemon, cut into thin ⅛-inch rounds
1½ cups Green Rice (page 88)
2 large ripe beefsteak tomatoes, cut into 4 slices each (seasoned with salt)

PREPARE THE HERB SEASONING

Add the tarragon, parsley, chives, Old Bay, garlic, butter, lemon juice, and wine to a small mixing bowl. Mix well until combined and a paste-like consistency is achieved. Set aside.

PREPARE THE BLUEFISH

Preheat the oven to 350°F.

Season the bluefish on both sides with salt and pepper. Using your fingers, rub the Herb Seasoning on both sides of the bluefish, reserving a little to use later.

Arrange each bluefish fillet on a sheet of aluminum foil. Top each fillet with a dollop of the remaining Herb Seasoning and a slice or two of the lemon rounds. Seal the foil creating four foil packets. Bake for 15 to 20 minutes, or until the fish is opaque and cooked through.

FINISHING THE DISH

Open the foiled packets and place on four large plates. Serve with Green Rice and freshly salted beefsteak tomatoes.

BEVERAGE SUGGESTION

Bluefish is mostly caught in the summer off Cape Cod. We prefer a Sam Adams lager or a dry French Chablis to complement the pronounced flavor of the bluefish and cut through the herb seasoning.

TARGETING STRIPED BASS—A FATHER AND SON TRADITION

Surfcasting for striped bass is a family tradition of mine. I vividly remember the early morning or late-night outings at the Seabrook Inlet in New Hampshire and Nauset Beach on Cape Cod with my father. We'd time it so we could catch the incoming tide, often on a full moon with the crisp ocean air creeping down our necks. We'd wade knee-deep into surf, which was illuminated in a silvery glow from the moon. We'd cast a classic wooden plug or baited hook into the froth. The tugs on our line usually started with small, immature two-to-three-pound stripers (schoolies), which we'd haul into shore and throw back so they could live another day. But when a big fish hit, it was a sudden and heavy strike. Our line would sizzle out under a light drag as the fish made a powerful run. After a heart-pounding battle of pumping and winding, we'd drag a tired striper onto shore, which often tipped the scales between twenty and forty pounds. The experience of fighting such a formidable fish under the moonlit sky remains one of my most cherished memories of times spent with my father. Today, I continue the same tradition with my children, surfcasting the beaches along New England for stripers, New Jersey for weakfish, and Florida for pompano. These nostalgic memories capture the essence of surfcasting and the thrill of the hunt, the beauty of nature, the bond between anglers, and the timeless pursuit of the perfect catch.

PAN-SEARED STRIPED BASS A L'AMATRICIANA

Because striped bass have a mild, slightly sweet flavor with a firm yet flaky texture, they're an excellent table fish. The flesh is white and moist, making a striper a versatile species that pairs well with various seasonings and cooking methods. Stripers are often compared to other mild-flavored fish like sea bass or halibut, which you can use as a substitute if you cannot locate wild striped bass at your local fishmonger or market. There's also fantastic quality-farmed striped bass available. At the restaurant, we have many popular ways to cook striped bass. Our favorite is to pan-sear skin-on fillets since the skin cooks up crisp and delicious, which is what you'll find in this recipe.

SERVES 4

L'AMATRICIANA SAUCE
MAKES 3½ CUPS

2 teaspoons extra-virgin olive oil
¼ cup finely chopped pancetta
½ cup chopped yellow onion
⅛ teaspoon crushed red pepper flakes
3 garlic cloves, peeled and minced
¼ teaspoon kosher salt, divided
2 cups heirloom grape tomatoes, quartered
1 teaspoon balsamic vinegar
2 cups arugula

STRIPED BASS

4 (8-ounce) fresh striped bass fillets, skin on
Kosher salt and fresh cracked black pepper, to taste
1 teaspoon olive oil
1 tablespoon chopped fresh Italian flat-leaf parsley, for garnish, optional

PREPARE THE L'AMATRICIANA SAUCE

Add the olive oil to a large nonstick skillet over medium-high heat. When heated and the oil is shimmering, add the pancetta. Cook for 1 minute, stirring occasionally. Add the onion, pepper flakes, garlic, and half the salt. Cook for 5 minutes, or until pancetta is browned, stirring occasionally. Add the tomatoes and vinegar. Cook, stirring frequently, for 3 minutes or until the tomatoes blister and soften, Add the remaining salt, stirring well. Remove from the heat and keep warm until ready to serve.

PREPARE THE STRIPED BASS

Season both sides of the striped bass fillets generously with salt and pepper and set aside. Add the olive oil to a large nonstick skillet over medium-high heat. When heated and the oil is shimmering, add the fillets, skin-side down. Cook for 4 minutes, or until the skin is crispy. Flip the fillets and cook for another 3 to 4 minutes, or until the fish is opaque and cooked through. Remove from the heat.

FINISHING THE DISH

Add the arugula to the warm sauce and toss to evenly coat and slightly wilt the arugula. Divide the arugula and pancetta mixture into 4 portions on four plates. Top the arugula mixture with a fillet of striped bass, skin-side up. Garnish with chopped parsley, if using, and serve.

BEVERAGE SUGGESTION

A light Pinot Noir complements the tomato and pancetta-based amatriciana sauce. We prefer Head High Pinot Noir from Sonoma, which we have partnered with to raise funds for the Sea Trees Foundation that focuses on the reforestation of kelp.

BAKED HADDOCK WITH BUTTERY RITZ CRACKER CRUMBS

Haddock, a member of the cod family, has a long and significant history in New England, playing a crucial role in the region's culture, economy, and cuisine. I find it virtually impossible to visit a restaurant and not find haddock on the menu or on the specials board. Growing up in New England, when my friends and I weren't surfcasting the beaches or inlets for stripers or flounder, we'd target haddock out of Seabrook, New Hampshire. We'd fish the Isle of Shoals aboard large party boats that also targeted cod and pollack. At the end of the day, I'd cart home burlap sacks of freshly caught haddock, cod, and pollack to clean and cook at my grandparents' beach house, and my grandmother would prepare this recipe that is ubiquitous in small-town restaurants and taverns throughout Eastern Massachusetts.

Baked haddock is particularly popular, often prepared with a simple combination of butter, cracker crumbs, and lemon juice. Haddock's mild flavor and firm texture make it a versatile fish often featured in community events and seafood festivals across New England that celebrate the region's maritime heritage and culinary traditions.

SERVES 4

BUTTERY RITZ CRACKER CRUMBS

1¼ cups Ritz crackers
¼ cup panko breadcrumbs
1 lemon, zested
½ teaspoon kosher salt
½ teaspoon fresh cracked black pepper
¼ cup finely chopped fresh Italian flat-leaf parsley
1 cup melted butter

HADDOCK

4 (8-ounce) fresh, skinless, boneless haddock fillets
½ lemon
½ cup dry white wine
1 teaspoon paprika
Finely chopped fresh Italian flat-leaf parsley, for garnish

PREPARE THE RITZ CRACKER CRUMB CRUST

Crush Ritz crackers to a fine breadcrumb consistency and add to a bowl. Add the panko, lemon zest, salt, pepper, and parsley. Mix well to combine, then stir in the melted butter.

PREPARE THE HADDOCK

Preheat the oven to 425°F.

Dry the haddock fillets with paper towel. Using a small ceramic baking dish or individual casserole dishes, sprinkle a thin layer of the cracker crumb mix on the bottom of the dish. Add the white wine and then the haddock to the top of the crumbs and wine. Squeeze some lemon juice over the fillets and then top them with the remaining crumb mixture. Dust the tops of the fillets with paprika. Bake on the top rack of the oven until crumbs brown and the internal temperature of the fish reaches 140°F,

15 to 18 minutes. Be careful not to overbrown the topping. Cover with a sheet of aluminum foil, if necessary, until the fish is cooked.

FINISHING THE DISH

Plate the fish, garnish with parsley, and serve. Seasonal sides that work well with the dish include asparagus and roasted cauliflower, carrots, or potatoes.

BEVERAGE SUGGESTION

An oaky Chardonnay from Napa like William Hill or Trefethen complements this dish with the richness of the buttery Ritz crumb mixture and the lemon.

SOUTHERN WATERFRONT & THE GULF

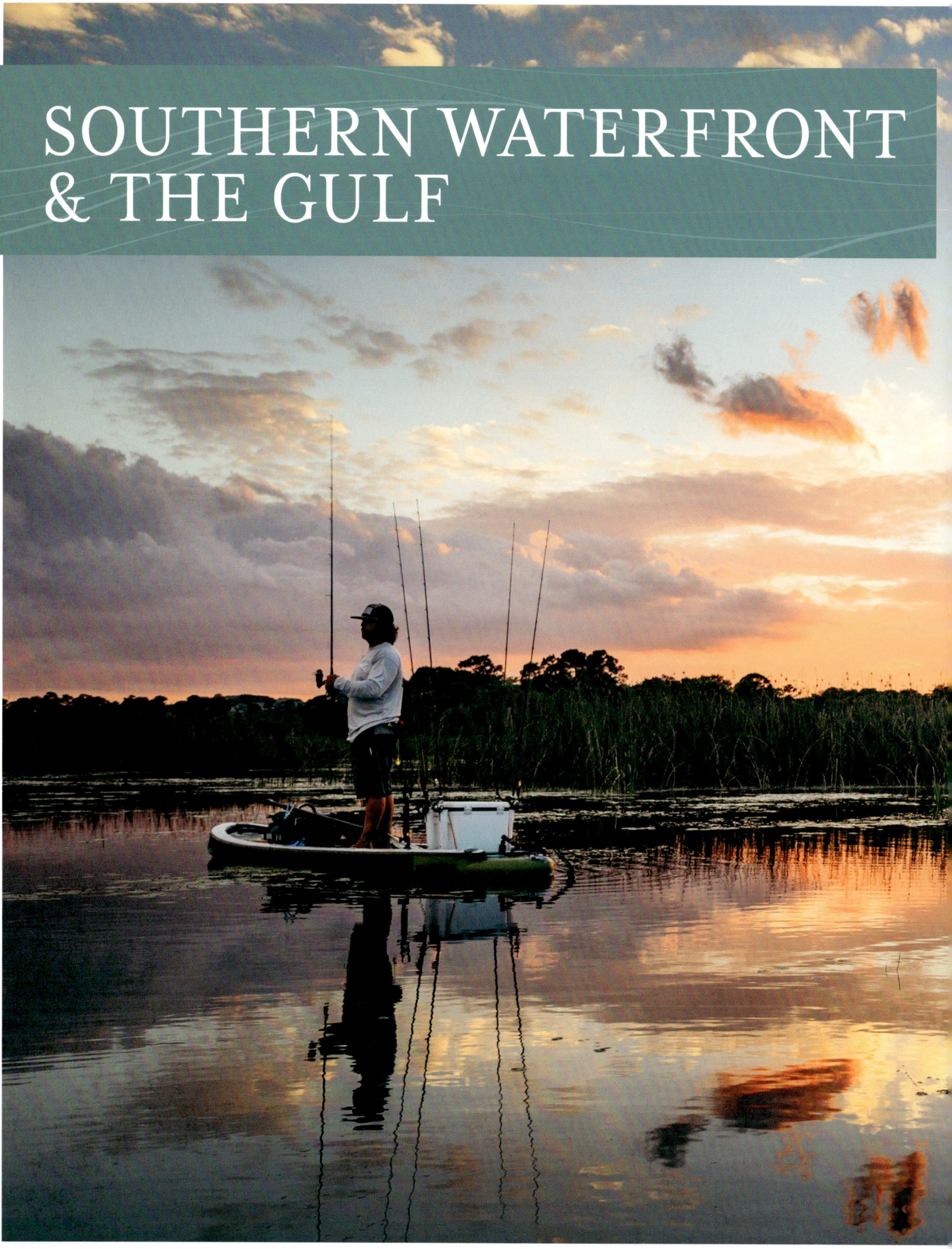

SOUTHERN WATERFRONT & THE GULF

Similar to the Atlantic seafood scene, the Southern waterfront and Gulf of Mexico offer a seafood experience equally rich in flavor, culture, and tradition. Stretching from the Florida Keys to Texas, this region is renowned for its warm waters, which provide an abundance of fresh and diverse seafood. Whether you're sitting down at a casual beachside restaurant or bringing the seafood home to a coastal kitchen, the fish and shellfish here are a culinary treasure. My mother and stepfather were engaged on Longboat key, just outside Tampa, on the west coast of Florida in 1971. We would return every few years to visit friends and go to famous Ybor City, the "Cigar Capital of the United States," and seafood restaurants like Shrimp & Company or Bern's Steakhouse with its famous wine cellar with 6,500 wines and 500,000 bottles and its 20 varieties of caviar.

There are many gastronomic highlights of this sun-drenched area, and one is the Gulf shrimp, known for its sweet, tender meat. Shrimp boils are a Southern tradition in which shrimp are boiled with corn, potatoes, and sausage, seasoned with spices, and enjoyed outdoors. What we like to do at Bluewater Grill is feature the shrimp in such favorites as our Salt and Pepper Fried Whole Shrimp as well as our New Orleans–Style Barbecue Shrimp, and we plunk them in our rich and flavorful gumbos and jambalayas.

Oysters are another standout along the Gulf Coast. In particular, the oysters from Apalachicola, or the Big Bend area of Florida, are renowned. Raw oysters on the half shell, drizzled with lemon or cocktail sauce, are a beloved appetizer. In Louisiana, charbroiled oysters—grilled with butter, garlic, and cheese—are a must-try delicacy, bursting with smoky, savory flavors. We'll take the oysters one step further and showcase them in our classic Oysters Rockefeller and Oysters Bienville.

The Southern Gulf waters are rich in fish like grouper, pompano, catfish, and redfish. You'll find all these delicious species in this chapter, which we prepare a number of ways, from sake- and soy-based marinades to blackened dishes that are highlighted with Creole- and Southern-based sides like our steamed mustard greens and étouffées.

Without question, the seafood along the Southern waterfront and Gulf of Mexico is not just about the food—it's about the laid-back coastal atmosphere, vibrant local culture, and fresh-from-the-sea meals that create an unforgettable dining experience, where the flavors of the ocean meet the warmth and hospitality of the South.

OYSTERS ROCKEFELLER

Oysters Rockefeller is a classic American dish first created in 1899 at Antoine's, a historic restaurant in New Orleans, by owner Jules Alciatore. Due to a shortage of escargot, he swapped in local oysters. Named after John D. Rockefeller, the wealthiest American at the time, the dish was designed to be rich and luxurious, reflecting Rockefeller's immense wealth. The recipe typically involves fresh oysters on the half-shell, topped with a rich mixture of butter, parsley, green herbs, and breadcrumbs, then baked until golden and bubbly. Some versions also include ingredients like spinach, garlic, and Pernod or anise-flavored liqueur to enhance the flavor. The precise original recipe is reputed not to contain spinach but instead watercress, parsley, or some other leafy vegetable to give the dish its signature green color. We will never know because Mr. Alciatoire took the original recipe to his grave. Today, the dish's signature richness and vibrant green color have made it a favorite for over a century. Oysters Rockefeller is often served as an appetizer and remains a symbol of opulence and indulgence in American cuisine. Its legacy continues to be celebrated in culinary circles, showcasing the enduring appeal of this sumptuous seafood dish. We pride ourselves on serving an authentic version of "Rockies" at Bluewater, and our guests are addicted to the rich creamed spinach and cheese topping.

SERVES 4 (4 OYSTERS EACH)

4 slices thick-cut bacon
5 tablespoons unsalted butter, divided
1 finely diced shallot
2 garlic cloves, peeled and finely chopped
1½ cups chopped fresh baby spinach + more for serving
1 teaspoon fresh cracked black pepper
2 tablespoons Pernod
1¼ cups freshly grated Romano cheese, divided
½ cup panko breadcrumbs
1 tablespoon finely chopped fresh Italian flat-leaf parsley + ¼ teaspoon for garnish
16 freshly shucked large oysters (page 103) with thick shell
Lemon wedges, for serving

PREPARE THE FILLING

Add the bacon to a sauté pan over medium heat and cook until crispy. Remove the bacon from the pan, drain on paper towels, then chop and set aside. Add 3 tablespoons of butter to the pan. When the butter is melted, add the shallot and garlic and cook, stirring often, for 1 minute. Add the spinach and black pepper and stir to combine. Add the Pernod and cook, stirring often, until the spinach is wilted, about 3 minutes. Add ¼ cup of the cheese. Stir in the chopped bacon. Cook for 2 minutes to thicken slightly. Remove from the heat and set aside.

PREPARE THE TOPPING

Add the remaining 2 tablespoons butter to the sauté pan over medium heat. When melted and the butter is foaming, add the breadcrumbs and parsley and mix thoroughly. Remove from the heat and set aside.

FILL AND COOK THE OYSTERS

Preheat the oven to 375°F.

Shuck the oysters, placing the meat in a bowl without any liquor (oysters should be dry). Set aside. Rinse the shells and dry them thoroughly. Fill half of each oyster shell with about 1 tablespoon of filling.

Place 1 shucked oyster on top of the filling and then top with the 1 tablespoon topping on each. Place the stuffed oysters on a wire rack in a roasting pan. (Note: This is important so the oven heat will circulate on top and bottom of the shell.) Bake on the top rack for 10 minutes, or until the cheese mixture is melted. Switch the oven to broil and broil for 1 minute for a little extra browning, but do not burn. Remove from the oven.

FINISHING THE DISH

Arrange the oysters on a platter with a bed of fresh spinach to support the uneven bottoms of the shells. Serve with small seafood forks and lemon wedges.

BEVERAGE SUGGESTION

A full-bodied Chardonnay or Viognier stands up well to the richness of the cheese and creaminess of the spinach-and-bacon filling in this dish. We prefer Hermit Crab Viognier/Marsanne from Australia.

OYSTERS BIENVILLE

Oysters Bienville is a classic Creole dish originating from New Orleans, named after the city's founder, French explorer Jean-Baptiste Le Moyne de Bienville. This Louisiana specialty highlights the rich culinary traditions of the region, particularly in seafood preparation. Oysters Bienville is often served as an appetizer or main course alongside crusty French bread or rice.

Oysters Bienville is believed to have been created in the early twentieth century at Antoine's Restaurant in New Orleans. Antoine's, established in 1840, is one of the oldest family-run restaurants in the United States and has been a cornerstone of Creole cuisine. The dish combines French culinary techniques with local Gulf Coast ingredients, particularly oysters, which are abundant in the region. Over the years, the recipe for Oysters Bienville has evolved and varied among chefs and restaurants, but it typically involves a rich and savory sauce that complements the briny flavor of the oysters. This recipe is our version.

When making at home, feel free to adjust the ingredients to your personal preferences. For example, try adding Gruyère or cheddar for added richness. Instead of shrimp, you can use crabmeat or a combination of seafood. You can also adjust the amount of hot sauce according to your preferred level of spiciness.

A NOTE ABOUT MAKING ROUX

Making roux is a fundamental technique in many cuisines, particularly in French, Creole, and Cajun cooking. Roux is a mixture of equal parts fat (usually butter, oil, or lard) and flour, cooked together to thicken sauces, soups, and stews. To make a roux, melt the fat in a pan over medium heat, then gradually whisk in the flour until smooth. Cook the mixture, stirring constantly, until it reaches the desired color—white, blonde, brown, or dark brown—each imparting different levels of flavor. The darker the roux, the richer and nuttier the taste, though it will have less thickening power.

SERVES 4 (6 OYSTERS EACH)

24 fresh oysters
6 tablespoons unsalted butter
¼ cup all-purpose flour
1 cup wild Gulf shrimp (16/20), peeled and finely chopped (see page 60 for sizing)
½ cup finely chopped onion
½ cup finely chopped green bell pepper
½ cup finely chopped celery
2 garlic cloves, peeled and minced
¼ cup dry white wine
1 cup heavy cream
¼ cup freshly grated Parmesan cheese
1 tablespoon Worcestershire sauce
1 tablespoon Tabasco sauce, or to taste
Kosher salt and fresh cracked black pepper, to taste
¼ cup chopped fresh Italian flat-leaf parsley, for garnish
Lemon wedges, for serving

PREPARE THE OYSTERS

Shuck the oysters, reserving their liquor (page 103). Arrange the oysters on a baking sheet or in a shallow baking dish. Set aside.

PREPARE THE SAUCE

Add the butter to a large skillet over medium heat. Add the flour and cook, stirring

constantly, for 2 minutes to make a roux. Add the shrimp, onion, bell pepper, celery, and garlic. Cook, stirring occasionally, until the vegetables are tender, and the shrimp turn pink, 5 to 7 minutes. Deglaze the skillet with the white wine, scraping up any browned bits from the bottom of the pan. Stir in the heavy cream and reserved oyster liquor. Cook, stirring occasionally, until the sauce thickens, about 5 minutes. Remove the skillet from the heat and stir in the grated Parmesan cheese, Worcestershire sauce, and Tabasco sauce. Season with salt and pepper to taste.

FINISHING THE DISH

Preheat the oven to 350°F.

Spoon the sauce over each oyster on the baking sheet, covering them generously. Bake for 15 to 20 minutes, or until the sauce is bubbly and lightly browned on top. Remove and garnish with chopped parsley. Serve the Oysters Bienville hot, with lemon wedges on the side for squeezing over the oysters.

BEVERAGE SUGGESTION

A crisp, acidic white wine or chilled sparkling wine wonderfully complements the rich flavors of this dish. The rich butter-based sauce needs the acidity to cut the fat and allow the flavor of the oyster to shine through. We enjoy Trimbach, Pinot Blanc from Alsace.

SALT AND PEPPER FRIED WHOLE SHRIMP

This recipe for salt and pepper fried whole shrimp, perfect as an appetizer or main dish, is a delightful way to enjoy shrimp with their shells on, which adds a pleasant crunch and extra flavor. For those who haven't tried these before, don't be shy. Simply grab the shrimp by the head, tear off the tail flippers, and eat the tail, shell and all. Once you finish the tail, crunch half the head and body, as all the flavor is in the shell. Meanwhile, the simplicity of the seasoning allows the natural taste of the shrimp to shine through. At our restaurant, our guests love the crispy texture of our succulent shrimp. We'll serve this savory dish with a side of steamed rice or a fresh garden salad for a complete meal.

SERVES 2 AS AN APPETIZER

1 pound wild Gulf shrimp (16/20), tail deveined, with head and shells on (see page 60 for sizing)
½ cup cornstarch
1 teaspoon sea salt
1 teaspoon fresh cracked black pepper
1 teaspoon white pepper
1 teaspoon garlic powder
1 teaspoon paprika, optional
Vegetable oil, for frying
2 green onions, finely chopped
2 garlic cloves, peeled and minced
1 or 2 red chilies thinly sliced, depending on your desired heat level, and optional
Fresh chopped cilantro, for garnish
Lemon or lime wedges, for serving

PREPARE THE SHRIMP

Pat the shrimp dry with paper towels and set aside. (Note: Leaving the shells on adds flavor and crunch, but make sure the shrimp are thoroughly cleaned. If you prefer, you can remove the shells and just keep the tails on.)

Add the cornstarch, salt, black pepper, white pepper, garlic powder, and paprika, if using, to a mixing bowl. Mix well to combine. Next, toss the shrimp in the mixture, making sure each shrimp is well coated. Shake off any excess cornstarch. Set aside.

Add 1 to 2 inches of vegetable oil to a large deep-sided skillet or wok over medium-high heat. Heat the oil until it reaches 350°F. Use a candy or digital thermometer to check the temperature. You can also test by dropping a small piece of shrimp in the oil. If the shrimp sizzles immediately, the oil is ready. (Note: Make sure to maintain the oil temperature between 350°F and 375°F during frying for optimal results. Too low and the shrimp will be greasy; too high and they may burn.)

Carefully add the shrimp to the hot oil in batches to avoid overcrowding. Fry each batch for 2 to 3 minutes, or until the shrimp are golden brown and crispy. Use a slotted spoon to transfer the fried shrimp to a plate lined with paper towels to drain excess oil.

In another pan, heat a small amount of oil over medium heat. When heated and the oil is shimmering, add the green onions, garlic, and red chilies, if using. (Note: You can also add a pinch of chili flakes for extra heat. Sauté for 1 to 2 minutes, or until fragrant.)

FINISHING THE DISH

Add the fried shrimp to the pan with the sautéed aromatics. Toss everything together to ensure the shrimp are well-coated. Transfer the shrimp to a serving platter. Garnish with fresh cilantro and serve with lemon or lime wedges.

BEVERAGE SUGGESTION

Wines with herbaceous citrus or tropical fruit flavors like a Voigner or Sauvignon Blanc pair well. We love Duckhorn's Decoy Sauvignon Blanc from California.

NEW ORLEANS–STYLE BARBECUE SHRIMP

When I was young and would visit friends at Tulane University, many of our nights kicked off with a visit to Bourbon Street, where we always found great food like these barbecue shrimp, great drinks, and great entertainment. Our guests at our restaurant also appreciate these New Orleans–style shrimp. Enjoy making them at home as a shared appetizer along with an ice-cold Dixie or Abita beer from Louisiana. It's important, but not critical, to purchase wild Gulf shrimp when making this recipe, and any others in this chapter, that call for shrimp. That's because wild Gulf shrimp are prized for their sweet, firm texture and rich flavor, harvested from the warm waters of the Gulf of Mexico. Unlike farmed shrimp, they thrive naturally, offering a distinctive taste influenced by their environment. Sought after by chefs and seafood lovers, they're a premium, sustainable choice. Just ask Bubba Gump.

SERVES 2 AS AN APPETIZER

CREOLE SEASONING
MAKES ABOUT 1/3 CUP

1 tablespoon kosher salt
½ teaspoon cornstarch
1 teaspoon cayenne pepper
1 teaspoon granulated garlic
1 teaspoon fresh cracked black pepper
1 teaspoon paprika
1 teaspoon celery salt
1 teaspoon Coleman's ground dry mustard
1 teaspoon dry basil
1 teaspoon granulated onion
½ teaspoon dry oregano
½ teaspoon dry thyme
1 teaspoon gumbo filé
1 tablespoon packed dark brown sugar

CREOLE BARBECUE SAUCE
MAKES 1½ CUPS

⅓ cup Worcestershire sauce
1 teaspoon Tabasco sauce
1 cups tomato juice
1 tablespoon fresh lemon juice
1 tablespoon apple cider vinegar

SHRIMP

10 wild Gulf shrimp (16/20), peeled, deveined, tail-on (see page 60 for sizing)
2 tablespoons extra-virgin olive oil
1 tablespoon + 1 teaspoon chopped garlic, divided
½ cup grape tomatoes, sliced in half
½ cup Creole Barbecue Sauce
1 tablespoon unsalted butter
1 tablespoon thinly sliced green onion, for garnish
Rustic bread, toasted with olive oil and chopped garlic, for serving

PREPARE THE CREOLE SEASONING

Add the salt, cornstarch, cayenne, granulated garlic, pepper, paprika, celery salt, dry mustard, basil, granulated onion, oregano, thyme, gumbo filé, and brown sugar to a food processor. Mix until combined. Set aside.

PREPARE THE CREOLE BARBECUE SAUCE

Add the Worcestershire sauce, Tabasco sauce, tomato juice, lemon juice, and apple cider vinegar to a bowl. Mix until combined. Set aside.

FINISHING THE DISH

Coat the shrimp with the Creole Seasoning and set aside.

Add the oil to a large deep-sided sauté pan over medium-high heat. When heated and the oil is shimmering, add the seasoned shrimp and 1 tablespoon of the garlic. Cook for 1 minute and add the tomatoes. Cook for 1 minute. Add the Creole Barbecue Sauce and stir to combine. Add the shrimp and when the shrimp are fully cooked, about 3 minutes, turn off the heat and mix in the remaining teaspoon of garlic along with the butter. Note: The sauce should not reduce.

Transfer the shrimp and sauce to a small serving dish. Garnish with the green onions and serve with a side of rustic bread for dipping into the sauce.

BEVERAGE SUGGESTION

A chilled Dixie or Abita beer from Louisiana is a great way to share this dish. The cold beer mixes well with the barbecue flavor.

SHRIMP AND CHICKEN GUMBO

This gumbo is a quintessential dish originating from Louisiana's Creole cuisine, representing the culinary practices of numerous cultures including African, French, Spanish, and the Native American Choctaw. The iconic stew, renowned for its rich flavors and hearty texture, combines succulent shrimp, tender chicken, and the "Holy Trinity" (celery, bell pepper, and onion) cooked in a savory broth. Gumbo is typically categorized by the type of thickener used. At the restaurant, we prefer filé powder (dried and ground sassafras leaf). Served over a bed of fluffy rice, this comforting gumbo offers a symphony of tastes that satisfies the palate while celebrating the vibrant culinary heritage of the American South. SEE PHOTO (page 253, shown with Fried Green Tomatoes).

SERVES 4

GUMBO AND SAUCE

8 tablespoons unsalted butter, divided
1 cup all-purpose flour
1 cup coarsely chopped celery
1 large yellow onion, peeled and coarsely chopped
1 large green bell pepper, coarsely chopped
2 cloves garlic, peeled and minced
1 pound andouille sausage, sliced
3 quarts water
6 cubes beef bouillon
1 tablespoon white sugar
Kosher salt, to taste
2 tablespoons hot pepper sauce (such as Tabasco), or to taste
½ teaspoon Tony Chachere's Creole Seasoning, or to taste
4 bay leaves
½ teaspoon dried thyme leaves
1 (14.5-ounce) can stewed tomatoes
1 (6-ounce) can tomato sauce
4 teaspoons filé (gumbo) powder, divided + more for garnish
2 (10-ounce) packages frozen cut okra, thawed
2 tablespoons distilled white vinegar
1 pounds boneless, skinless chicken thighs, cut into 1-inch pieces
2 pounds uncooked medium (16/20) Gulf shrimp, peeled and deveined (see page 60 for sizing)
2 tablespoons Worcestershire sauce
4 cups steamed white rice
Chopped fresh Italian flat-leaf parsley, for garnish

PREPARE THE GUMBO

Add 6 tablespoons butter in a large, heavy saucepan over medium-low heat and heat until melted. Using a whisk, blend in the flour and cook to a roux, whisking constantly, until the mixture turns a rich mahogany brown color, about 10 minutes. Watch the heat carefully and whisk constantly or the roux will burn. Remove from heat and continue whisking until the mixture stops cooking. Set aside.

Add the celery, onion, green bell pepper, and garlic to the bowl of a food processor and pulse until all the vegetables are very finely chopped.

Stir the vegetables into the roux and mix in the sliced sausage. Cook over medium-low heat, stirring constantly, until the vegetables are tender, 10 to 15 minutes. Remove from heat and set aside.

Combine the water and beef bouillon cubes in a large Dutch oven or soup pot and bring to a boil over medium-high heat. Stir until the bouillon cubes dissolve, then whisk the roux mixture into the boiling water. Reduce the heat to a simmer and mix in the sugar, salt, hot sauce, Creole seasoning, bay leaves, thyme, stewed tomatoes, and tomato sauce. Simmer the soup over low heat for 1 hour, then stir in 2 teaspoons of filé gumbo powder at the 45-minute mark.

Meanwhile, add the remaining 2 tablespoons butter in a skillet over medium heat. When melted, add the okra and vinegar and cook for 15 minutes. Remove the okra with a slotted spoon and stir into the simmering gumbo.

Add chicken, shrimp, and Worcestershire sauce, and simmer until the flavors have blended, about another 45 minutes. Stir in the remaining 2 teaspoons filé gumbo powder just before serving.

FINISHING THE DISH

Mound the rice in the middle of a large serving bowl. Divide the sauce, chicken, and shrimp equally around the rice. Top with the Gumbo Sauce, being careful to leave the rice intact. Garnish with a sprinkling of gumbo filé and parsley. Serve immediately.

BEVERAGE SUGGESTION

Beer from Abita or Faubourg Brewing Co (formerly Dixie) to celebrate the spirit of New Orleans. A French Chenin Blanc, Dry Rose, or Viognier also pairs well.

CREOLE JAMBALAYA WITH BLACKENED SHRIMP

Like Gumbo, Jambalaya is a beloved dish from Louisiana, deeply rooted in the state's Creole and Cajun cultures. It's a one-pot meal that brings together a hearty mix of flavors and ingredients, making it a staple of Southern cuisine and at our restaurant. The dish typically starts with a base of the "Holy Trinity"—onions, bell peppers, and celery—sautéed in oil. To this, garlic, tomatoes, and a mix of proteins such as chicken, sausage (usually andouille), and shrimp are added, along with rice and a variety of spices.

The origins of jambalaya are a reflection of Louisiana's diverse cultural influences, combining Spanish paella, French techniques, and African and Native American culinary traditions. There are two main styles: Creole jambalaya, which includes tomatoes, and Cajun jambalaya, which does not. The dish is cooked slowly until the rice absorbs all the rich flavors, creating a comforting, flavorful meal. Jambalaya is often served at gatherings and celebrations, embodying the spirit of sharing and community central to Southern hospitality.

SERVES 4

JAMBALAYA RICE
MAKES 4 CUPS

¼ cup canola or safflower oil
1 cup (¼-inch diced) yellow onion
1 cup (¼-inch diced) green bell pepper
1 cup (¼-inch diced) celery
1 tablespoon chopped garlic
1 cup canned diced tomato
1 cup parboiled long-grain white rice
½ tablespoon minced fresh thyme
1½ tablespoon Tony Chachere's Creole Seasoning
½ tablespoon paprika
1 quart vegetable stock

BLACKENED SHRIMP

2 tablespoons canola or safflower oil
20 wild Gulf shrimp (16/20), peeled and deveined (see page 60 for sizing)
1 tablespoon Tony Chachere's Creole Seasoning
1 tablespoon canola or safflower oil

JAMBALAYA

2 tablespoons canola or safflower oil
16 ounces boneless, skinless chicken thighs, large dice
1 cup sliced andouille sausage
4 cups Jambalaya Rice
Green onion, julienned, for garnish

PREPARE THE JAMBALAYA RICE

Add the oil to a stockpot over medium-high heat. When heated and the oil is shimmering, add the onion, bell pepper, and celery and sweat, stirring often, until softened, 5 to 7 minutes. Add the garlic and cook for 2 minutes. Stir in the tomatoes, rice, thyme, Creole seasoning, paprika, and vegetable stock. Bring to a boil, then reduce the heat to low, cover, and simmer for 20 minutes until all water is absorbed. Remove from the heat.

PREPARE THE BLACKENED SHRIMP

Place 5 shrimp each on four bamboo skewers. Season both sides of the shrimp with Creole seasoning. Set aside. Preheat a large skillet to high heat. When hot, add the oil. When hot and shimmering, add the shrimp skewers and sear both sides until shrimp are fully cooked, about 3 minutes per side. Set aside and keep warm.

PREPARE THE JAMBALAYA

Add the oil to a large deep-sided sauté pan over medium-high heat. When heated and the oil is shimmering, add the chicken and sausage and cook until both are cooked through, about 6 minutes. Add the Jambalaya Rice to the pan and stir well until chicken and sausage are evenly distributed. Set aside.

FINISHING THE DISH

Ladle the Jambalaya in serving bowls and mound the Jambalaya Rice in the middle, on top of the Jambalaya. Place a cooked shrimp skewer on top of the rice off to one side. Garnish with green onions and serve.

BEVERAGE SUGGESTION

A reserve Rioja melds with the smoky, meaty flavors of jambalaya. We love the reserve Rioja from Marques de Riscal.

372 LBS.

196LBS

SAKE AND SOY FLORIDA GROUPER WITH ENGLISH CUCUMBER SALAD

Florida, with its vast coastline and numerous wrecks, offers a haven for grouper, a delicious, easy-to-prepare fish, which is popular among anglers. Recognized by their large mouths and heavy robust bodies, groupers are widely distributed in tropical seas. They are often found in shallow and deepwater reefs, foraging for any prey they can stuff whole into their cavernous mouths. Growing up as a child, my family and I would take vacations to Florida where I would fish for grouper and later enjoy them at the dinner table. Grouper is a staple on many restaurant menus throughout the Sunshine State. A trip to Florida would not be complete without a starter of Grouper Fingers (lightly breaded strips served with a dipping sauce) or a fresh piece simply baked, grilled, fried, or in a more upscale preparation. At our restaurant, we like to serve fresh grouper in mirin, sake, and soy. We find the Asian components complement the fish's light, mild flavor, and firm texture, while a crisp cucumber salad adds the perfect accompaniment with a crunch.

SERVES 4

GARNISH

½ cup chopped fresh cilantro
⅓ cup chopped fresh chives
1 teaspoon black sesame seeds, plus more, as needed, for garnish
1 red bell pepper, sliced into thin strips

ENGLISH CUCUMBER SALAD

1 seedless English cucumber, peeled and cut in half
1 medium carrot, peeled
1 small daikon radish, peeled

SAKE & SOY DRESSING

3 tablespoons seasoned rice vinegar
1 tablespoon Junmai or other cooking sake
3 tablespoons reduced-sodium soy sauce
1 tablespoon mirin
2 teaspoons whole-grain mustard
1 garlic clove, peeled
6 tablespoons (3 ounces) canola or safflower oil

GROUPER

4 (8-ounce) boneless, skinless grouper fillets
Fine sea salt and fresh cracked black pepper, as needed
1 medium shallot, peeled and thinly sliced
2 garlic cloves, peeled and roughly chopped
3 tablespoons canola or safflower oil

PREPARE THE GARNISH

Add the cilantro, chives, and sesame seeds to a small bowl. Mix well and set aside along with the pepper.

PREPARE THE ENGLISH CUCUMBER SALAD

Using a mandolin or sharp kitchen knife, slice half of the cucumber lengthwise in flat 4- to 6-inch strips. Julienne (short, thin strips like matchsticks), the remaining cucumber half along with the carrot and radish. In a small bowl, add the julienned vegetables and toss. Set aside with the cucumber strips.

PREPARE THE SAKE & SOY DRESSING

Add the vinegar, sake, soy sauce, mirin, mustard, and garlic to a food processor or kitchen blender. Process while slowly adding the oil until the mixture is smooth. Set aside.

PREPARE THE GROUPER

Season the grouper steaks on each side with salt and pepper and set aside. Add the oil to a large sauté pan or cast-iron pan over high heat. When heated, add the shallots and garlic and sauté for 1 or 2 minutes, or until lightly brown. Remove the shallots and garlic from the pan and set aside. Reduce the heat to medium and add the seasoned grouper steaks to the pan. Sear for 3 or 4 minutes, or until golden brown. Carefully turn the fillets over and cook the other side for 2 to 3 minutes, or until the flesh is slightly opaque in the middle. If desired, use a food thermometer and remove the fillets from the heat when the center reaches 130°F. (Note: The fish will continue to cook after it's removed from the heat.)

FINISHING THE DISH

Organize the reserved components on the kitchen counter with four warm dinner plates set in a row. Place 1 tablespoon of Sake & Soy Dressing in the center of each plate. Use the back of the spoon to spread the dressing into a 4-inch circle. Next, divide the strips of cucumber and fold them on top of the dressing. Place one grouper steak on top of the cucumber, evenly divide the julienned vegetable mixture, and place on top of each piece of grouper. Drizzle the top of the grouper with the remaining dressing. Garnish each plate with the fried garlic, shallots, cilantro, chives, and bell pepper. Finish with a small sprinkle of black sesame seeds and serve.

BEVERAGE SUGGESTION

In keeping with the sake in this recipe, we enjoy a premium Junmai Sake like Kikusui Ginjo "Chrysanthemum Water" served chilled.

PAN-SEARED POMPANO WITH LEMON AND BEURRE MONTE

Recreational pompano fishing is a popular pastime for locals and tourists alike. The Florida pompano is prized for its fight and delicate, delicious flavor. Growing up and spending my holidays in Florida, pompano was an ubiquitous menu item at many restaurants and country clubs. I often surfcasted for pompano in front of our house with my father and later my children. Recognizable by its silvery body and forked tail, the Florida pompano typically inhabits coastal waters, including sandy beaches, bays, and estuaries. They are known for their speed and strength, making them a fun catch for anglers, like us. We'd collect live sand fleas and bait them on a hook with a weighted line and small float to keep the sand fleas off the bottom (a classic pompano rig). It didn't take long to land a mess of pompano. Pompano can be caught year-round in Florida, but the best times are during the spring (March to May) and fall (September to November) migrations. Sandy beaches, especially along the Gulf Coast and the Atlantic coast, are prime spots for pompano fishing. Surf fishing is particularly effective. We'd end our day by bringing our catch home and cleaning the fish before pan-frying them whole. The result is a golden and crispy skin with a moist and flaky inside, highlighting the fish's natural flavors and making them a welcome addition in many coastal kitchens like ours.

SERVES 2

BEURRE MONTE
MAKES ½ CUP

- 3 tablespoons water
- ½ cup chilled unsalted butter, cut into 8 equal pieces
- 1 tablespoon gochujang (Korean fermented red chili paste)
- 2 teaspoons fresh lime juice
- Kosher salt, to taste
- Fresh cracked black pepper, to taste
- ¼ teaspoon sugar

POMPANO

- 1 cup all-purpose flour
- 2 tablespoons sea salt, divided
- 2 tablespoons fresh cracked black pepper, divided
- 2 (1–2-pound) whole pompanos, cleaned
- 2 tablespoons Clarified Butter (page 72)
- 2 lemons, thinly sliced

PREPARE THE BEURRE MONTE

Add 3 tablespoons of water to a medium saucepan over medium-high heat. Bring to a simmer then reduce heat to maintain a gentle simmer. Whisk in the butter, one piece at a time, about every 20 to 30 seconds. When all butter is added and has a consistency of gravy, whisk in the gochujang, lime juice, kosher salt, pepper, and sugar. Lower heat to the minimum setting and keep warm. (Note: The sauce can be held up to 4 hours on a very low setting. When ready to use, whisk briskly to incorporate any solids that have developed.)

PREPARE THE SEASONED FLOUR

Add the flour to a large bowl and season with salt and pepper. Mix to combine.

PREPARE THE POMPANOS

With a sharp knife, make a series of diagonal cuts in a diamond-shaped pattern, 1 inch apart and ¼ inch deep, on both sides of the fish. Season each fish with ¼ tablespoon of salt and pepper on both sides. Dredge each pompano in the seasoned flour, gently shaking off the excess flour. Set aside.

Add the Clarified Butter to a large deep-sided sauté pan over medium-high heat. When heated, add the pompanos to the pan. (Note: You may need to cook the fish in two batches, depending on the pan and fish size.) Cook for 8 to 10 minutes, or until golden brown. Carefully turn the fish over and cook another 8 or 10 minutes, or until golden brown. Remove from the heat and drain on paper towels.

FINISHING THE DISH

Place the pompano in the center of two serving plates. Place the fresh lemon slices on top, drizzle about ¼ cup of Beurre Monte over the lemons and fish per plate and serve.

BEVERAGE SUGGESTION

Pompano is rich and elegant, so you need a bright wine like a white burgundy or Bordeaux Blanc with its structured acidity to focus every bite. We especially like Barton & Gustier Bordeaux Blanc from France.

CATFISH

Catfish, which are high in omega-3, are typically thought of as a southern dish, fried whole or served with hush puppies and fried collard greens smothered in butter. At our restaurant, we feature a farmed product from Mississippi which tastes much cleaner and has a higher protein than wild-caught catfish. Our preferred method of cooking catfish at Bluewater Grill is to blacken boneless, skinless fillets and serve with lemon and simple side dishes like steamed collard, turnip, or mustard greens.

CATFISH FARMING INDUSTRY

The farming industry for catfish is a significant sector within the aquaculture industry, particularly in the United States. It involves the breeding, raising, and harvesting of catfish in controlled environments.

Catfish farming in the United States began in the 1960s in the Southern states, primarily in Mississippi, Alabama, and Arkansas. The industry's growth was driven by the increasing demand for catfish as a source of affordable, high-quality protein. By the 1980s and 1990s, catfish farming had expanded significantly, with advances in breeding, feed technology, and disease management. Today, the United States remains one of the largest producers of farm-raised catfish in the world.

The taste difference between farmed and wild catfish can be attributed to several factors, including diet, environment, and handling practices. Farmed catfish are fed a controlled diet, typically consisting of high-quality, formulated feed that includes grains, soybeans, and fish meal. This consistent diet leads to a milder, cleaner flavor in the fish. The food floats so the fish eat on the surface, rather than the bottom. Wild catfish have a varied diet that can include small fish, aquatic plants, insects, and sometimes even mud or detritus from the bottom of lakes or rivers. This diverse diet can result in a stronger, sometimes muddy or fishy taste. Catfish farms maintain controlled water quality to ensure the health of the fish. This involves regular monitoring and cleaning of the ponds or tanks to keep them free of pollutants and off-flavors. Wild catfish live in natural water bodies that can be subject to varying environmental conditions. If the water quality is poor or contains high levels of organic matter, it can affect the taste of the fish, often giving it a more earthy or muddy flavor. Farmed catfish are raised in a controlled environment where factors such as diet, water quality, and growth rates are monitored closely. This results in a more consistent product with predictable taste and texture. The quality of wild catfish can vary significantly depending on the specific body of water they come from and the time of year they are caught. This variability can lead to inconsistencies in flavor and texture. Farm-raised catfish are typically harvested and processed quickly to ensure freshness. Farmed catfish tend to have a higher fat content due to their diet and controlled growth environment, which contributes to a richer, more tender texture and a milder flavor. Wild catfish may have a leaner body composition, resulting in a firmer texture and a more pronounced flavor that some people may find less appealing.

BLACKENED CATFISH WITH STEAMED MUSTARD GREENS

Blackened catfish is a flavorful dish that uses a blend of spices and high heat to create a deliciously crispy and spicy crust on the fish. This recipe is straightforward and quick, perfect for a weeknight dinner or a special occasion.

SERVES 4

MUSTARD GREENS

2 cups chopped mustard greens
1 tablespoon lemon juice

BLACKENING SEASONING MAKES ABOUT ½ CUP

1 tablespoon paprika
1 teaspoon onion powder
1 teaspoon garlic powder
1 teaspoon dried thyme
1 teaspoon dried oregano
1 teaspoon cayenne pepper, or to taste
1 teaspoon fresh cracked black pepper
1 teaspoon white pepper
1 teaspoon kosher salt

CATFISH

4 boneless, skinless catfish fillets
4 tablespoons melted unsalted butter
Lemon wedges, for serving
Chopped fresh Italian flat-leaf parsley, for garnish

PREPARE THE STEAMED MUSTARD GREENS

Add the chopped leaves to a steamer basket and place in boiling water for 5 to 7 minutes. Remove the leaves and press with paper towels to remove excess water. Drizzle with lemon juice, set aside, and keep warm.

PREPARE THE BLACKENING SEASONING

Add the paprika, onion powder, garlic powder, thyme, oregano, cayenne, black pepper, white pepper, and salt to a small bowl. Mix well to ensure the spices are evenly distributed. Set aside or store in an airtight container until ready to use.

PREPARE THE CATFISH

Pat the catfish fillets dry with paper towels. Brush both sides of each fillet with the melted butter. Generously sprinkle the Blackening Seasoning over both sides of the fillets, pressing lightly to help the seasoning adhere.

Place a large cast-iron skillet over high heat and heat until extremely hot, about 5 minutes. (Note: It's crucial to use a cast-iron skillet because the skillet retains heat and helps achieve the desired blackened crust.) Once the skillet is very hot, add the fillets. Cook the fillets for 2 to 3 minutes on each side, or until the fish is cooked through and has a blackened crust. The fish should flake easily with a fork when done. (Note: Be cautious of the smoke; it's best to use a vent or open a window.)

FINISHING THE DISH

Transfer the blackened catfish fillets to a serving platter or individual plates. Garnish with fresh parsley and serve with lemon wedges and steamed mustard greens.

BEVERAGE SUGGESTION

We love to drink a nice beer from Louisiana like Dixie or Abita. The Cajun spice of the blackened fish is mellowed by the cold carbonation of a nice beer.

BLACKENED REDFISH WITH SHRIMP ÉTOUFFÉE AND CREOLE RICE

Like the Blackened Catfish recipe, here's another popular Cajun dish that originated in Louisiana. Chef Paul Prudhomme popularized this dinner special, known for its bold flavors and crispy texture, at his famous K-Paul's in New Orleans. At our restaurant, we'll serve redfish from time to time to offer our guests a flavorful and aromatic celebration of Southern cooking. SEE PHOTO (PAGE 252).

SERVES 6

SHRIMP ÉTOUFFÉE

3 tablespoons unsalted butter
¼ cup all-purpose flour
1 cup chopped yellow onion
½ cup chopped green bell pepper
½ cup chopped celery
½ tablespoon minced garlic
½ cup diced tomatoes
½ teaspoon kosher salt
¼ teaspoon cayenne pepper
1 bay leaf
1½ tablespoons (or to taste) Tony Chachere's Creole Seasoning, divided
1 cup seafood or shrimp stock
¾ pound medium shrimp (21–25 per pound), peeled and deveined (see page 60 for sizing)
2 tablespoons chopped fresh Italian flat-leaf parsley

CREOLE RICE
MAKES 5 CUPS

2 tablespoons unsalted butter
¾ cup diced celery
¾ yellow onion, peeled and diced
¾ cup diced red bell pepper
2 tablespoons Tony Chachere's Creole Seasoning
1 (14-ounce) can diced tomatoes with juice
2 cups uncooked white rice
3½ cups water
¾ cup diced green onion

BLACKENED REDFISH

6 boneless, skinless redfish fillets
4 tablespoons melted unsalted butter
Blackening Seasoning (page 248)
6 cups Shrimp Etouffee
6 cups Creole Rice, for serving
Chopped fresh Italian flat-leaf parsley, for garnish
Lemon wedges, for serving

PREPARE THE SHRIMP ÉTOUFFÉE

Add the butter to a Dutch oven or stockpot over medium heat. When the butter is melted, add the flour, stirring continuously with a whisk to form a roux. Whisk for 5 to 7 minutes, or until the roux is light brown. Add the onion, bell pepper, celery, and garlic and cook, stirring occasionally, until softened, about 8 to 10 minutes. Add the tomatoes, salt, cayenne, bay leaf, and half the Creole seasoning. Cook for 3 minutes and whisk in the stock. Bring to a boil then reduce the heat to a simmer. Cook, stirring occasionally, for 45 minutes. Add the shrimp and season the étouffée with the remaining Creole seasoning. Cook 5 to 7 minutes, or until the shrimp are cooked through. Add the parsley and stir to combine. Set aside and keep warm.

PREPARE THE CREOLE RICE

Add the butter to a saucepot over medium heat. When the butter is melted, add the celery, onion, bell pepper, and Creole seasoning. Sauté, stirring occasionally, until the vegetables are soft, 8 to 10 minutes. Add the diced tomatoes, rice, and water. Stir well and bring to a boil. When boiling, reduce the heat to low and cover. Cook until the rice is tender, and all the liquid has absorbed, about 25 minutes. Set aside and keep warm. Fluff with a fork and garnish with the green onions just before serving.

PREPARE THE REDFISH

Pat the redfish fillets dry with paper towels. Brush both sides of each fillet with the melted butter. Generously sprinkle the Blackening Seasoning over both sides of the fillets, pressing lightly to help the seasoning adhere.

Place a large cast-iron skillet over high heat and heat until extremely hot, about 5 minutes. (Note: It's crucial to use a cast-iron skillet because the skillet retains heat and helps achieve the desired blackened crust.) Once the skillet is very hot, add the fillets. Cook the fillets for 2 to 3 minutes on each side, or until the fish is cooked through and has a blackened crust. The fish should flake easily with a fork when done. (Note: Be cautious of the smoke; it's best to use a vent or open a window.)

FINISHING THE DISH

Transfer the blackened redfish fillets to a serving platter or individual plates. Top with the Shrimp Étouffée and serve with a side of Creole Rice. Garnish with fresh parsley and lemon wedges and serve.

BEVERAGE SUGGESTION

A light-bodied red wine like a Pinot Noir or Rioja enhances the flavor of the fish and neutralizes the spice of the blackening. My favorite is Castle Rock Pinot Noir since it is light, high in alcohol, and not jammy.

AUSTRALIA, OCEANIA & THE HAWAIIAN ARCHIPELAGO

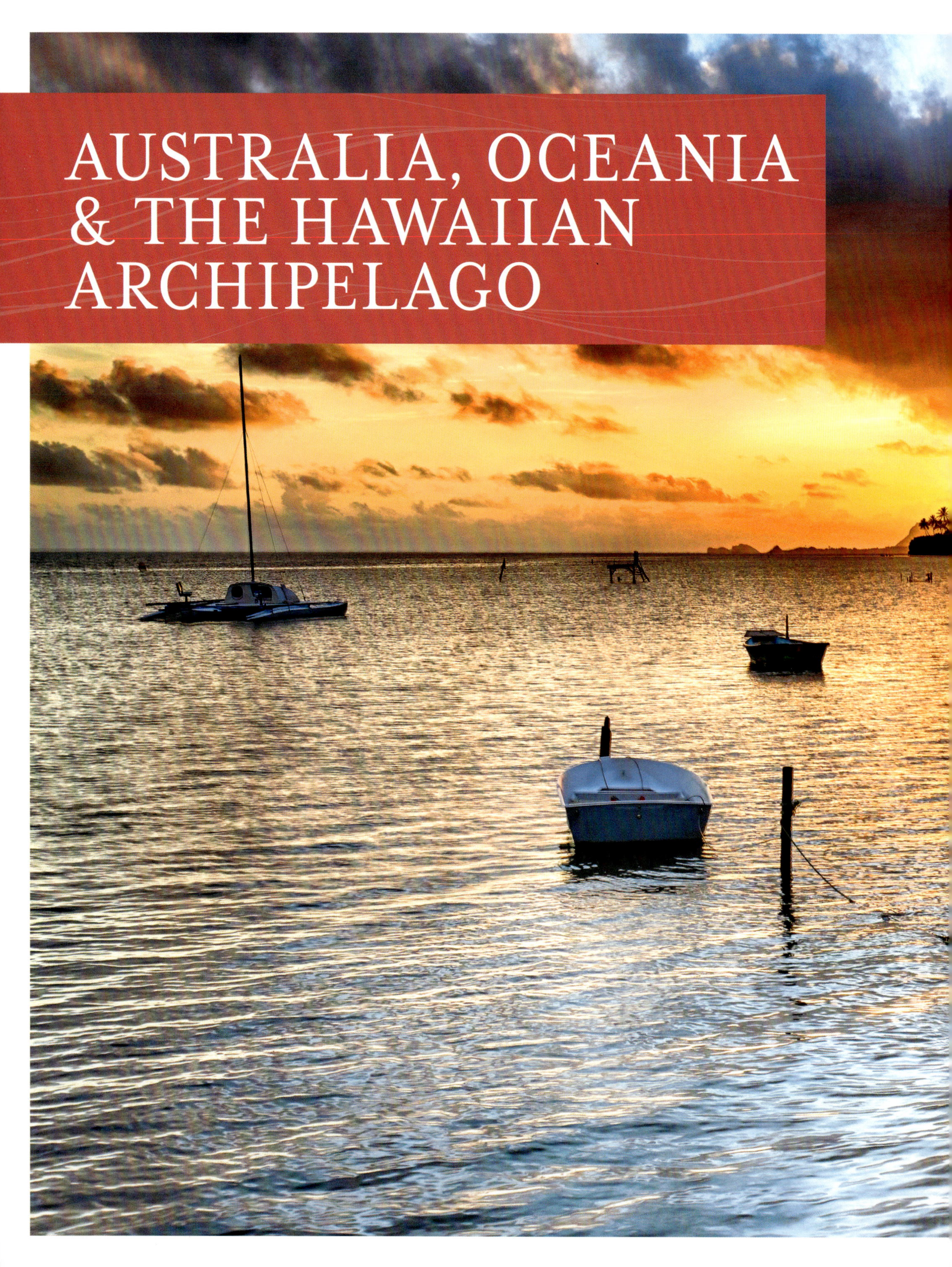

AUSTRALIA, OCEANIA & THE HAWAIIAN ARCHIPELAGO

Australia, New Zealand, Oceania, and the Hawaii Archipelago are culinary havens for seafood lovers, each offering a unique array of locally sourced fish, including Australia's tiger prawns and barramundi, New Zealand's Ōra salmon, and Hawaii's diverse catch of tuna, mahi mahi, ono, and snapper.

In Australia, barramundi is a true icon. Found in both salt water and fresh water, this sportfish has a mild, buttery flavor with a firm texture, making it versatile for a variety of dishes like our Barramundi with Crab and Arugula, Coconut Rice, and Jalapeño Lime Vinaigrette. Barramundi is also terrific pan-fried, grilled, poached, or deep-fried for such dishes as our Australian Beer-Battered Fish. You can have the pleasure of enjoying barramundi, aside from our restaurant, in cities like Sydney and Melbourne, as well as the coastal towns in Queensland, where barramundi is often served in fusion or traditional Australian dishes.

Over in neighboring New Zealand, the locally renowned fish is Ōra king salmon, considered one of the best-tasting salmon varieties in the world. Farmed sustainably in the clean, cold waters of New Zealand's Marlborough Sounds, Ōra salmon is sought after for its rich, oily flesh and vibrant color. We like to serve it with a spicy Hatch Green Chile Ponzu and a Sunchoke Salad. If you're ever in New Zealand, Auckland and Wellington boast some of the finest markets and restaurants where you can enjoy Ōra salmon in a variety of styles, often paired with the country's fresh produce and award-winning wines.

In Hawaii, a tropical paradise we visit, the local seafood scene is extremely vibrant, with a variety of mouthwatering seafood including ahi tuna, mahi mahi, ono (wahoo), and Opakapaka, better known as Hawaiian pink snapper. Ahi tuna is the cornerstone of Hawaiian cuisine, and one we always feature at Bluewater Grill, such as our Seared Ahi Tuna with Soy Mirin and Crispy Rice, Yellowfin Ahi Tuna with Miso Butter Sauce and Coconut Ginger Rice, and our Ponzu Ahi Tuna Poke. Mahi mahi is another favorite of mine, with its firm flesh and mild flavor, often grilled or blackened. Ono and snapper, known for their light, flaky textures, are also enjoyed grilled or in tropical-style dishes like our Opakapaka with Macadamia Nut Crust and Pineapple Salsa.

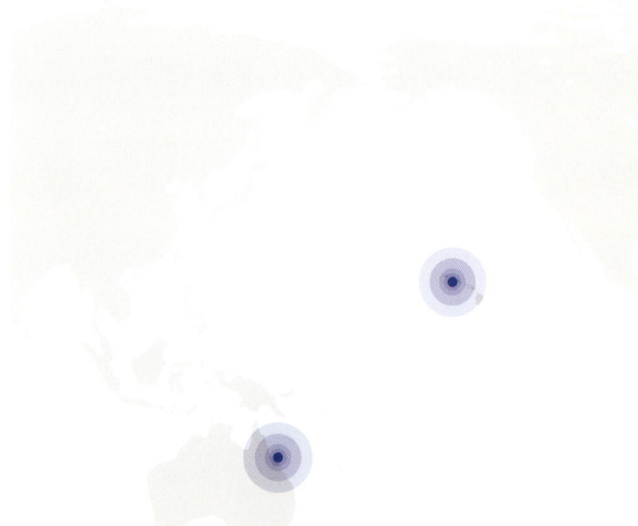

GARLIC BUTTER AUSTRALIAN TIGER PRAWNS

Australian prawns, which are integral to Australian culinary traditions, particularly during festive seasons and celebrations such as Christmas and Easter, play a central role in dining. They are very special and highly sought after due to their excellent quality and superior flavor. Their meat is sweet, succulent, and firm, which is a result of the pristine waters they inhabit and the careful handling and processing practices used in Australia. Australia is home to a variety of prawn species, each with its own unique characteristics and flavors. Australian prawns are often sold under the name of king prawns, tiger prawns, banana prawns, and endeavor prawns. Because Australia has stringent fisheries management and sustainability practices in place, the prawns are harvested responsibly to maintain healthy populations while protecting the marine environment. At the restaurant, we enjoy cooking tiger prawns because they are versatile and can be prepared in a number of ways, including grilling, barbecuing, frying, steaming, and as ingredients in soups, curries, salads, and seafood platters. Their robust flavor and firm texture make them ideal for both simple and complex dishes. Without question, Australian prawns have earned a reputation for excellence worldwide, with exports to markets across Asia, Europe, and North America. Their premium quality and consistent supply make them highly desirable among consumers and chefs like us. Growing up in Australia, we would often enjoy prawns cooked in myriad ways, not just "on the barbie."

SERVES 2 (3 LARGE PRAWNS EACH)

6 (12-ounce) whole tiger prawns with head, tail, and legs
3 teaspoons olive oil
3 tablespoons unsalted butter, divided
2 garlic cloves, peeled and minced
1 tablespoon dry white wine
Sea salt and fresh cracked black pepper, to taste
¼ cup chopped fresh Italian flat-leaf parsley, for garnish

With a pair of scissors, trim away the sharp point on the head. Remove the legs, if desired, then carefully cut open the back of the shell with a knife to expose the black vein that runs down the middle. Remove the vein and rinse the shrimp. Pat dry with paper towels. Repeat with the remaining shrimp and set aside.

Add the oil and half the butter to a large sauté pan over medium-high heat. When the oil is shimmering and the butter is bubbling, add the prawns and pan-fry for 4 minutes on one side. Flip and sauté the other side for 2 minutes; do not overcook. Add the garlic, wine, and remaining butter. Cover and cook for 1 minute, or until the prawns are just cooked through. Remove from the heat and transfer the prawns to a serving platter. Season with salt and pepper, garnish with parsley, and serve.

BEVERAGE SUGGESTION

Prawns are a sweet-tasting food so following the rule that wine must be sweeter than the dish it is paired with guides us to an off-dry Riesling or Pinot Gris like Jim Barry's Watervale Riesling from the Clare Valley in Australia.

AUSTRALIAN BEER-BATTERED FISH

Australian fish-and-chips are a beloved staple of coastal life, embodying the nation's deep connection to the ocean. Typically served in casual eateries and takeaway shops, this dish consists of freshly caught local fish, like barramundi or flathead, which is lightly battered or crumbed, then deep-fried until golden and crispy. Americans tend to over-batter fish and create a "corndog" effect. The proper batter is just thick enough to coat the fish and then enough you can almost see the color of the fish underneath. The fish is traditionally paired with thick-cut, perfectly seasoned chips (fries), often served with a wedge of lemon and a side of tartar sauce or tomato sauce for dipping. Since chips are difficult to do without a deep fryer, we recommend you serve with your favorite side dishes. Some places add a unique twist with seasonings or extras like potato cakes and dim sums.

What makes Australian fish-and-chips special is the quality of the ingredients, with the fish being locally sourced and sustainably caught. The experience is often enjoyed outdoors, whether at the beach, in a park, or on a picnic, with the smell of the sea in the air. This dish is more than just a meal—it's a cherished part of Australian culture, evoking memories of summer, sunshine, and simple pleasures by the ocean.

SERVES 4

BEER BATTER
MAKES 1¾ CUPS

- 1¼ cups all-purpose flour
- 2 tablespoons cornstarch
- 1 tablespoon paprika
- 1 teaspoon garlic powder
- 1 teaspoon seasoning salt
- ½ teaspoon fresh cracked black pepper
- 1 large egg, beaten
- 1 cup Australian beer (Coopers, Carlton, Fosters, or Tooheys)

FISH

- 4 cups canola or safflower oil, for frying
- 2 pounds fresh barramundi, snapper, cod, or halibut, cut into 1 by 3-inch strips
- Sea salt and fresh cracked black pepper, to taste
- 12 lemon wedges, for serving
- 1½ cups Tartar Sauce (page 62), for serving
- Malt vinegar, for serving

PREPARE THE BEER BATTER

Add the flour, cornstarch, paprika, garlic powder, seasoning salt, and pepper to a large mixing bowl. Mix well to combine. Add the egg and mix until incorporated. Slowly add the beer while mixing until a pancake batter–like consistency is achieved. Set aside.

PREPARE THE FISH

Add the oil to a heavy-bottomed 2-quart pot over medium-high heat. There should be at least 3 inches of oil in the pot. Heat the oil until it reaches 375°F. Use a candy or digital thermometer to check the temperature.

While the oil is heating, pat the fish dry thoroughly with paper towels, then season each piece of fish with salt and pepper. Dredge the fish in the batter, allowing the excess batter to drip back in the bowl. Working in batches as not to overcrowd the pot, place the first batch of fish into the hot oil and cook for 3 to 4 minutes, or until the fish is golden brown. Remove the fish and drain on paper towels. Continue with the remaining fish.

FINISHING THE DISH

Arrange the fish on a platter and serve with lemon wedges, Tartar Sauce, and a side of malt vinegar.

BEVERAGE SUGGESTION

Since most beer comes in a 12-ounce bottle and the recipe only calls for 8, it would be alcohol abuse not to finish off the remainder of the Australian beer you used in the recipe. Of course, you never buy just one bottle, so it's fun to finish off the six-pack when enjoying your fish-and-chips.

AUSTRALIAN FISH PIE

Australian fish pie is a hearty and comforting dish, deeply rooted in the country's coastal cuisine. Typically, it features a variety of fresh seafood, such as whitefish, prawns, and sometimes scallops, all sourced from Australia's abundant waters. These are cooked in a rich, creamy white sauce, often flavored with onions, garlic, and herbs. The filling is then encased in a flaky pastry or topped with a golden-brown mashed potato crust, offering a satisfying contrast in textures. Some variations include the addition of vegetables, such as peas or leeks, adding to the dish's heartiness.

Australia has embraced the meat pie as part of the culture, and of course, seafood pie is an expected extension. The pie reflects Australia's diverse culinary influences, blending British traditions with local ingredients and flavors. It's a popular dish in many households, especially during colder months when comfort food is most appreciated. Whether served at a family gathering or enjoyed in a seaside café, Australian fish pie showcases the nation's love for seafood and its creative approach to classic dishes, making it a beloved staple in Australian cuisine.

When making this pie at home, feel free to add chopped fresh herbs like parsley or dill to the filling for added flavor. You can also sprinkle grated cheese over the pastry before baking for a cheesy crust. SEE PHOTO (PAGE 264, BOTTOM).

SERVES 4

2 tablespoons unsalted butter
¼ cup sliced leek
¼ cup diced carrot
2 tablespoons all-purpose flour
1 cup fish or vegetable stock
½ cup cream or milk
1 tablespoon Dijon mustard
1 tablespoon lemon juice
Sea salt and fresh cracked black pepper, to taste
1 pound boneless, skinless fish fillets (barramundi or cod), cut into 1-inch pieces
½ pound cooked shrimp, peeled and deveined
1 cup frozen peas
1 sheet puff pastry, thawed if frozen
1 egg, beaten

Preheat the oven to 400°F.

Add the butter to a large saucepan over medium heat. When the butter is melted and foaming, add leek and carrot. Cook until softened, about 5 minutes. Stir in the flour and cook, stirring frequently, for 2 minutes to make a roux. Gradually add the fish stock and cream, stirring constantly, to avoid lumps. Add the mustard and lemon juice, then bring the mixture to a simmer. Cook for 5 to 7 minutes, or until the sauce has thickened. Season with salt and pepper. Add the fish fillets, shrimp, and frozen peas. Gently stir to combine and cook for another 3 to 5 minutes, or until the fish is just cooked through and the shrimp are pink and opaque. Remove from heat. Transfer the fish and shrimp mixture to a baking dish (about 8 by 8 inches) and set aside.

Roll out the puff pastry on a lightly floured surface until it's slightly larger than the baking dish. (Note: Instead of puff pastry, you can top the fish pie with mashed potatoes for a more traditional Australian twist known as "fisherman's pie.") Place the puff pastry over the filling, pressing down gently around the edges to seal. Trim any excess pastry and crimp the edges with a fork to create a decorative border. Brush the top of the pastry with the beaten egg to create a golden crust. Place the fish pie in the oven and bake for 25 to 30 minutes, or until the pastry is puffed and golden brown. Remove and let cool for several minutes before serving. Serve hot, accompanied by a side salad or steamed vegetables.

BEVERAGE SUGGESTION

The creamy sauce of the fish pie is the dominant flavor, and it should be matched with a lightly oaked Chardonnay. It needs something to stand up to the big flavors while cutting through the creaminess. We like Lindeman's or Jacob's Creek from Southeastern Australia.

LAGER

BARRAMUNDI WITH CRAB, ARUGULA, COCONUT RICE, AND JALAPEÑO LIME VINAIGRETTE

This dish features succulent Australian barramundi, a popular and sustainable whitefish, known for its mild flavor and delicate texture. The barramundi is pan-seared to perfection, then served over a bed of fragrant Coconut Rice, which adds a subtle sweetness and richness to the dish.

The highlight of this meal, aside from the moist barramundi, is the crab and arugula dressed with a Jalapeño Lime Vinaigrette, which brings a zesty and spicy kick to the plate. The vinaigrette, made from fresh jalapeño, lime juice, olive oil, honey, and a touch of mayonnaise, perfectly balances the richness of the fish and the creaminess of the coconut rice.

At the restaurant, we like to garnish this special with a drizzle of unagi (eel) sushi sauce for an extra punch of flavor. We love this vibrant, tropical-inspired dish, perfect for a light yet satisfying meal. SEE PHOTO (PAGE PAGE 264, TOP).

SERVES 4

COCONUT RICE
MAKES 4 CUPS

2 cups jasmine rice
2 kaffir lime leaves, crush but keep the leaves intact
1¾ cups unsweetened coconut milk
2 tablespoons sugar
½ teaspoon sea salt
1 tablespoon toasted coconut

JALAPEÑO LIME VINAIGRETTE
MAKES ABOUT ¾ CUP

2 limes, juiced
1 jalapeño, seeded and diced
1 tablespoon honey
¼ cup extra-virgin olive oil
2 tablespoons mayonnaise
¼ teaspoon sea salt
¼ teaspoon fresh cracked black pepper

CRAB AND ARUGULA

4 cups wild arugula, washed and destemmed
½ cup crabmeat
½ cup thinly sliced red bell pepper

BARRAMUNDI

2 tablespoons olive oil
4 (8-ounce) boneless, skinless barramundi fillets
Sea salt and fresh cracked black pepper, to taste
¼ cup Unagi (Eel) Sushi Sauce

PREPARE THE COCONUT RICE

Rinse the rice in water until clear to remove any excess starch. Then soak the rice in water for 1 hour, and drain. Transfer the rice to an 8 × 8–inch ceramic dish and add the crushed lime leaves on top. Set aside.

Preheat the oven to 400°F.

Add 1 cup of water to a 4-quart stockpot. Add the coconut milk, sugar, and salt. Mix to combine. Bring to a boil then remove from the heat. Pour the hot mixture over the rice and stir to incorporate. Cover the dish with foil and bake for 40 minutes. Remove and let rest, covered, for 15 minutes to ensure all the liquid is absorbed. Remove the lime leaves. Top the rice with the toasted coconut and fluff with a rubber spatula. Keep warm.

PREPARE THE JALAPEÑO LIME VINAIGRETTE

Add the lime juice, jalapeño, honey, oil, mayonnaise, salt and pepper to a food processor. Blend for 30 seconds, or until smooth. Taste and adjust with salt and honey, as needed. Set aside.

PREPARE THE CRAB AND ARUGULA

Add the arugula, crab, bell pepper, and ¾ cup of the Jalapeño Lime Vinaigrette to a bowl. Lightly toss and refrigerate until ready to serve.

PREPARE THE BARRAMUNDI

Lightly season both sides of the barramundi fillets with salt and pepper. Set aside.

Add the oil to a large sauté pan over medium-high heat. When heated and oil is shimmering, add the barramundi fillets and lightly sear the fish on both sides until the fish reaches an internal temperature of 140°F, about 6 minutes per side. Remove and set aside.

FINISHING THE DISH

Place 1 scoop of Coconut Rice in each bowl or plate. Place a barramundi fillet on top of the rice.

Evenly divide the Crab and Arugula and place on top of each fillet. Garnish with eel sauce and serve.

BEVERAGE SUGGESTION

Barramundi's clean, buttery flavor and meaty texture call for a mid-weight and fragrant white wine from Australia like a Lindeman's, Oxford Landing, or Yellow Tail.

ORA KING SALMON

Ora king salmon is a premium brand of New Zealand salmon farmed exclusively in the pristine waters of the Marlborough Sounds at the top of the South Island. The salmon are raised in a sustainable and carefully managed environment, benefiting from the cold, clean waters of the region. As a result, the salmon is known for its exceptional quality and taste. The salmon's diet and environment contribute to its distinctive flavor, which is often described as clean and oceanic with a subtle sweetness. The vibrant orange-red flesh is rich and buttery with a firm and oily texture. The salmon are selectively bred to ensure consistent quality and desirable characteristics, such as high fat content and marbling, which contribute to its superior quality.

From a cooking perspective, Ora king salmon is versatile and can be prepared in various ways, including grilling, pan-searing, baking, smoking, or enjoyed raw as sashimi or sushi. In the recipe that follows, we pair Ora king salmon with sunchokes and black rice along with a ponzu sauce made with Hatch green chiles for a little kick.

ORA KING SALMON WITH HATCH GREEN CHILE PONZU AND SUNCHOKE SALAD

SEE PHOTO (PAGE 265).

SERVES 4

HATCH GREEN CHILE PONZU
MAKES 1 CUP

½ cup soy sauce
¼ cup seasoned rice vinegar
¼ cup mirin
¼ cup sugar
¼ cup yuzu juice, or Meyer lemon juice
¼ cup roasted Hatch chiles, peeled, seeded, and chopped

SUNCHOKE SALAD
MAKES 1½ CUPS

1 cup sunchokes, scrubbed
1 teaspoon olive oil
Kosher salt, to taste
Fresh cracked black pepper, to taste
½ cup cooked black rice
Rice vinegar, to taste

SALMON ABURI

4 teaspoons mayonnaise, divided
1 pound Ora King salmon, or other salmon, cut into 12 equal portions
Kosher salt and fresh cracked black pepper, to taste
Fresh herbs and edible flowers, for garnish
Serrano chili, very thinly sliced, for garnish
Lime zest, for garnish
Fresh grated ginger, for garnish
Lemon extra-virgin olive oil, for drizzling

PREPARE THE HATCH GREEN CHILE PONZU

Add the soy sauce, rice vinegar, mirin, sugar, and yuzu juice to a medium-sized bowl and whisk to combine. Add the chiles and use a blender to puree. Set aside.

PREPARE THE SUNCHOKE SALAD

Preheat the oven to 350°F.

Add the sunchokes to a small bowl and season with the oil, salt, and pepper. Toss to combine. Spread on a baking sheet and bake until fork-tender, about 40 minutes. Remove and let cool, then dice.

Add the diced sunchokes to the bowl along with the cooked black rice. Season with salt and pepper and a splash of rice vinegar and set aside.

PREPARE THE SALMON

Spread the mayonnaise in a thin layer on the 12 pieces of salmon. Using a crème brûlée torch, lightly char the surface of the fish until a light crust forms. (Note: If you don't have a torch, place the salmon under the broiler until the mayonnaise is bubbly and golden brown.)

FINISHING THE DISH

Form ½ cup rice into a 1 × ¼ × 3–inch rectangle. Make 4 rectangles and place one on the side of each dinner plate. Puddle 1 tablespoon of the Hatch Green Chile Ponzu next to the rice. Lay 3 pieces of the fish on top of the Ponzu plate. Garnish with a sprinkle of herbs and edible flowers and the sliced chili, lime zest, grated ginger. Drizzle with olive oil and serve.

BEVERAGE SUGGESTION

Pair with a New Zealand wine with high acidity and herbaceous notes from Marlborough County, like The Landing, Boathouse Sauvignon Blanc.

SEARED (AHI) TUNA WITH SOY MIRIN AND CRISPY RICE

Ahi grade tuna refers to the quality and freshness of tuna, particularly yellowfin or bigeye species, that meet stringent standards for eating it raw, such as in sashimi, sushi, or quickly seared. Ahi is Hawaiian for yellowfin tuna, but it is commonly used in the United States to describe both yellowfin and bigeye tunas. Interesting story: The word ahi literally means "fire" in the Hawaiian dialect and dates back to ancient times when these powerful fish would pull the lines out so fast, they would smoke against the canoes of the Hawaiian fisherman.

Ahi grade tuna is characterized by its vibrant, deep-red color, firm texture, and a rich, clean flavor. To be classified as "ahi grade," the tuna must be extremely fresh, often caught and processed quickly to maintain its quality. The fish is typically flash-frozen right after being caught to preserve its flavor and texture.

The grading process involves assessing the tuna's color, fat content, and overall freshness. Ahi grade tuna is prized for its high quality, making it ideal for raw dishes like this one where the flavor and texture of the fish can truly shine.

SERVES 4 APPETIZER PORTIONS

SOY MIRIN SAUCE
MAKES 1½ CUPS

½ cup soy sauce
½ cup mirin
½ cup seasoned rice wine vinegar

CRISPY RICE
MAKES 1 CUP

1 cup cold cooked rice
1 cup canola or safflower oil

RADISH AND CUCUMBER SALAD

½ cup julienned peeled English cucumber
½ cup julienned daikon radish
½ cup julienned red radish

AHI TUNA

2 tablespoons 90/10 olive oil/canola blend
4 (4-ounce) portions ahi tuna loin, trimmed and cut into a 1½ × 1½ × 4–inch block
Sea salt and fresh cracked black pepper, to taste
½ cup fresh Italian flat-leaf parsley + 4 whole leaves, for garnish
Chive Oil (page 82), for garnish
Sesame seeds, for garnish
4 fresh cilantro leaves, for garnish
4 fresh mint leaves, for garnish

PREPARE THE SOY MIRIN SAUCE

Add the soy sauce, mirin, and seasoned rice wine vinegar to a small bowl. Whisk until combined. Set aside.

PREPARE THE CRISPY RICE

Add the oil to a large sauté pan over medium-high heat. While the oil is heating, spread out the rice, separating the rice kernels as best as possible. When heated and the oil is shimmering, add the rice, continuing the spread out the kernels with a rubber spatula. What

94
112

we're trying to do is crisp each rice kernel as much as possible; this will not be achieved by just dumping the clumped rice in the pan. The more you can spread it out, the better. Fry the rice while stirring and separating the kernels until the rice is crisp and oil has stopped bubbling, about 2 minutes. Remove the rice, drain on paper towels, and set aside to cool.

PREPARE THE RADISH AND CUCUMBER SALAD

Add the cucumber, daikon, and red radish to a small bowl. Toss to combine and set aside.

PREPARE THE AHI TUNA

Add the oil to a medium-sized sauté pan over high heat. While the oil is heating, season the ahi with salt and pepper and roll in the chopped parsley. When heated and the oil is shimmering, add the ahi and quickly sear on all sides, about 15 seconds per side. Remove from the pan.

FINISHING THE DISH

Arrange the Radish and Cucumber Salad lengthwise down the center of a platter. Slice each portion of the ahi into eight slices and layer on top of salad in a shingled fashion. Top the ahi with a couple tablespoons of Soy Mirin Sauce, garnish with Chive Oil, Crispy Rice, sesame seeds, and parsley, cilantro, and mint leaves and serve.

BEVERAGE SUGGESTION

Seared ahi tuna pairs well with a dry Riesling or French rosé to balance the rich umami flavors and tender texture.

YELLOWFIN (AHI) TUNA WITH MISO BUTTER SAUCE AND COCONUT GINGER RICE

Seared ahi tuna with miso butter sauce is a delightful fusion of flavors that brings out the best in this premium cut of fish. The ahi tuna, known for its firm texture and rich, meaty taste, is seared to perfection, leaving the inside rare and tender. The searing process enhances the tuna's natural flavors while giving it a slightly crispy outer layer.

At the restaurant, we believe the Miso Butter Sauce is the perfect complement, blending the savory, umami notes of miso with the richness of butter. This sauce adds depth and a touch of sweetness to the dish, balancing the slight saltiness of the seared tuna. A hint of coriander and peppercorn add another layer of complexity.

We like to serve this dish with a side of Coconut Ginger Rice and Sautéed Green Beans for a visually appealing and flavor-packed dish. For me, it's a dish that feels both luxurious and comforting, perfect for a special occasion or a simple yet elegant weeknight dinner.

SERVES 4

COCONUT GINGER RICE
MAKES 3 CUPS

2½ cups warm water
1 teaspoon vegetable base (Better Than Bouillon)
1¼ cups coconut milk
1½ cups parboiled rice (page 234)
1 tablespoon minced fresh ginger
1 tablespoon kosher salt
¼ teaspoon white pepper
1 cup chopped fresh cilantro

SAUTÉED GREEN BEANS

1 quart water
1 pound trimmed green beans
Salt and fresh cracked black pepper, as needed, to taste

MISO BUTTER SAUCE
MAKES 2½ CUPS

½ cup mirin
1 cup sake
½ cup rice wine vinegar
2 tablespoons soy sauce
2 tablespoons white miso paste
1 tablespoon coriander seeds
1 tablespoon whole black peppercorns
1½ cups heavy cream
4 sticks (1 pound) unsalted butter

YELLOWFIN AHI TUNA

3 tablespoons togarashi spice
4 (8-ounce) center cut yellowfin ahi tuna steaks
2 tablespoons canola or safflower oil
1½ tablespoons bonito flakes
¼ cup sliced green onions
4 daikon radish sprouts, for garnish

PREPARE THE COCONUT GINGER RICE

Preheat the oven to 350°F.

Add 2½ cups warm water to a medium-sized mixing bowl along with the vegetable base and coconut milk. Stir to combine and until the vegetable base has dissolved.

Add the parboiled rice to a 9 × 9–inch greased baking dish, then pour the vegetable base mixture evenly over the rice. Sprinkle the ginger, salt, and pepper over the top. Cover the pan with plastic wrap then foil and bake for 1 hour, or until the rice is fully cooked. Remove and stir the rice to fluff. Mix in the cilantro and keep warm until ready to use.

PREPARE THE SAUTÉED GREEN BEANS

Add 1 quart of water to a pot over high heat. Bring to a boil. Add the trimmed green beans and cook for 3 minutes, or until al dente. Remove from the heat, drain, and add the beans to an ice water bath. Once chilled, drain the beans and set aside. Before serving, reheat the beans by placing them in a skillet over medium-high heat. Season with a little salt and pepper and toss until heated through.

PREPARE THE MISO BUTTER SAUCE

Add the mirin, sake, vinegar, soy sauce, miso paste, coriander, and peppercorns to a medium saucepot over medium heat. Stir to combine. Let cook until the mixture reduces by half, about 10 minutes. Add the heavy cream and reduce again until the mixture reduces by half, about 10 minutes. Slowly add the butter while stirring until fully incorporated. Reduce the heat to very low and keep warm until ready to use.

PREPARE THE YELLOWFIN "AHI" TUNA

Add the togarashi to a bowl. Coat the 4 tuna steaks with the oil and then dip each steak in the togarashi. Set aside.

Add the oil to a large cast-iron skillet over high heat. When heated, add the tuna steaks and quickly sear for 1 to 2 minutes to char the spice while leaving the center of the tuna raw. Turn the steaks over and sear for another 1 to 2 minutes to char the other side. Remove the tuna steaks from the heat and set aside.

FINISHING THE DISH

Arrange four warm plates on the counter. Divide the Miso Butter Sauce and add to the center of each plate. Slice each tuna steak in half on the bias to expose the raw center and place slightly off center on top of the sauce. Divide the Coconut Ginger Rice and place next to the tuna. Divide the Sautéed Green Beans and arrange on top of the rice. Garnish with the green onions and daikon sprout and sprinkle with bonito flakes and serve.

BEVERAGE SUGGESTION

Seared ahi tuna pairs well with a dry Riesling or French rosé to balance the rich umami flavors and tender texture. We recommend Chateau d'Esclans Whispering Angel from Provence.

PONZU AHI TUNA POKE

Ahi tuna poke is a traditional Hawaiian dish consisting of diced raw tuna in a savory ponzu sauce. The word *poke* means "to slice" or "to cut crosswise into pieces" in Hawaiian. Ahi tuna, prized for its deep red color and buttery texture, is the star ingredient of this refreshing and flavorful dish. At the restaurant, we serve this as an appetizer or a light meal, accompanied by house-made wonton chips.

SERVES 1 OR 2

PONZU

½ cup reduced-sodium soy sauce
¼ cup mirin
¼ cup rice wine vinegar
2 tablespoons orange juice
1 tablespoon lime juice
1 tablespoon bonito flakes

AHI TUNA

¼ cup vegetable oil
2 wonton wrappers, sliced in 2-inch strips
4 ounces fresh sashimi-grade ahi, diced into ½-inch cubes
1 tablespoon paper-thin sliced sweet onion, rinsed in water and drained
Sea salt, as needed
1 tablespoon ponzu, recipe follows
½ avocado, pitted, peeled, and sliced
Green onion, very thinly sliced or julienned, placed in cold water to curl, for garnish

PREPARE THE PONZU

Add the soy sauce, mirin, vinegar, orange juice, lime juice, and bonito flakes to a saucepot over medium-high heat. Bring to a boil, then remove from the heat and let cool. When cool, strain into a container, cover with a lid, and refrigerate until ready to use.

PREPARE THE AHI TUNA POKE

Add the oil to a sauté pan over medium-high heat. When heated, add the wonton wrappers and fry until crispy and slightly browned. Remove the wrappers from the pan and drain on paper towel.

Add the tuna and sliced onion to a bowl. Mix to combine.

FINISHING THE DISH

Mound the tuna mixture in the middle of a serving bowl. Lightly season with sea salt. Drizzle the ponzu around the tuna. Add slices of avocado to the edges of the tuna. Garnish with the green onion and serve with the reserved wonton chips.

BEVERAGE SUGGESTION

We love to serve a cold sake with raw tuna. It has a light, fresh taste and fruity aroma and the sweetness complements the umami of the tuna tossed in ponzu. We prefer a premium Junmai Sake like Kikusui Ginjo "Chrysanthemum Water" served chilled.

にごり酒
CRÈME de SAKE

MAHI MAHI WITH LEMON PEPPER CRUST AND CILANTRO CHILI HOLLANDAISE

"Mahi Mahi, a name so nice, we say it twice." The name derives from the Hawaiian word for "strong,' so it translates to "strong, strong." Also called "Dolphin-fish" in Florida and "Dorado" in Mexico, these fish are prized among sport fishermen. On trips to Florida, Baja, or the Bahamas, we like to target "sandwich" mahi mahi, which is one that yields fillets that are the perfect size for fish sandwiches and tacos. Catching mahi mahi is an electrifying experience as the fish will flash vivid colors of blue, green, and gold. Considered a sustainable species, mahi mahi have one of the fastest reproduction cycles and are prized for their lean sweet flavor and firm flesh that cooks up moist and tender.

SERVES 4

LEMON PEPPER CRUST
MAKES ABOUT 1 CUP

2 cups panko breadcrumbs
2 tablespoons fresh lemon zest
2 tablespoons finely chopped fresh Italian flat-leaf parsley
1 tablespoon kosher salt
2 tablespoons fresh cracked black pepper

CILANTRO CHILI HOLLANDAISE
MAKES 2½ CUPS

2 egg yolks
½ tablespoon Dijon mustard
1 teaspoon Worcestershire sauce
½ teaspoon Tabasco sauce
2 cups Clarified Butter (page 72)
1 tablespoon fresh lemon juice
2 tablespoons finely chopped fresh cilantro leaves
1 tablespoon sambal
1 teaspoon kosher salt

MAHI MAHI

4 boneless, skinless mahi mahi fillets
1 cup all-purpose flour
Egg wash (2 large eggs + 1 tablespoon water)
¼ cup canola or safflower oil
Cilantro Chili Hollandaise, for serving
Scalloped Potatoes, for serving (page 126)
Sautéed spinach, for serving
Chopped fresh Italian flat-leaf parsley, for garnish

PREPARE THE LEMON PEPPER CRUST

Add the breadcrumbs, lemon zest, parsley, salt, and pepper to a mixing bowl. Mix well until well incorporated and there aren't any lumps from the lemon zest. Set aside until ready to use.

PREPARE THE CILANTRO CHILI HOLLANDAISE

Add the egg yolks, mustard, Worcestershire sauce, and Tabasco sauce to a double boiler and whisk to combine. Slowly cook until the yolks begin to thicken. Slowly whisk in the Clarified Butter until emulsified. Remove from heat and whisk in the lemon juice, cilantro, and sambal. The sauce should be smooth

and creamy. To adjust the thickness of the sauce, add a little water as necessary. Keep warm until ready to use.

PREPARE THE MAHI MAHI

Set up a dredging station by filling one bowl with the flour. Add the egg wash to a second bowl, and the Lemon Pepper mixture to a third bowl.

Dredge the mahi mahi first in the seasoned flour, gently shaking off the excess flour. Then dredge in the egg wash, allowing the extra egg to drip back into the bowl. Then place in the Lemon Pepper mixture and use your fingers to help coat both sides of the fish. Set aside.

Add the oil to a large deep-sided sauté pan over medium-high heat. When heated, add the breaded mahi mahi in the pan. Reduce the heat to medium-low and cook until golden brown, about 6 minutes. Carefully turn the fish over and cook or until golden brown and the fish is cooked through, about another 6 minutes. Remove from the heat.

FINISHING THE DISH

Place some sautéed spinach and Scalloped Potatoes in the center of each serving plate. Top with the mahi mahi. Spoon the Cilantro Chili Hollandaise over the fish, garnish with the parsley, and serve.

BEVERAGE SUGGESTION

A nice French Sauvignon Blanc with crisp acidity pairs well with the bright, lemony pepper flavor in the panko coating without overwhelming the fish. We recommend B&G Bordeaux Blanc from France.

HAWAIIAN ONO

Also known as wahoo, ono is a popular game fish found in tropical and subtropical waters worldwide, particularly in the regions of Hawaii, Florida, the Caribbean, Mexico, and parts of the Indian Ocean. I love fishing for ono, particularly in Florida and Mexico. That's because the ono is known for its speed and agility in the water, making them a challenging catch for anglers like me. Once hooked, they often swim at high speeds, making powerful runs when hooked. They can also grow to impressive sizes, with adults commonly reaching lengths of 4 to 5 feet and weights exceeding 50 pounds. Their large size and strong fighting abilities make them a thrilling target. When I fish for them, I'll use a variety of techniques, including trolling with artificial lures or natural baits, such as ballyhoo or squid, and at varying depths. They often respond well to high-speed trolling tactics.

From a culinary aspect, the ono is highly valued in Pacific Rim cuisines. If I'm fortunate to land one while at sea, I'll prepare some ono sashimi right on deck after it's caught, which I find absolutely delicious. Back at home and at the restaurant, I'll prepare ono in a variety of ways to accentuate the ono's delicious flesh, which has a mild, slightly sweet flavor with firm, white flesh that is lean and delicate. If you've never had fresh ono, you're in for a real treat. Ono is prized for its versatility in cooking. It can be grilled, baked, pan-seared, or used in ceviche and sushi preparations. Its firm texture also holds up well to grilling and lends itself to a wide range of seasoning and marinades.

Today, ono fisheries are well-managed and sustainable, with efforts to maintain healthy populations through responsible fishing practices and conservation measures. Ono has also gained popularity beyond Hawaiian cuisine and is appreciated by seafood enthusiasts and chefs worldwide for its quality, taste, and cooking versatility.

GRILLED HAWAIIAN ONO WITH COCONUT LIME SAUCE

This recipe offers a delightful blend of flavors that highlight the natural sweetness of the fish with a creamy, tangy sauce. Enjoy the taste of the islands right at your table. SEE PHOTO (PAGE 295, TOP).

SERVES 4

COCONUT LIME SAUCE
MAKES 1 CUP

½ cup coconut milk
1 lime, zested and juiced
2 tablespoons soy sauce
2 tablespoons honey or maple syrup
1 tablespoon grated fresh ginger
2 garlic cloves, peeled and minced
Sea salt and fresh cracked black pepper, to taste

ONO

4 (8-ounce) boneless, skinless ono fillets
Sea salt and fresh cracked black pepper, to taste
2 tablespoons olive oil
Fresh cilantro or Italian flat-leaf parsley leaves, for garnish

PREPARE THE COCONUT LIME SAUCE

Add the coconut milk, lime zest, lime juice, soy sauce, honey, ginger, garlic, salt, and pepper to a saucepot. Mix well to combine. (Note: Adjust the sweetness of the sauce by adding more or less honey or maple syrup according to your taste preference.) Bring to a simmer over medium heat, stirring occasionally. Cook for 3 to 4 minutes, or until slightly thickened. Remove and set aside.

PREPARE THE ONO

Preheat an outdoor grill to medium-high heat. Note: Ensure the grill grates are clean and well-oiled before placing the fish to prevent sticking. While the grill is heating, pat the ono dry with paper towels and season both sides with salt and pepper. Brush the fillets lightly with olive oil to prevent sticking on the grill. Place the ono on the grill. Grill for 4 to 5 minutes on each side, or until the ono is opaque and easily flakes with a fork. (Note: Cooking time may vary depending on the thickness of the fillets.)

FINISHING THE DISH

Transfer the grilled ono fillets to serving plates. Drizzle the Coconut Lime Sauce over each fillet. Garnish with chopped cilantro or parsley. Serve with coconut rice, steamed jasmine rice, or a fresh mango salad for a complete Hawaiian-inspired meal.

BEVERAGE SUGGESTION

Off-dry Rieslings like Dr. Loosen pair well with chili-laden coconut milk–based sauces.

OPAKAPAKA WITH MACADAMIA NUT CRUST AND PINEAPPLE SALSA

Opakapaka, also known as Hawaiian pink snapper, is a prized fish in Hawaiian cuisine, celebrated for its delicate flavor and firm, pink flesh. Found in the deep waters around the Hawaiian Islands, opakapaka is a member of the Lutjanidae family, typically inhabiting depths of 180 to 600 feet. The fish is highly sought after by both commercial and recreational fishermen, particularly during the winter months when it is most abundant.

In the kitchen, opakapaka is very versatile and often steamed, baked, or grilled, allowing its mild, sweet flavor to shine through. It is also a popular choice for sashimi due to its tender texture. In Hawaiian culture, opakapaka holds a special place, featured in traditional feasts and celebrations. As a result, opakapaka remains a cherished ingredient in Hawaiian and Pacific Rim cuisines, embodying the rich marine heritage of the islands. At the restaurant, we like to highlight the snapper's firm texture and mild, sweet flavor with the crunch of macadamia, adding a tropical twist to the delightful dish.

SERVES 4

PINEAPPLE SALSA
MAKES 2 CUPS

1 cup diced fresh pineapple
½ cup diced red bell pepper
¼ cup finely chopped red onion
1 jalapeño, seeded and finely chopped
2 tablespoons chopped fresh cilantro
1 lime, juiced
Kosher salt and fresh cracked black pepper, to taste

OPAKA

4 (8-ounce) boneless, skinless opaka fillets
Sea salt and fresh cracked black pepper, to taste
¼ cup all-purpose flour
2 eggs, beaten
1 cup macadamia nuts, finely chopped or crushed
½ cup panko breadcrumbs
2 tablespoons olive oil
Fresh cilantro leaves, for garnish

PREPARE THE PINEAPPLE SALSA

Add the pineapple, bell pepper, onion, jalapeño, cilantro, lime juice, salt, and pepper to a small bowl. Mix well. Cover and refrigerate until ready to serve.

PREPARE THE FISH

Preheat the oven to 375°F.

Season the fillets with salt and pepper on both sides.

Set up a dredging station by adding the flour to a shallow dish or plate. Add the egg wash to a bowl, and the macadamia nuts and panko to another shallow dish or plate.

Dredge the opaka first in the flour, gently shaking off any excess flour. Then dredge in the egg wash, allowing the extra egg to drip back into the bowl. Then place in the macadamia-panko mixture and use your fingers to help coat both sides of the fish. Set aside.

Add the oil to a large, deep-sided oven-safe sauté pan over medium-high heat. When heated, add the opaka to the pan and cook for 2 to 3 minutes, or until lightly golden and crispy. Transfer the pan to the oven and bake for an additional 8 to 10 minutes, or until the opaka is cooked through and flakes easily with a fork.

FINISHING THE DISH

Remove the fillets from the oven and transfer to serving plates. Spoon the Pineapple Salsa over top of the fish. Garnish with cilantro and serve with coconut rice or a fresh garden salad.

BEVERAGE SUGGESTION

Since snapper is a lean whitefish, a light wine like a New Zealand Sauvignon Blanc with a fruit-forward palate pairs nicely with the opaka and complements the pineapple salsa. We enjoy any Marlborough County New Zealand Sauvignon Blanc, but Cloudy Bay is renowned.

FARAWAY COASTLINES

FARAWAY COASTLINES

I love exploring seafood abroad because it takes me on a culinary journey across faraway coastlines, where unique local traditions and ingredients create unforgettable flavors.

In Spain, where seafood is a central part of the cuisine, dishes like octopus and seafood paella define coastal dining. Galicia, in the northwest, is renowned for its octopus, and we feel we've represented this delicacy in our Spanish Octopus with Brava Sauce and Garlic Aioli. In Valencia, seafood paella, which you'll also find in this chapter, brings together fresh mussels, shrimp, and squid with saffron-infused rice, creating a rich, comforting dish that captures the essence of the Mediterranean.

Speaking of the Mediterranean, the region is home to branzino, a favorite along the coasts of Italy, Greece, and Turkey. This white-fleshed sea bass is often grilled whole, which is how we prepare it at Bluewater Grill for our Branzino with Sautéed Spinach, Mushrooms, and Balsamic Glaze. The flavor is light yet flavorful, making it a perfect dish for a seaside meal.

In the United Kingdom, Dover sole is prized for its delicate, mild flavor and firm texture. Often prepared with classic European techniques like meunière (pan-fried in butter and lemon), this fish is a staple in upscale seafood restaurants, especially along the southern coast of England.

In Brazil, coastal cuisine features hearty seafood stews, like Bahia Seafood Stew with Brazilian Coconut, which we included in this chapter. One bite and you'll see why. The dish vividly captures the vibrant, tropical flavors of Brazil's coastal regions. Same with our Bouillabaisse, a quintessential seafood dish of Provence. This rich French stew combines a variety of seafood, including cod, clams, mussels, scallops, and shrimp, with a fragrant broth flavored with fennel, leek, saffron, and a bit of orange peel.

Finally, Italy offers Zuppa di Pesce, the classic rustic seafood stew made with local seafood, simmered in a tomato-based broth with garlic and white wine, a simple yet rich dish that reflects Italy's coastal charm—perfect for concluding this international chapter.

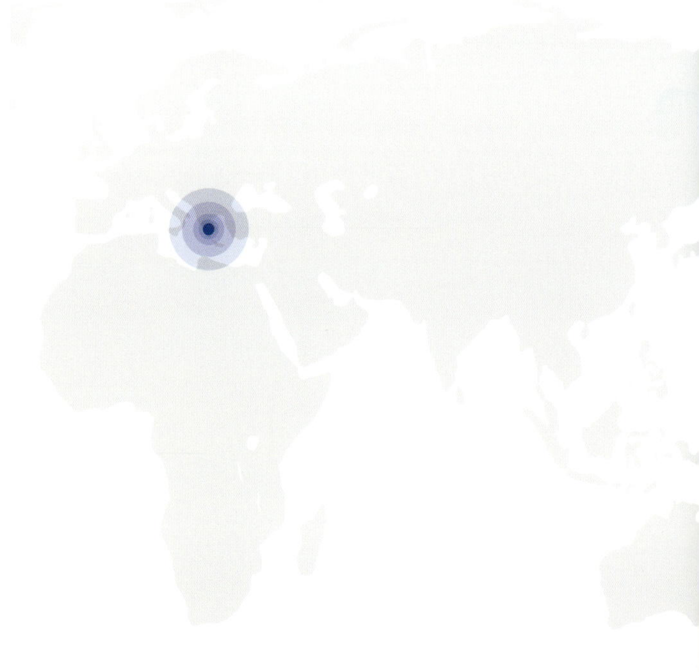

SPANISH OCTOPUS WITH BRAVA SAUCE AND GARLIC AIOLI

Spanish octopus, or *pulpo*, is a highly prized seafood delicacy in Spain, known for its tender texture and rich flavor. Found primarily in the coastal waters of the Atlantic Ocean, especially near the Galician coast, this cephalopod is a staple in Spanish cuisine. Thankfully, Spanish fishermen use sustainable practices to harvest octopus, ensuring the species' long-term viability.

The traditional dish *pulpo a la Gallega* features boiled octopus seasoned with olive oil, coarse salt, and smoky paprika, often served on wooden plates alongside potatoes. Octopus is celebrated for its versatility; it can be grilled, stewed, or added to paellas and salads. The octopus is also culturally significant, often featured in festivals and local celebrations.

Octopus can be a little tricky to prepare, but when perfectly cooked, octopus offers the perfect balance of tenderness and flavor, making it a favorite among chefs and food enthusiasts. This recipe is not just a delicious meal our guests enjoy; the dish is a symbol of Spain's rich maritime heritage and culinary tradition, reflecting the deep connection between the sea and their culture.

SERVES 2 AS AN APPETIZER

ROASTED MARBLED POTATOES

1½ pounds mixed marbled potatoes (cut in half)
2 tablespoons olive oil
1 tablespoon kosher salt
2 teaspoons fresh cracked black pepper

BRAVA SAUCE
MAKES 1¼ CUP

1 tablespoon Spanish extra-virgin olive oil
1 garlic clove, peeled and sliced
1 arbol chili
1 tablespoon sugar
1 tablespoon Spanish sherry vinegar
1 tablespoon tomato paste
1 (10-ounce) can pureed tomatoes
1 tablespoon smoked paprika
Kosher salt, to taste

OCTOPUS

1 small (1-pound) octopus, cleaned
Spanish olive oil, as needed
Sea salt and fresh cracked black pepper, for seasoning
½ cup Brava Sauce
1 tablespoon Garlic Aioli (page 50)
4 Italian flat-leaf parsley sprigs, for garnish

PREPARE THE ROASTED MARBLED POTATOES

Preheat the oven to 350°F.

Add the potatoes to a mixing bowl and toss with the olive oil, salt, and pepper. Arrange on a baking sheet lined with parchment paper. Roast for 30 minutes or until fork-tender. Remove and set aside.

PREPARE THE BRAVA SAUCE

Add the oil to a medium-size saucepot over medium heat. When the oil is hot and shimmering, add the garlic and chili and sauté, stirring often, until the vegetables begin to

brown (do not burn). Add the sugar and stir until it melts. Stir in the vinegar and tomato paste and cook for 3 minutes. Add the pureed tomatoes and stir to incorporate. Reduce the heat to low and allow to simmer until the mixture is almost dry. Add the paprika and adjust the seasoning with salt, if necessary. Remove from the heat, discard the chili, set aside and keep warm.

PREPARE THE OCTOPUS

Preheat the oven to 375°F.

Coat the octopus lightly with olive oil and season with salt and pepper. Place on a baking sheet and roast for 45 minutes. Remove and let cool. When cool, slice the tentacles into 2- to 3-inch sections cut on the bias. Set aside.

FINISHING THE DISH

Preheat an outdoor grill to medium-high heat.

Place the octopus on the grill and sear the tentacles on all sides until hot and crispy, about 3 minutes.

Brush the Brava Sauce on a serving platter or individual plates. Top with the Roasted Marbled Potatoes, charred Octopus, and Garlic Aioli. Garnish with parsley and serve.

BEVERAGE SUGGESTION

This classic Spanish dish is great served with a Spanish Tempranillo. The light red stands up well to the hearty octopus and rich tomato Brava Sauce. We recommend the Spanish Ribera del Duero Tempranillo from Protos.

SEAFOOD PAELLA VALENCIANA

Here's a renowned Spanish dish that we make at the restaurant, which hails from the region of Valencia. Celebrated for its rich and flavorful ingredients, paella is traditionally cooked in a wide, shallow pan called a *paellera*. This seafood specialty showcases a bounty from the sea, such as clams, mussels, shrimp, and squid (although we don't add squid to our version).

The key to a perfect seafood paella is the rice, which is infused with saffron—a spice that gives the dish its distinctive golden color and earthy flavor. The rice also absorbs the broth made from simmering seafood and vegetables like tomatoes, bell peppers or pimentos, and onions, creating a harmonious blend of taste and texture.

Paella Valenciana is a festive dish, often served at gatherings and special occasions. While the original Valencian paella included rabbit, chicken, and snails, this seafood variation has gained widespread popularity, especially along Spain's coastal regions. Like most paellas, preparing this recipe requires patience and precision, particularly in achieving the coveted *socarrat*—a crispy layer of rice at the bottom of the pan that adds an extra dimension of flavor and texture. Whether dining at our restaurant or cooked at home, enjoy this genuine taste of Mediterranean cuisine, embodying the rich culinary traditions of Spain.

SERVES 4–6

1 tablespoon smoked paprika
1½ teaspoons minced fresh thyme
1 teaspoon ground cumin
2 teaspoons dried oregano
1 pound chicken breast and thigh meat, ½-inch diced
¼ cup extra-virgin olive oil
1 cup yellow onion, peeled and diced
4 garlic cloves, peeled and chopped
1 bunch chopped fresh Italian flat-leaf parsley (reserve ¼ for garnish)
1 (15-ounce) can whole tomatoes, drained and hand crushed
4 cups Valencia rice
3 cups clam juice
3 cups water
½ pound Spanish chorizo sausage, cut into ⅛-inch-thick slices on the bias
1½ teaspoons saffron threads
20 Manila clams, scrubbed
20 black mussels, scrubbed and debearded (page 162)
20 (16/20) shrimp, deveined with tails on (see page 60 for sizing)
½ cup frozen peas, thawed and drained
1 cup pimentos, drained and chopped
1 lemon, cut into wedges, for serving

PREPARE THE PAELLA

Add the smoked paprika, thyme, cumin, and oregano to a small bowl. Mix to combine. Add the chicken and rub the spice mixture on all sides, then refrigerate.

Add the oil to a paella pan over medium heat. When the oil is heated, add the onion, garlic, and parsley. Cook for 3 minutes. Add the tomatoes and cook for another 3 minutes. Add the rice and stir to coat the rice. Add the clam juice and 3 cups water. Simmer for 10 minutes, or until the rice has absorbed

all the liquid. Add the chicken, chorizo, and saffron. Add the clams and mussels, tucking them under the rice so the shellfish is covered. Do not stir the rice or disturb the dish at this stage. Cook for 5 minutes and add the shrimp evenly on top. Continue to cook until the rice is al dente, about another 10 minutes. Add the peas and pimentos evenly on top and cook for 1 minute. The rice should be fluffy and fully cooked at this stage. Increase the heat to high and cook untouched for 1 minute to "toast" the bottom layer of rice. This will create a slightly crispy, savory crust known as the socarrat.

FINISHING THE DISH

Remove from the heat, garnish with the additional parsley, and serve directly in the pan with a serving spoon, pair of tongs, and a side of lemon wedges.

BEVERAGE SUGGESTION

Spanish Abadia de San Campio Albarino is a natural selection to pair with Paella, the national dish of Spain. The citrus and stone fruit notes of the wine enhance the seafood flavor and complement the intensity of the saffron.

CATALONIAN "ZARZUELA" SEAFOOD STEW

Catalonia, a medieval region on the Mediterranean Sea in northeast Spain, is home to "Zarzuela." This dish, a seafood stew slowly simmered in a savory tomato saffron broth, gets its name from the Spanish theater featuring storytelling, song, and dance. Like live musical theatre, zarzuela is exciting and vibrant, with a medley of ingredients that elevate this stew in the culinary tradition of Spain. If you've ever prepared a seafood stew, you know each fish has a different cooking time even though it's all prepared in the same pot. To achieve uniform doneness, make sure to add the seafood in the correct order, with items that have the quickest cook times last. You can also make the broth ahead of time, cutting your final prep to 10 to 15 minutes. To keep with Spanish tradition, select a white wine and brandy from Catalonia. SEE PHOTO (PAGE 312).

SERVES 4

WINE MIXTURE

1 cup Spanish dry white wine
2 tablespoons Spanish brandy
1 tablespoon lemon juice
¼ teaspoon dried saffron threads

ALMOND MIXTURE

½ cup slivered almonds
⅓ cup finely chopped fresh parsley

TOMATO SAFFRON BROTH

2 large tomatoes (or one 14.5-ounce can whole peeled tomatoes, drained and finely chopped)
⅓ cup Spanish extra-virgin olive oil
1 large yellow onion peeled and finely diced
1 red bell pepper, chopped into ½-inch dice
¼ teaspoon sea salt
2 garlic cloves, peeled and finely chopped
1 teaspoon smoked paprika
¼ teaspoon red pepper flakes
2 cups clam juice
½ cup manzanilla green olives, pitted and chopped

SEAFOOD & GARNISH

1 pound cod, haddock, or similar white flaky fish, cut into 1-inch pieces
12 (16/20) shrimp, peeled, deveined, and tails removed (see page 60 for sizing)
8 ounces whole squid, cleaned, bodies cut into 1-inch rings, tentacles left whole
¾ teaspoon sea salt
1 pound Mediterranean black mussels, scrubbed and debearded (page 162)
1 lemon, cut in 8 wedges
1 tablespoon chopped Italian flat-leaf parsley, plus 4 parsley sprigs for garnish

PREPARE THE WINE MIXTURE

Add the white wine, brandy, lemon juice, and saffron threads to a small bowl. Mix well and set aside.

PREPARE THE ALMOND MIXTURE

Add the almonds to a food processor and pulse 15 to 20 times. Add the parsley and pulse 10 times, or until finely ground. Remove the contents and transfer to a small bowl. Set aside.

PREPARE THE TOMATO SAFFRON BROTH

Remove the seeds from the tomatoes. Using a box grater, grate the tomatoes until finely grated. Do not grate the skins, which should be discarded. Set aside.

Add the olive oil to a cast-iron enameled casserole dish (Le Creuset is our brand of choice) over medium-high heat. Add the onion, bell pepper, and salt. Cook, stirring occasionally, until the vegetables are soft, 7 to 8 minutes. Add the garlic, paprika, and pepper flakes. Cook for 1 more minute. Add the reserved Wine Mixture and cook until mostly evaporated, 5 to 6 minutes. Add the reserved Almond Mixture, grated tomato, clam juice, and olives. Simmer, uncovered, until the liquid has thickened slightly and reduced by 25 percent, 6 to 8 minutes. Continue with the next step if you plan to serve immediately. Otherwise, set the casserole aside and reserve until ready to prepare. You can also refrigerate the broth overnight to use the next day.

FINISHING THE DISH

Add the fish, shrimp, and squid to a large bowl. Add the salt and toss to evenly coat. Set aside.

Bring the Tomato Saffron Broth in the cast-iron casserole dish to a low boil over medium-high heat. Add the mussels and cook for 4 minutes, or until the shells start to release. Add the seafood mixture and stir to ensure the mixture is covered by liquid. Cover the pot and remove from heat. Let stand for 10 minutes, gently stir, replace the lid, and allow the seafood to rest for another 5 minutes.

Arrange four warm soup/pasta bowls in a row on the kitchen counter. Evenly divide the mussels, shrimp, and fish pieces in each bowl, discarding any unopen mussels. Ladle the remaining broth on top. Squeeze a lemon wedge on each portion, and garnish with chopped parsley, parsley sprigs, and remaining lemon wedges. Serve with a large soup spoon and rustic bread, if desired, for dipping.

BEVERAGE SUGGESTION

Catalonia boasts many world-class white and red wines. Part of the fun of preparing regional foods is to source wine from that region. For this dish, we recommend a Catalonian dry white wine, like Penedés, Macabeo, or Xarel-lo.

ZUPPA DI PESCE

Zuppa di Pesce, also known as Italian fish soup, is a rich and flavorful dish rooted in coastal Italian cuisine. Traditionally made by fishermen, it's a hearty meal that utilizes the catch of the day, often a mix of clams, mussels, shrimp, squid, and various fish. The seafood is historically simmered in a broth of tomatoes, garlic, white wine, and olive oil, creating a fragrant and savory base. The dish is then enhanced with fresh herbs like parsley and a hint of red pepper flakes for subtle heat.

The origins of Zuppa di Pesce are humble, reflecting the resourcefulness of Italian fishermen who used whatever seafood was available. Over time, this simple dish has become a beloved staple in Italian households and restaurants, like ours, celebrated for its vibrant flavors and the way it brings together the best of the sea in one pot. Often served with crusty bread to soak up the rich broth, Zuppa di Pesce is a comforting and satisfying dish that captures the essence of Italian coastal cooking.

At our restaurant, we enjoy offering this hearty stew to our guests, especially during the Christmas holidays when we'll pair the dish with a nice Italian red wine. When making at home, don't be afraid to wear a bib and get your hands dirty with this one.

SERVES 8 TO 10

- 8 ounces dry Barilla or Di Cecco linguine (2 ounces of dry pasta per person)
- 3 tablespoons extra-virgin olive oil, plus more for garnish
- 1 medium fennel bulb, diced
- 1 small yellow onion, peeled and diced
- 1 tablespoon chopped fresh garlic
- 2 tablespoons crushed red pepper flakes
- 1 cup dry white wine
- 2 (28-ounce) cans San Marzano crushed tomatoes
- 2 (6.5-ounce) cans chopped sea clams
- 1¼ cups clam juice
- 1 pound calamari tentacles and tubes, cut into 1-inch pieces
- 2 pounds Manila clams (about 24), scrubbed
- 2 pounds black mussels (about 24 mussels), scrubbed and debearded (page 162)
- 2 pounds (16/20) shrimp, peeled and deveined with tails on (see page 60 for sizing)
- 1 teaspoon sea salt, or to taste
- 2 pounds (U8) sea scallops (about 16 scallops; see page 60 for sizing)
- 1 teaspoon dried oregano
- 1 teaspoon dried parsley
- Chopped fresh parsley, for garnish
- ¼ cup olive oil
- Crusty bread, for serving

PREPARE THE PASTA

Prepare the pasta according to package directions. Cook until al dente, about 10 minutes. Drain but reserve a small amount of the pasta water. Set aside.

PREPARE THE STEW

Add the olive oil to a large deep-sided sauté pan or Dutch oven over medium-low heat. When the oil is heated, add the fennel and onion, and cook, stirring occasionally, until soft, 5 to 7 minutes. Add the garlic and cook for 3 minutes. Add the red pepper flakes and cook for 30 seconds. Add the wine and increase the heat to high for 1½ minutes to evaporate the alcohol. Lower the heat to medium-low again and add the crushed tomatoes, chopped clams, and clam juice. Bring to a simmer. Add the calamari. Cover and simmer for 10 minutes. Add the clams, cover, and cook for 5 minutes, or until they begin to open. Add the mussels and shrimp, cover, and cook for 5 minutes, or until the mussels start to open. Taste and adjust with salt, if necessary. Add the scallops along with oregano, parsley, and salt. Give the stew a good stir and turn off the heat. Cover and let sit for 5 minutes. The scallops should be slightly opaque in the middle when served.

FINISHING THE DISH

Divide the cooked pasta into four bowls and divide the shellfish, shrimp, and scallops evenly, discarding any unopen clams or mussels. Top with the sauce and garnish with the parsley and a drizzle of olive oil. Serve with slices of crusty bread along with pasta spoons, shell bowls, and bibs.

BEVERAGE SUGGESTION

Italy boasts many world-class wines so naturally we recommend a Chianti Classico, which pairs exceptionally well with this dish. We like Marchesi Antinori Villa Antinori Riserva Chianti Classico from central Tuscany.

BOUILLABAISSE WITH ROUILLE

Bouillabaisse is a traditional Provençal fish stew originating from the port city of Marseille in southern France. This dish, which dates back to the ancient Greeks, was originally a humble meal prepared by fishermen using the unsold or bony fish, such as rascasse, conger, and gurnard. Over time, bouillabaisse evolved into a more elaborate dish, incorporating a variety of seafood like mussels, crabs, and even lobster, as well as aromatic herbs and spices like saffron, garlic, fennel, and bay leaves.

The preparation of bouillabaisse is both an art and a ritual, with the fish being added to the broth in a specific order based on cooking time. The broth itself, rich and fragrant, is often served separately with slices of toasted bread and rouille, a garlicky saffron-infused mayonnaise. Bouillabaisse is more than just a stew; it's a reflection of Marseille's cultural melting pot, embodying the essence of Mediterranean cuisine and the connection between the sea and the people who live by it. SEE PHOTO (PAGE 317).

SERVES 4

ROUILLE

2 medium-sized red bell peppers, roasted and seeds removed
1 jalapeño, roasted and seeds removed
9 garlic cloves, peeled
1 tablespoon kosher salt
4 ounces (convert to cups) French bread (soaked in warm water and squeezed out)
1½ cups extra-virgin olive oil

BOUILLABAISSE FISH STOCK

2½ pounds whitefish bones
¼ cup 90/10 olive oil/canola blend
2 tablespoons chopped fresh garlic
1 fennel bulb, diced
1 medium yellow onion, peeled and diced
1 medium orange peel, cut in 1-inch strip
½ bunch Italian flat-leaf parsley
1 tablespoon fresh thyme leaves chopped
1 bay leaf
1 teaspoon whole black pepper corns
1 cup clam juice
2 tablespoons clam base
1 gallon water

1 leek, white and green parts cut into ½-inch pieces
⅛ cup Pernod
1 (10-ounce) can crushed tomatoes
½ teaspoon saffron threads (soaked in ¼ cup water)
1¼ quarts Bouillabaisse Fish Stock
1-pound boneless, skinless cod fillets, cut into pieces
24 live Manila clams, scrubbed
24 live black mussels, scrubbed and debearded (page 162)
8 scallops (U10/15) scallops (see page 60 for sizing)
12 (16/20) shrimp, peeled and deveined, with tails on (see page 60 for sizing)
¼ cup Rouille
4 fresh Italian flat-leaf parsley sprigs, for garnish
4 thick slices toasted baguette, for serving

PREPARE THE ROUILLE

Add the bell peppers, jalapeño, garlic, salt, and bread to a food processor. Mix until smooth, then slowly drizzle in the olive oil until fully combined. Set aside.

PREPARE THE BOUILLABAISSE FISH STOCK

Add the fish bones to a bowl of cold water and soak for 30 minutes. Drain and set aside. Add the oil to a large stockpot over medium heat. When the oil is heated, add the garlic, fennel, and onion and sauté, stirring occasionally, until the onion is soft and translucent, about 10 minutes. Add the fish bones, orange peel, parsley, thyme, bay leaf, pepper corns, clam juice, clam base, along with 1 gallon (16 cups) of water. Increase the heat to medium-high and bring to a boil, then reduce to a simmer and cook for 1 hour. (Note: Make sure to skim the stock as it cooks.) Remove from the heat and strain the stock through a chinois or fine-mesh strainer and return the strained stock to a clean stockpot over medium-high heat. Add the leeks, Pernod, tomato, saffron, and simmer for 20 minutes. Remove from the heat and strain the stock again, then place in an ice bath to cool.

PREPARE THE BOUILLABAISSE

Add the Bouillabaisse Fish Stock to a large deep-sided sauté pan over medium-low heat. When the stock is heated, add the cod, clams, and mussels, cover and cook for 2 minutes. Add the scallops and shrimp, cover, and cook until the clams and mussels open, about 6 minutes. Remove from the heat.

FINISHING THE DISH

Divide the seafood and shellfish equally among four large pasta bowls, discarding any unopen clams or mussels. Add the stock then add the Rouille in the center. Garnish with the parsley and a piece of sliced baguette. Serve with side bowls for the shells along with cocktail forks and soup spoons.

BEVERAGE SUGGESTION

France boasts many world-class wines so naturally we recommend a Chablis, which pairs exceptionally well with this dish. We enjoy William Febvre Vallions Chablis from France.

BAHIA SEAFOOD STEW WITH BRAZILIAN COCONUT

Bahia, a coastal state in Brazil, derives its heritage from the Portuguese settlers who arrived in 1500. Its seaside location and tropical climate coupled with a vibrant culture provide the ingredients for this exotic and flavorful stew, which is accentuated with a light, citrusy coconut broth that doesn't overpower the succulent grouper and shrimp nestled within. You can always make the broth ahead of time to facilitate finishing this dish, which only takes 10 to 15 minutes to assemble.

SERVES 4

COCONUT BROTH

2 tablespoons canola or safflower oil
1 small onion, peeled and chopped to ½ inch dice
1 red bell pepper, chopped to ½ inch dice
½ cup medium shallots, peeled and chopped
2 garlic cloves, peeled and finely chopped
1 tablespoon peeled and finely minced fresh ginger
1 stalk lemongrass, trimmed of outside leaves and pounded
1 cup fresh tomato, seeded and chopped to ¼ inch dice
1 cup unsweetened coconut milk
Sea salt and fresh cracked black pepper, as needed, to taste

SEAFOOD STEW

1 pound skinless, boneless grouper fillet, cut into 1-inch pieces
1 pound raw shrimp (16/20), peeled, deveined, and tails removed (see page 60 for sizing)
Sea salt and fresh cracked black pepper, as needed
½ cup chopped fresh cilantro, plus 4 sprigs for garnish
2 medium-sized limes (enough to produce 2 tablespoons of juice)
White rice and rustic bread, for serving
8 lime wedges, for serving

PREPARE THE COCONUT BROTH

Add the oil to a cast-iron enameled casserole dish (Le Creuset is our brand of choice) over medium heat. Add the onion, bell pepper, shallots, garlic, ginger, and lemongrass. Cook until the vegetables have turned soft and translucent, 6 to 9 minutes. Add the tomatoes, unsweetened coconut milk, and season with salt and pepper. Cook for another 3 minutes. Continue with the next step if you plan to serve immediately. Otherwise, set the broth aside and reserve until ready to prepare. You can also reserve the broth in the refrigerator overnight for use the next day.

FINISHING THE DISH

Season the grouper and shrimp with salt and pepper. Add the shrimp and cilantro to the simmering broth. Cover and cook for 2 minutes, or until the shrimp turn translucent. Add the grouper and cook for another 3 minutes. Remove the casserole dish from the heat. Using a lime squeezer, add the 2 tablespoons of lime juice. To assemble, arrange 4 warm soup/pasta bowls in a row on the kitchen counter. Evenly divide the grouper and shrimp in each bowl. Discard the lemongrass stalk and ladle the broth on top and garnish with the cilantro sprigs. Serve with a large soup spoon, white rice, and rustic bread for dipping, if desired, and the lime wedges.

BEVERAGE SUGGESTION

The Caipirinha is the national drink of Brazil and features cachaca, an alcohol from Brazil made from sugarcane, fresh lime, and sugar. Or pair with a hearty Chardonnay from Argentina or Chile.

BRANZINO

Branzino, also known as European sea bass, is a prized fish found in the Mediterranean Sea and along the eastern Atlantic coast. Renowned for its delicate, mild flavor and tender, flaky white flesh, branzino is a popular choice in seafood cuisine. Its skin is often silver, with a streamlined body that makes it appealing for grilling, roasting, or baking. The fish is typically served whole with its skin intact, which helps retain moisture and flavor during cooking. Branzino is celebrated for its versatility and is commonly prepared with simple seasonings like lemon, herbs, and olive oil to highlight its natural taste. Its low fat content and clean taste make it a favorite among chefs and health-conscious diners. In recent years, branzino has gained popularity in global cuisine, appearing in various dishes from fine-dining restaurants to home kitchens.

Due to its high demand, branzino is now often extensively farmed. Aquaculture has made the fish more accessible while helping to manage wild populations, contributing to sustainable seafood practices. Farmed branzino is widely available in markets, ensuring a consistent supply throughout the year.

At our restaurant, we serve our branzino whole and will instruct our guests how best to debone the fish. Simply remove the fins from the top and bottom and peel back the fillet from the central spine. When finished enjoying the first side, remove the central bone whole and set aside and eat the second half below.

BRANZINO WITH SAUTÉED SPINACH, MUSHROOMS, AND BALSAMIC GLAZE

SERVES 2

BALSAMIC GLAZE
MAKES 1 CUP

1 cup balsamic vinegar
¼ cup honey
2 teaspoons fresh orange juice
2 sprigs fresh thyme

BRANZINO

1 whole branzino, cleaned
1 teaspoon sea salt
1 teaspoon fresh cracked black pepper
¼ cup 90/10 oil blend
2 cups fresh spinach
2 cups sliced cremini mushrooms
4 slices lemon
2 fresh thyme sprigs
1½ ounces Balsamic Glaze, for garnish
1 Grilled Lemon Half (page 65), for garnish
Micro greens, for garnish

PREPARE THE BALSAMIC GLAZE

Add the vinegar, honey, orange juice, and thyme to a small saucepan over medium-high heat. Stir to incorporate and bring to a boil. Once boiling, reduce heat to low and let simmer until reduced by half, 15 to 20 minutes. (Note: The consistency should resemble maple syrup.) Remove and strain. Set aside until ready to use or store in an airtight container in the refrigerator up to 2 weeks.

PREPARE THE BRANZINO

Preheat an outdoor grill to medium-high heat.

Rinse the branzino and pat dry with paper towels. Using a kitchen knife, score both sides of the fish and then season both sides with salt and pepper. Fill the fish's cavity with the lemon slices and thyme sprigs and drizzle both sides of the fish with olive oil. Set aside.

Add 1 tablespoon of olive oil to a large skillet over medium-high heat. When heated, add the spinach and sauté until wilted, about 2 minutes. Remove the spinach and keep warm. Add the mushrooms to the skillet and sauté until the mushrooms are soft and tender, about 8 minutes. Remove the mushrooms and keep warm.

Place the fish on the grill and cook for 6 to 8 minutes. Turn the fish over and cook for 4 to 6 minutes, or until the fish is cooked through and reaches an internal temperature of 140°F. Remove the fish.

FINISHING THE DISH

Arrange the sautéed spinach and mushrooms in the center of a plate. Drizzle the Balsamic Glaze across the vegetables. Place the branzino on top of the vegetables. Garnish with the Grilled Lemon and micro greens and serve.

BEVERAGE SUGGESTION

When pan-searing Branzino, a nice Chardonnay with vanilla and buttery flavors like Trefethen Chardonnay pair well.

DOVER SOLE WITH LEMON BUTTER SAUCE

Dover sole is a highly prized flatfish known for its delicate flavor and fine texture. Found primarily in the North Atlantic and Mediterranean Sea, this fish is celebrated in European cuisine, particularly in France and the United Kingdom. The fish's name originates from the town of Dover on England's southeast coast, where it was historically abundant. Dover sole is relatively small, typically weighing between one and two pounds, with a smooth, brown skin. It is considered a luxury seafood item, often commanding a high price due to its limited availability and the labor-intensive methods required to catch it sustainably.

Dover sole has a light, firm, yet tender flesh that holds up well to various cooking methods, including grilling, poaching, and pan-frying. Its mild, sweet taste is complemented by simple, classic preparations, often involving butter, lemon, and herbs. Whether served whole or filleted, Dover sole is a gourmet delicacy that continues to be a favorite among chefs and seafood lovers alike.

SERVES 2

LEMON BUTTER SAUCE

2 tablespoons unsalted butter
1 lemon, juiced
2 tablespoons chopped fresh Italian flat-leaf parsley

DOVER SOLE

2 (1-pound) whole Dover sole, scaled and cleaned
½ cup all-purpose flour
Sea salt and fresh cracked black pepper, to taste
2 tablespoons vegetable oil
2 tablespoons unsalted butter
1 lemon, cut into wedges, for serving

PREPARE THE LEMON BUTTER SAUCE

Add 2 tablespoons of butter to a small skillet over medium heat. Allow the butter to melt and turn a light brown color, creating a nutty aroma (called beurre noisette), about 3 minutes. Remove from the heat and stir in the lemon juice and chopped parsley. Swirl the skillet to combine the ingredients. Set aside and keep warm.

PREPARE THE DOVER SOLE

Pat the sole dry with paper towels and set aside. Add the flour to a bowl and season with salt and pepper. Dredge each sole in the seasoned flour, lightly coating both sides of the dish. Shake off any excess flour and set aside.

Add the oil to a large skillet over medium-high heat. When heated, add half the butter (2 tablespoons). When the butter is melted and starts to foam, add the sole, one at a time. Cook for 2 to 3 minutes, or until golden brown. Gently turn the sole over and cook for another 2 or 3 minutes, until golden brown and cooked through. (Note: Be gentle when flipping the sole to avoid breaking the fish.) Remove the sole and keep warm. Repeat the cooking process with the second sole.

DEBONING THE SOLE

Place the cooked sole on a cutting board or serving platter. Use a kitchen knife to make a shallow incision along the backbone, from the head to the tail. If not already removed, peel away the skin from both sides of the fish. Start at the head end and gently pull the skin toward the tail. Using a knife or fish spatula, carefully lift the flesh from one side of the backbone. Start at the head and work your way down to the tail, following the natural line of the bones. Repeat this process for the other side of the backbone. Next, gently lift the backbone, starting from the head and pulling it toward the tail. The bones should come away cleanly from the flesh. If the head is still attached, you can cut it off along with the backbone. Inspect the fillets for any remaining small bones and remove them with tweezers or your fingers.

FINISHING THE DISH

Once deboned, the sole fillets are ready to be served on warm plates. You can also reassemble them on the plate to resemble the whole fish for presentation. Pour the Lemon Butter Sauce over the cooked fillets. Serve with lemon wedges on the side.

BEVERAGE SUGGESTION

A nice White Burgundy pairs well with the firm flesh and butter sauce. Growing up and spending winters in Florida, my parents enjoyed Lousi Jadot Premier Cru Pouilly Fuisse at the Ocean Club, and I have continued the tradition to this day.

ACKNOWLEDGMENTS

The authors would like to personally thank the incredible Bluewater Grill family-kitchen teams, service staff, and management. Your passion and dedication bring every plate to life.

To our Executive Chef Albert Serrano who worked painstakingly to adapt our many recipes for the home chef.

To our suppliers for always saving the best quality for us.

To the cookbook production team, particularly James O. Fraioli and Culinary Book Creations, photographers Tucker + Hossler, Jim Randall Photography, and Palm & Ocean, Alan Hebel and Ian Koviak of The Book Designers, Senior Editor Nicole Frail, Senior Editor Jesse McHugh, and the teams at Skyhorse Publishing and Simon & Schuster. Your patience, guidance, and professionalism is appreciated and applauded.

To our spouses for all your love and support.

And to our parents, who taught us the value of hard work, love for great food, and creating the memories that these recipes bind us to . . . thank you for inspiring us to create something meaningful.

This book is for you!

METRIC CONVERSIONS

If you're accustomed to using metric measurements, use these handy charts to convert the imperial measurements used in this book.

Weight (Dry Ingredients)

1 oz		30 g
4 oz	¼ lb	120 g
8 oz	½ lb	240 g
12 oz	¾ lb	360 g
16 oz	1 lb	480 g
32 oz	2 lb	960 g

Oven Temperatures

Fahrenheit	Celsius	Gas Mark
225°	110°	¼
250°	120°	½
275°	140°	1
300°	150°	2
325°	160°	3
350°	180°	4
375°	190°	5
400°	200°	6
425°	220°	7
450°	230°	8

Volume (Liquid Ingredients)

½ tsp.		2 ml
1 tsp.		5 ml
1 Tbsp.	½ fl oz	15 ml
2 Tbsp.	1 fl oz	30 ml
¼ cup	2 fl oz	60 ml
⅓ cup	3 fl oz	80 ml
½ cup	4 fl oz	120 ml
⅔ cup	5 fl oz	160 ml
¾ cup	6 fl oz	180 ml
1 cup	8 fl oz	240 ml
1 pt	16 fl oz	480 ml
1 qt	32 fl oz	960 ml

Length

¼ in	6 mm
½ in	13 mm
¾ in	19 mm
1 in	25 mm
6 in	15 cm
12 in	30 cm

INDEX

C

R

S

T

U

V